# PROBLEMS IN TAX ETHICS

∎ ∎ ∎

By

## Donald B. Tobin
*Frank E. and Virginia H. Bazler Designated*
*Professor in Business Law and Associate Dean for Faculty*
*Moritz College of Law, The Ohio State University*

## Richard Lavoie
*Associate Professor of Law*
*The University of Akron School of Law*

## Richard E. Trogolo\*
*Managing Counsel, Cincinnati*
*Office of Chief Counsel for Internal Revenue Service*
*Adjunct Professor of Law, Capital University Law School*

## AMERICAN CASEBOOK SERIES®

## WEST®
A Thomson Reuters business

\* For identification purposes only. The views expressed herein are solely those of the author and are not the views of the Internal Revenue Service.

Mat #40333689

*American Casebook Series* is a trademark registered in the U.S. Patent and Trademark Office.

© 2009 Thomson Reuters
  610 Opperman Drive
  St. Paul, MN 55123
  1–800–313–9378
Printed in the United States of America

**ISBN:** 978–0–314–15899–4

To Alex and Anne, may you always love books

DBT

———

To Patricia, Jeremy and Torianna, with all my love

RLL

———

To my loving wife, Joan

RET

# Preface

Why this book? We have been teaching or working in the area of tax ethics for a combined total of over 40 years. The ethical issues and problems facing tax lawyers and tax professionals have become increasingly complex, and the general rules of professional responsibility do not always provide clear answers to these types of problems. We believe that people studying in this area of law need a text designed to deal with specific problems that arise often in the tax field. This book also considers the model rules of professional conduct and discusses those rules in the context of tax problems.

As much as possible, this book uses a problem format. We want students to recognize how the rules of professional responsibility apply in real world situations. Most practitioners believe they are acting ethically, but the practice of law generally, and tax law specifically, often encourages lawyers to push the envelope. In addition, sometimes professional responsibility rules conflict with our normative notions of ethical conduct. It is our hope that this book will help students understand their ethical obligations by examining these obligations in the context of tax law.

This book is set up with problems and scenarios. We chose this method so students could get a feel for the ethical problems they may face if they are in tax practice. The problems are designed to be constructive possible real life conflicts. It is our hope that by working through those conflicts now, students will be better able to identify and work through similar problems when they are practicing tax law. The scenarios are designed to be more detailed problems that also give students a chance to work through both tax problems and ethical issues in taxation. They are designed to work as class exercises, group projects, or as independent projects.

The book is also designed to be a starting point for the study of ethical issues in taxation. The book can be used for a course in tax ethics, or as a supplement to a basic federal income tax course. We have placed additional information that we believe may be helpful to students on our web site at www.taxethics.com.

There are special rules and standards that apply to tax lawyers and this book examines those provisions in depth. But, the goal of this book is also to introduce students to ethical problems that are related to the problems they will face in practice. We examine the Model Rules of Professional Conduct with an eye towards someone who is going to be practicing tax law.

We would like to thank The Moritz College of Law, The Ohio State University, and The University of Akron School of Law for their outstanding support. We would also like to thank Arthur Greenbaum and Barry Broden for their helpful thoughts and comments and our research assistants Sidra Khwaja and Zachery Keller and for their help with this project. In addition, Anita Bratcher at the Moritz College of Law was essential in helping bring this book to print.

Cases and opinions in the book are edited for ease of use. Citations are often omitted from the edited cases. Footnotes contained within cases are from the original work unless [ed. note] appears in the footnote.

One of the co-authors of this book, Richard Trogolo, works at the Internal Revenue Service. His thoughts, comments, and insights were incredibly important to the book and are his own. They in no way reflect positions of the Internal Revenue Service.

We would also like to thank the American Bar Association, University of Virginia Tax Review, American Law Institute, the Washington Law Review, and the Tax Lawyer for granting permission to reprint material contained in their publications.

December 2009

# Summary of Contents

# Table of Contents

# Table of Cases
# ABA Statements and Opinions

---

Cases cited or discussed in
the text are listed below.
Cases cited in principal cases
are not included.

# PROBLEMS IN TAX ETHICS

# Chapter 1

## Tax Preparer Rules and Obligations

———————

There is a wonderful law review article by George Cooper that highlights the ethical problems facing tax lawyers.[1] In the article, Professor Cooper sets out a hypothetical exchange of memos between an aggressive associate and a more ethically sensitive partner. The associate recommends transactions that all appear to have at least some support under the letter of the law. Many of the transactions, however, are very aggressive and highly questionable. The senior partner believes that in making these recommendations the associate has violated the ethical rules that govern the legal profession. The associate believes that he has an ethical duty to the client to recommend these aggressive transactions because they are not based on a frivolous reading of the statute. As you can imagine, at the end of the story the associate leaves the firm and gets the client.

The tension between the lawyer as an aggressive planner for the client, and the lawyer as a guardian of the law and our system of justice has only increased since Professor Cooper wrote his law review article in 1980. Tax and accounting malfeasance at Enron, WorldCom, Tyco, and Arthur Anderson to name just a few have increased national attention on ethical issues in tax practice. Lawyers and accountants have played a major role in assisting companies in defrauding consumers, investors, stock holders, and regulators. Some lawyers were all too willing to push the envelope and to craft or employ creative and sometimes ludicrous tax avoidance schemes.

The ethical issues facing tax lawyers are very complex. To whom do lawyers owe their duty and to what degree? What is the role of a tax lawyer when giving tax advice? Is a lawyer's obligation solely to the client, or do lawyers have some obligation to society? How aggressive can lawyers be when they recommend a client take a particular tax position?

———————

[1] George Cooper, The Avoidance Dynamic: A Tale of Tax Planning, Tax Ethics, and Tax Reform, 80 Column. L. Rev. 1553 (1980).

In the famous opinion, Gregory v. Helvering, the Court stated "[t]he legal right of a taxpayer to decrease the amount of what otherwise would be his taxes, or altogether avoid them, by means which the law permits, cannot be doubted."[2] If it is legal for a taxpayer to avoid tax by means which the law permits, lawyers should be able to aid taxpayers in doing so. In *Gregory*, however, the Court, while recognizing the right to decrease ones taxes, found against the taxpayer. The Court noted, "the question for determination is whether what was done, apart from the tax motive was the thing the statute intended."[3] In other words, the Court faced the same quandary that we still face today. How do we differentiate between taxpayers who are legally trying to reduce their taxes, and taxpayers who are pushing the envelope too far and using creative arguments to avoid paying their fair share?

In many ways, a tax lawyer's role is special in our legal system. Because we have a system of taxation that is based on voluntary compliance, and because audit rates are so low, the system itself depends on honest reporting by taxpayers. Generally, a lawyer has an obligation not to file a claim or take a position if the claim or position is frivolous. But if we used a frivolous standard in the tax field, attorneys would have every incentive to recommend that their clients take very aggressive tax positions. After all, only a few returns are ever audited, and it is easy to justify a position as "not frivolous." Such an attitude, however, would destroy the idea of voluntary compliance.

Tax attorneys generally have two different functions and the ethical standards may be different depending on the role the attorney is playing at the time. Sometimes a lawyer acts as an advisor. In this role, the lawyer advises his client in various ways. He may advise a client whether a position is justified, how to set up a transaction, or how to take advantage of a loophole in the tax law. He may even be part of a company that creates and sells "tax preferred" packages designed to reduce his client's tax bill. Since, as we will see later, reliance on an accountant or an attorney may shield a taxpayer from penalties, the attorney plays a role here as a check on abuse. He provides, in a sense, a seal of approval. When he is acting in this capacity, it may be fair to require that the attorney have a higher level of certainty when he recommends a position to a client.

---

[2] 293 U.S. 465, 469, 55 S. Ct. 266 (1935).
[3] *Id.*

A tax lawyer, however, may also be the taxpayer's advocate. If the Internal Revenue Service ("IRS" or "Service") disputes an item on a taxpayer's return, the taxpayer enters into an adversary proceeding with the IRS (first, usually with an IRS agent or an appeals officer, and later in court). This can happen in several different ways but usually takes one of two tracks. First, a taxpayer files a return, and the return is accepted as filed by the IRS. The IRS later questions that position. If the IRS and the taxpayer cannot agree on the treatment of the position after an audit, the taxpayer may pay the tax and sue for a refund (either in District Court or the U.S. Court of Federal Claims) or, after receiving a notice of deficiency from the IRS,[4] he may file an action in the Tax Court without paying the tax.

Once the taxpayer's position is questioned by the Service, the attorney's role changes. The attorney is now an advocate for the client. Once he is an advocate, he has the same ethical responsibilities of every attorney to be honest to the court and to not take any position that is frivolous. He has, however, the obligation to represent his client aggressively and thoroughly. He has no greater ethical responsibility than any other attorney representing a client in court.

In this book we often talk about ethical standards, but these standards are not necessarily *moral* standards. Instead, they are rules and standards promulgated by different authorities that have some power over tax practitioners. We are talking about regulated ethics here, not your own moral values.

Lawyer conduct in tax practice is regulated in many ways. First, the general ethics rules and requirements set out by state bars apply to tax lawyers. State bar decisions and rules are often significantly influenced by the ABA Model Rules and by ABA Formal Opinions, but the ABA rules and opinions are not binding on state bars. Second, the Department of Treasury regulates the conduct of professionals who practice before the IRS. These regulations

---

[4] Section 6212 of the Internal Revenue Code of 1986, as amended (the Code) provides that if the Service determines that there is a deficiency in the tax paid by a taxpayer, the Service should send notice to the taxpayer. This notice is called a "Notice of Deficiency," or in tax circles a "90 day letter." Once a taxpayer receives the notice, she has 90 days to file a petition in Tax Court. If the taxpayer fails to file the petition, the deficiency can be assessed. If the taxpayer wants to contest the deficiency at that point, she must pay the tax, file a claim for refund, and if the claim for refund is denied, she may file suit in either District Court or the U.S. Court of Federal Claims.

generally apply to lawyers, accountants, and enrolled agents who represent clients before the IRS. Finally, Congress has at times stepped in and created specific rules regulating tax professionals.[5]

The following sections discuss rules that are specific to tax practitioners when they are advising a taxpayer on positions the taxpayer may take on his tax return.

## A.  Standards for Advising Taxpayers on Return Positions

### 1.    ABA OPINIONS

In devising the ethical standards for tax lawyers, the ABA has grappled with the conflict between the lawyer as an advisor and the lawyer as an advocate. The Model Rules of Professional Conduct do not have any provisions dealing specifically with tax lawyers. The ABA has, however, attempted to set standards for tax lawyers based on the Canons of Ethics and the Model Rules of Professional Conduct.

## ABA FORMAL OPINION 314[*]
### Tax Return Advice
### April 27, 1965

[ABA Formal Opinion 314 starts with a recitation of the Canons of Professional Ethics that might apply in this situation]

* * * [A] lawyer who is asked to advise his client in the course of the preparation of the client's tax returns may freely urge the statement of positions most favorable to the client just as long as there is reasonable basis for those positions. Thus where the lawyer believes there is a reasonable basis for a position that a particular transaction does not result in taxable income, or that certain

---

[5] For an interesting look at the early development of Ethics in Tax Practice see Barry Charles Broden, Ethics in Tax Practice, (Dec.12, 1977)(Ph.D. dissertation). Broden also examines the early literature on compliance with ethical norms.

expenditures are properly deductible as expenses, the lawyer has no duty to advise that riders be attached to the client's tax return explaining the circumstances surrounding the transaction or the expenditures. * * *

In all cases, with regard both to the preparation of returns and negotiating administrative settlements, the lawyer is under a duty not to mislead the Internal Revenue Service deliberately and affirmatively, either by misstatements or by silence or by permitting his client to mislead. The difficult problem arises where the client has in fact misled but without the lawyer's knowledge or participation. In that situation, upon discovery of the misrepresentation, the lawyer must advise the client to correct the statement; if the client refuses, the lawyer's obligation depends on all the circumstances.

Fundamentally, subject to the restrictions of the attorney-client privilege imposed by Cannon 37 [Model Rule 1.6], the lawyer may have a duty to withdraw from the matter. * * *

But as an advocate before a service which itself represents the adversary point of view, where his client's case is fairly arguable, a lawyer is under no duty to disclose its weaknesses, any more than he would be to make such a disclosure to a brother lawyer. * * *

So long as a lawyer remains within these limitations, and so long as his duty is "performed within and not without the bounds of the law", he "owes 'entire devotion to the interest of the client, warm zeal in the maintenance and defense of his rights and the exertion of his utmost learning and ability,' to the end that nothing be taken or be withheld from him, save by the rule of law, legally applied" in his practice before the Internal Revenue Service, as elsewhere.

## Questions and Comments:

1.  How tough is this standard? If you were a lawyer advising a client based on Opinion 314, what standard do you think you need to use?

2.  The Opinion says a lawyer may "freely urge" a position most favorable to a client as long as there is a "reasonable basis" for the position. What does reasonable basis mean to you? Does that mean that a lawyer may take a position as long as it is not frivolous?

3.  If reasonable basis means something more than not frivolous, how can a higher standard be justified under the Model Rules?

ABA formal opinion 314 did not prove extremely helpful to those trying to determine the appropriate standard for a return position.  At the request of the ABA Section of Taxation, the ABA tried again.

# ABA FORMAL OPINION 85-352[*]
Tax Return Advice; Reconsideration of Formal Opinion 314
July 7, 1985

The Committee has been requested by the Section of Taxation of the American Bar Association to reconsider the "reasonable basis" standard in the Committee's Formal Opinion 314 governing the position a lawyer may advise a client to take on a tax return. * * *

The Committee is informed that the standard of "reasonable basis" has been construed by many lawyers to support the use of any colorable claim on a tax return to justify exploitation of the lottery of the tax return audit selection process.  The view is not universally held, and the Committee does not believe that the reasonable basis standard, properly interpreted and applied, permits this construction.

However, the Committee is persuaded that as a result of serious controversy over this standard and its persistent criticism by distinguished members of the tax bar, IRS officials and members of Congress, sufficient doubt has been created regarding the validity of the standard so as to erode its effectiveness as an ethical guideline.  For this reason, the Committee has concluded that it should be restated. * * *

This position reconsiders and revises only that part of Opinion 314 that relates to the lawyer's duty in advising a client of positions that can be taken on a tax return. * * *

---

The ethical standards governing the conduct of a lawyer in advising a client on positions that can be taken in a tax return are no different from those governing a lawyer's conduct in advising or taking positions for a client in other civil matters. Although the Model Rules distinguish between the roles of advisor and advocate, both roles are involved here, and the ethical standards applicable to them provide relevant guidance. In many cases a lawyer must realistically anticipate that the filing of the tax return may be the first step in a process that may result in an adversary relationship between the client and the IRS. This normally occurs in situations when a lawyer advises an aggressive position on a tax return, not when the position taken is a safe or conservative one that is unlikely to be challenged by the IRS.

Rule 3.1 of the Model Rules, which is in essence a restatement of DR 7-102(A)(2) of the Model Code, states in pertinent part:

> A lawyer shall not bring or defend a proceeding, or assert or controvert an issue therein, unless there is a basis for doing so that is not frivolous, which includes a good faith argument for an extension, modification or reversal of existing law.

Rule 1.2(d), which applies to representation generally, states:

> A lawyer shall not counsel a client to engage, or assist a client, in conduct that the lawyer knows is criminal or fraudulent, but a lawyer may discuss the legal consequences of any proposed course of conduct with a client and may counsel or assist a client to make a good faith effort to determine the validity, scope, meaning or application of the law.

On the basis of these rules and analogous provisions of the Model Code, a lawyer, in representing a client in the course of the preparation of the client's tax return, may advise the statement of position most favorable to the client if the lawyer has a good faith belief that those positions are warranted in existing law or can be supported by a good faith argument for an extension, modification or reversal of existing law. A lawyer can have a good faith belief in this context even if the lawyer believes the client's position probably will not prevail. However, good faith requires that there be some realistic possibility of success if the matter is litigated.

This formulation of the lawyer's duty in the situation addressed by this opinion is consistent with the basic duty of the lawyer to a client, recognized in ethical standards since the ABA Canons of Professional Ethics, and in the opinions of this Committee: zealously and loyally to represent the interests of the client within the bounds of the law. * * *

In the role of advisor, the lawyer should counsel the client as to whether the position is likely to be sustained by a court if challenged by the IRS, as well as of the potential penalty consequences to the client if the position is taken on the tax return without disclosure. Section 6661 of the Internal Revenue Code imposes a penalty for substantial understatement of tax liability which can be avoided if the facts are adequately disclosed or if there is or was substantial authority for the position taken by the taxpayer. Competent representation of the client would require the lawyer to advise the client fully as to whether there is or was substantial authority for the position taken in the tax return. If the lawyer is unable to conclude that the position is supported by substantial authority, the lawyer should advise the client of the penalty the client may suffer and of the opportunity to avoid such penalty by adequately disclosing the facts in the return or in a statement attached to the return. If after receiving such advise [sic] the client decides to risk the penalty by making no disclosure and to take the position initially advised by the lawyer in accordance with the standard stated above, the lawyer has met his or her ethical responsibility with respect to the advice.

In all cases, however, with regard both to the preparation of returns and negotiating administrative settlements, the lawyer is under a duty not to mislead the Internal Revenue Service deliberately, either by misstatements or by silence or by permitting the client to mislead. Rules 4.1 and 8.4(c); DRs 1-102(A)(4), 7-102(A)(3) and (5).

In summary, a lawyer may advise reporting a position on a return even where the lawyer believes the position probably will not prevail, there is no "substantial authority" in support of the position, and there will be no disclosure of the position in the return. However, the position to be asserted must be one which the lawyer in good faith believes is warranted in existing law or can be supported by a good faith argument for an extension, modification or reversal of existing law. This requires that there is some realistic possibility of success if the matter is litigated. * * *

## Questions and Comments:

1. The ABA opinion indicates that this is a restatement of Opinion 314. Opinion 314 uses the terminology "reasonable basis." The ABA notes that some people claimed "reasonable basis" meant any colorable claim. The ABA appears to reject that notion, but what does Opinion 314 actually say on this matter?

2. In order to clarify the standard, the ABA restated it in Formal Opinion 85-352. Is the "realistic possibility of success" standard any better than the reasonable basis standard? Formal Opinion 85-352 implies that submitting a return may be the first step in an adversarial process. What standard applies in an adversarial process? See Model Rule 3.1. Does this mean that the standard for advising a client on a return is the same as the standard for the lawyer as an advocate? If so, does an attorney involved in civil litigation need a "realistic possibility of success?" Or does it mean that an attorney advising a taxpayer on a return position only needs a colorable claim? Did the ABA spend a lot of time and effort reaching the conclusion that tax lawyers advising a taxpayer have the same obligations of all other lawyers?

3. It turns out Formal Opinion 85-352 still did not clarify the standard for lawyers when advising a taxpayer on a return position. There was still significant room for doubt about what "realistic possibility of success" meant. In fact, although the opinion appears to claim otherwise, a fair reading of both opinions would be that a lawyer may advise a client to take a position on a return as long as the position was not frivolous.

After the issuance of ABA Opinion 85-352, the ABA Tax Section believed that the realistic possibility of success standard was significantly stronger than merely not frivolous. Some of the leading academics and lawyers in the tax ethics field were the drafters of the following report:[6]

---

[6] Paul J. Sax, Chairman, James P. Holden, Theodore Tannenwald, Jr., David E. Watts, and Bernard Wolfman are listed as the drafters of the report.

# REPORT OF THE SPECIAL TASK FORCE ON FORMAL OPINION 85-352[7][*]

39 Tax Law. 635

\* \* \* This Report examines Opinion 85-352 and how it will apply to tax practice. It concludes that Opinion 85-352 properly rejects a low standard of tax reporting, reduces some of the potential for misuse of the governing ethical standard, and, properly interpreted and implemented, should work to improve the reliability of tax advice furnished by members of the bar.

### Background

\* \* \*

The Standards of Tax Practice Committee was directed to undertake a study, and reported to Council in July 1983 a form of proposed revision to Opinion 314 intended to elevate the ethical standard by elimination of the "reasonable basis" standard. \* \* \* The proposal was then forwarded by the Section Chairman to the ABA Committee, which agreed with the position of the Tax Section that the "reasonable basis" standard required revision and, after correspondence and deliberation, issued its conclusion as Opinion 85-352. \* \* \* [Note: The ABA did not necessarily agree with the Tax

---

[7] The publication of the Special Task Force Report appeared in *The Tax Layer*. *The Tax Lawyer* is published by Georgetown University Law Center and is the official publication of the ABA Tax Section. The Tax Section often publishes important papers and guidance in the *Tax Lawyer*. As part of the publication of the report, the following history was included.

> At meetings in San Diego on February 1 and 2, 1986, a prior draft of the Special Task Force Report was adopted by the Committee on Standards of Tax Practice and approved by the Council of the Section of Taxation with the request that it be published in *The Tax Lawyer*. Thereafter, changes were made in the Report that the Special Task Force believes are clarifications only, so that the final Report is wholly consistent with the adoption of the Report by the Committee on Standards of Tax Practice and its approval by the Council of the Section of Taxation. The Report has not been reviewed by the ABA Standing Committee on Ethics and Professional Responsibility, and its publication does not in any way imply approval by the Standing Committee.

Section's proposed revision of the standard. In fact, the ABA appears to have rejected the stronger standard urged by the Tax Section].

*Reasons for Revision*

Opinion 85-352 explains that as a result of serious controversy over the "reasonable basis" standard, and also as a result of persistent criticism by distinguished members of the tax bar, IRS officials, and members of Congress, sufficient doubt had been created regarding the validity of the "reasonable basis" standard as to erode its usefulness as an ethical guideline.

Formal Opinion 85-352 restates the lawyer's duty in advising a client as to positions that can be taken on a tax return. The same principles should apply to all aspects to tax practice to the extent tax return positions would be involved. For example, it should govern the lawyer's duty as to tax advice in the course of structuring transactions that will involve tax return positions, including tax advice in the course of preparing legal documents such as employee benefit trusts, wills, and business buy-sell agreements. However, Opinion 85-352 does not address a lawyer's duty and responsibilities in negotiation and settlement procedures with the Internal Revenue Service, which are the subject of discussion in Opinion 314, and which continue to be governed by Opinion 314. Nor does Opinion 85-352 address the lawyer's duties and responsibilities in tax litigation.

\* \* \*

*"Good Faith" as an Objective Standard*

The Opinion restates relevant passages of applicable guidelines to the effect that the lawyer, in advising a client in the course of preparation of the client's tax return, may advise the statement of positions most favorable to the client if the lawyer has a good faith belief that those provisions are warranted in existing law, or can be supported by a good faith argument for an extension, modification, or reversal of existing law. It states expressly that a lawyer can have a good faith belief even if the lawyer believes the client's position probably will not prevail.

The Opinion does not, however, leave "good faith" open to subjective interpretation. It instead applies an objective standard to the determination of whether good faith is present. The Opinion explains:

"However, good faith requires that there be some realistic possibility of success if the matter is litigated."

The result is an objective standard which can be enforced. A lawyer cannot advise taking a tax return position unless there is a realistic possibility of success, if litigated. * * *

*Role of the Audit Lottery*

The standard adopted by Opinion 85-352 does not permit taking into account the likelihood of audit or detection in determining whether the ethical standard is met. Whether the return will be audited or not is simply of no consequence to the application of the new standard. The determination of whether there is a realistic possibility of success is made without regard to the reality of the audit lottery, and assumes that the issue is in court and to be decided.

*Comparison of "Some Realistic Possibility of Success If Litigated" With "Reasonable Basis"*

Doubtless there were some tax practitioners who intended "reasonable basis" to set a relatively high standard of tax reporting. Some have continued to apply such a standard. To more, however, if not most tax practitioners, the ethical standard set by "reasonable basis" had become a low one. To many it had come to permit any colorable claim to be put forth; to permit almost any words that could be strung together to be used to support a tax return position. Such a standard has now been rejected by the ABA Committee. The Opinion expressly states that to the extent "reasonable basis" had been construed to support the use of any colorable claim on a tax return or to justify exploitation of the lottery of the tax return audit selection process, the construction was an improper interpretation and application of what was meant by "reasonable basis."

More important to differentiating between "reasonable basis" and the standard articulated by Opinion 85-352 is that the new standard requires not only that there be some possibility of success, if litigated, rather than merely a construction that can be argued or that seems reasonable, but also that there be more than just any possibility of success. The possibility of success, if litigated, must be "realistic." A possibility of success cannot be "realistic" if it is only theoretical or impractable. This clearly implies that there must be a substantial possibility of success, which when taken together with the assumption that the matter will be litigated, measurably elevates what had come to be widely accepted as the minimum ethical standard.

A position having only a 5% or 10% likelihood of success, if litigated, should not meet the new standard. A position having a likelihood of success closely approaching one-third should meet the standard. * * *

*If the Position Falls Below the Standard*

If the standard is not met, the position may be advanced by payment of the tax and claim for refund, which necessarily sets forth in detail each ground upon which a refund is claimed. A position may be advanced in litigation if it is not frivolous. The lawyer may bring a proceeding, and assert an issue therein, if there is a basis for doing so that is not frivolous, which includes a good faith argument for an extension, modification, or reversal of existing law. In such a context good faith does not require that there be a possibility of success that is "realistic." Model Rule 3.1; DR 7-102(A)(2).

If the client determines to proceed to assert a position in a tax return that is not supported by a realistic possibility of success if litigated, the lawyer must withdraw from the engagement, at least to the extent it involves advice as to the position to be taken on the return, subject to usual rules governing withdrawal. Model Rule 1.16(a) provides that a lawyer shall not represent a client, or having done so shall withdraw from the representation of the client, if "the representation will result in violation of the Rules of Professional Conduct or other law. . . ." To avoid conflict with obligations imposed upon tax return preparers, the lawyer should first determine whether the position meets the ethical standard. If not, the lawyer must counsel the taxpayer not to assert the position, and, unless this advice is accepted by the client, the lawyer may not prepare the return, and pursuant to Rule 1.16(a) must withdraw from further representation involving advice as to the position taken on the return. Only if the position meets the standard may the lawyer prepare the return, sign it, and present it to the client.

* * *

*Tax Returns Are Not Adversarial Proceedings*

Opinion 85-352 makes the new ethical standard applicable to return preparation in all cases. Although the Opinion recognizes that the taking of aggressive positions on tax returns may be the first step in development of an adversarial relationship between the client and the Internal Revenue Service, the lawyer, nevertheless, may not advise the taking of such positions in disregard of the new ethical standard. * * *

The Opinion does not state that the general ethical guidelines governing advocacy in litigation are determinative, or suggest that tax returns are adversarial proceedings. To the contrary, a tax return initially serves a disclosure, reporting, and self-assessment function. It is the citizen's report to the government of his or her relevant activities for the year. The Opinion says that because some returns, particularly aggressive ones, may result in an adversary relationship, there is a place for consideration of the ethical considerations regarding advocacy. Thus, the Opinion blends the ethical guidelines governing advocacy with those applicable to advising, from which the new ethical standard is derived.

The Opinion recites that the ethical guidelines governing tax return positions are no different from those applicable to advising on civil matters generally. But the *standard* to be derived from the guidelines necessarily depends on the facts and circumstances relevant to the particular application of the guidelines. Good faith is the touchstone for derivation of the standard under both the Model Rules and the Model Code. Good faith, though to be employed and interpreted objectively, may produce different outcomes in different settings. Good faith in advising a client not to perform a contract, for example, if based upon conduct of the other party, may be quite different from good faith in advising that a position be taken on a tax return. In the context of a tax return, good faith requires an objective determination that there is "some realistic possibility of success, if litigated."

* * *

## Questions and Comments:

1. Does the Special Task Force report clarify the realistic possibility of success standard?

2. Re-examine ABA Formal Opinion 85-352. Does the conclusion reached by the Special Task Force necessarily come from the Opinion? Could you craft a different standard than that advocated by the Special Task Force?

3. The Special Task Force Report recognizes that Opinion 85-352 provides that "the ethical guidelines governing tax return positions are no different from those applicable to advising on civil matters generally." It then claims, however, that the *standard* to be derived depends on the facts and circumstances. Can and should good faith mean different things depending on the situation? Can I proceed with a tort suit with a 20% chance of success, but not take a return position with the same chance of success? Why or why not?

4. The Special Task Force Report indicates that "The Report has not been reviewed by the ABA Standing Committee on Ethics and Professional Responsibility, and its publication does not in any way imply approval by the Standing Committee." If the report has not been reviewed by the ABA Standing Committee on Ethics and Professional Responsibility, what is the weight of the report?

5. The Special Task Force Report is clear and provides far more guidance to tax practitioners than the ABA Formal Opinion. Why wasn't similar language included in the ABA Formal Opinion?

6. The ABA Section of Taxation originally proposed a stricter version of the ethics rule to the ABA. The Tax Section proposed that attorneys not advise taxpayers to take a position unless it was meritorious.[8] Does the difference between "meritorious" and "some realistic possibility of success" make any difference? What would the difference be between a "meritorious claim" and one that had "some realistic possibility of success"?

7. If you were trying to argue that an attorney could not advise a client to take a position unless it was "meritorious," how would you

---

[8] See ABA Section of Taxation Proposed Revision to Formal Opinion 314, May 21, 1984, reprinted in Wolfman and Holden, Ethical Problems in Federal Tax Practice 71-73 (2d ed. 1985).

craft the argument under the Model Rules?    See Model Rules 1.16(b)(2), (4), 2.1, 3.1, 3.3(a)(3), 3.3(b).

8. The proposal by the Tax Section also provided that a tax return is not a submission in an adversary proceeding. Is a tax return the first step in an adversarial proceeding? If so, is a filing with the Federal Election Commission or the Securities and Exchange Commission also the first step in an adversarial proceeding? For background on the formation of Formal Opinion 85-352 see Theodore C. Faulk, *Tax Ethics, Legal Ethics, and Real Ethics: A Critique of ABA Formal Opinion 85-352*, 39 Tax. Law 643 (1986).

9. What if an attorney advises his client that she could avoid penalties by disclosing the position on her return? Can an attorney advise a taxpayer to take a position that lacks a realistic possibility of success as long as the position is disclosed to the IRS?

10. What would the policy arguments be in favor of allowing a lawyer to advise a taxpayer to take a position that lacks a realistic possibility of success as long as there is adequate disclosure? Why would we not want lawyers to give such advice even with disclosure?

11. The Tax Section appears to have modified its advice on this issue. The Report of the Special Task Force indicates that an attorney cannot advise a taxpayer to take a position that lacks a realistic possibility of success even if the position is disclosed. (The Report states "the new standard cannot be met by disclosure or 'flagging' of the position in the return.") In a later statement, however, the Tax Section, Committee of Standards of Tax Practice, stated that "[g]iven the legislative and regulatory refinements to the accuracy-related penalty since the issuance of ABA Opinion 85-352, we believe that it may fairly be read to permit a lawyer to advise a position not meeting the realistic possibility standard as long as that position is adequately disclosed on the return and satisfies the not frivolous standard * * *." See Standards of Tax Practice Statement 2000-1.

## 2.     TREASURY AND IRS PRONOUNCEMENTS

Congress provides the U.S. Department of Treasury with the authority to regulate the practice of representatives before its various entities, including the IRS. These requirements are contained in regulations promulgated by Treasury (see 31 C.F.R.

§ 10). The IRS publishes these rules in something referred to as Circular 230. So in this book, and in tax practice, you will likely see the rules by reference to Circular 230 or by reference to Treasury Regulations. Both references are to the same rules that provide guidance for tax practitioners who practice before the IRS.

The Treasury only has the authority to regulate attorneys that practice before the IRS, so an important question is, what does it mean to practice before the IRS? Does advising a taxpayer on the tax ramifications of a transaction count? The IRS has taken a fairly liberal position regarding the definition of "practice before the IRS."

Circular 230 defines it as "all matters connected with a presentation to the Internal Revenue Service . . . relating to a taxpayer's rights, privileges, or liabilities. . . " This includes "preparing and filing documents, corresponding and communicating with the Internal Revenue Service, rendering written advice with respect to any entity, transaction, plan or arrangement. . . ."

Some rules in Circular 230 apply generally to all individuals who practice before the IRS, and some rules are limited to specific circumstances.

The Code provides the Treasury with the authority to impose monetary penalties on both the individual who violates Circular 230 and on the firm where he works. The monetary amount may be up to the amount received by the practitioner or the firm "derived from the conduct giving rise to the penalty." Circular 230, § 10.50. The IRS may also censure, suspend, or reprimand a practitioner for violation of the rules.

Circular 230 also provides special rules and obligations on lawyers, and others, who advise taxpayers on taking positions on a tax return. This section discusses the IRS rules in relation to advising a client on a return position.

These rules are statutory ethical responsibilities. In the previous section, we discussed the responsibilities of tax lawyers based on the rules of professional conduct that apply to lawyers and the preceding discussion involved the ABA's and the Tax Section of the ABA's views regarding the ethical obligations of tax lawyer's based on the ABA model rules. As we will see, the Executive Branch and Congress also have the ability to regulate the obligations of tax lawyers. Circular 230's requirements may be influenced by the model rules, but are a separate, and very important, means of enforcing norms in tax practice.

One of the most important set of rules in Circular 230 are the standards lawyers, accountants, and preparers must follow when advising a taxpayer to take a position on their return.  The IRS originally followed the realistic possibility of success standard.  This was the standard used in the penalty provisions of the code (discussed in subsection C) and by the ABA.  The IRS quantified what the realistic possibility of success standard meant in percentage terms and determined that a lawyer must have a 1/3 chance of success on the merits to meet the standard.

As of the writing of this book, Congress modified the standard under the penalty provisions to require a practitioner have substantial authority to avoid penalty before recommending a position on a return.  The substantial authority standard is a standard higher than the realistic possibility of success standard and lower than the MLTN standard.  It is generally believed that a practitioner must have around a 40% chance of success on the merits to satisfy the substantial authority standard.

After the statutory change to the penalty provision, the IRS then issued a new version of Circular 230 and reserved the section that previously defined the realistic possibility of success standard, for new regulations (We assume this will be where the Service adopts a substantial authority requirement instead of a realistic possibility of success standard).  The current standard under Circular 230 is that a practitioner may not advise a client to take a position unless the position is not frivolous.  Lawyers, however, are still bound to a higher standard by ethical rules and by the statutory penalty provisions discussed in subsection C.

Because we believe there is a very strong likelihood that new guidance will be issued adopting the substantial authority standard in much the same way the previous standard was adopted, we have reproduced the old provision below.  Read it substituting "substantial authority" for "realistic possibility of success."  The Circular 230 definition of realistic possibility of success also gives us some guidance on the how such a standard might be interpreted in other context.

# IRS CIRCULAR 230 (31 C.F.R. §§10.00-10.93)
Standards for advising with respect to tax return
positions and for preparing or signing returns.
31. C.F.R. § 10.34

(a) Realistic possibility standard. A practitioner may not sign a tax return as a preparer if the practitioner determines that the tax return contains a position that does not have a realistic possibility of being sustained on its merits (the realistic possibility standard) unless the position is not frivolous and is adequately disclosed to the Internal Revenue Service. A practitioner may not advise a client to take a position on a tax return, or prepare the portion of a tax return on which a position is taken, unless—

(1) The practitioner determines that the position satisfies the realistic possibility standard; or

(2) The position is not frivolous and the practitioner advises the client of any opportunity to avoid the accuracy-related penalty in I.R.C. § 6662 by adequately disclosing the position and of the requirements for adequate disclosure.

(b) Advising clients on potential penalties. A practitioner advising a client to take a position on a tax return, or preparing or signing a tax return as a preparer, must inform the client of the penalties reasonably likely to apply to the client with respect to the position advised, prepared, or reported. The practitioner also must inform the client of any opportunity to avoid any such penalty by disclosure, if relevant, and of the requirements for adequate disclosure. * * *

(c) Relying on information furnished by clients. A practitioner advising a client to take a position on a tax return, or preparing or signing a tax return as a preparer, generally may rely in good faith without verification upon information furnished by the client. The practitioner may not, however, ignore the implications of information furnished to, or actually known by, the practitioner, and must make reasonable inquiries if the information as furnished appears to be incorrect, inconsistent with an important fact or another factual assumption, or incomplete.

(d) Definitions. For purposes of this section—

(1) Realistic possibility. A position is considered to have a realistic possibility of being sustained on its merits if a reasonable and well informed analysis of the law and the facts by a person knowledgeable in the tax law would lead such a person to conclude that the position has approximately a one in three, or greater, likelihood of being sustained on its merits. The authorities described in I.R.C. 6662, or any successor provision, of the substantial understatement penalty regulations may be taken into account for purposes of this analysis. The possibility that a tax return will not be audited, that an issue will not be raised on audit, or that an issue will be settled may not be taken into account.

## Questions and Comments:

1. The former version of Circular 230 appears to provide more clarity regarding the realistic possibility of success standard than the ABA opinions. The ABA Tax Section Task Force Report indicates that a 33% chance of success would satisfy the standard and a 5% to 10% chance likely would not. Former Circular 230 picks up on the idea of a percentage standard and sets it at 33%. Does this solve the problem?

2. How do attorneys determine if they meet a standard? How do they know if there is a 33% or 40% chance of success? Is it an objective or subjective standard?

3. Why should an attorney advise a taxpayer to take a position that the attorney believes will more likely fail than succeed? Both the realistic possibility of success standard and the substantial authority standard allow an attorney to advise on a position which the attorney believes there is less than a 50% chance of success on the merits.

4. Why is a lawyer prohibited from taking the chance of an audit into account when giving her advice? Can the lawyer tell the client that there is very little chance of audit?

## 3. CODE PROVISION

### (a) Section 6694

Section 6694 provides for a penalty for the preparer of a return when there is an understatement on a taxpayer's return. Specifically, if there is an understatement of liability on any return or claim for refund, and the understatement is due to a position on the return for which there was not substantial authority, the preparer must pay a $1,000 penalty. The preparer is only subject to the penalty if he knew or had reason to know the taxpayer took such a position, and the item was not properly disclosed on the return.

The preparer is subject to a $5,000 penalty under § 6694(b) if the understatement was due to willful or reckless conduct, or to an intentional disregard of rules or regulations. Under the current regulations, the preparer will not be subject to the penalty if the position is disclosed and there is a reasonable basis for the position.[9] In addition, when a position is contrary to a revenue ruling or notice, the position will not be reckless or an intentional disregard of the rules if there is substantial authority for the position.[10]

Section 6694 has been amended twice between 2007-2008 and the regulations have not kept pace with these changes. In 2007, Congress changed the standard under § 6694 from the realistic possibility of success standard to the more-likely-than-not (MLTN) standard. Therefore between 2007 and 2008, if there was a substantial understatement of tax, practitioners would be subject to the penalty under § 6694 unless the practitioner reasonably believed that the position would more-likely-than-not succeed. Practitioners complained about this change on many grounds, but principally because taxpayers had a different and slightly lower standard and this difference created a possible conflict between the preparer and the taxpayer (the taxpayer would have an incentive to be more aggressive than the preparer). Congress responded in 2008 by lowering the standard for preparers from the more-likely-than-not (MLTN) standard to the substantial authority standard. The taxpayers and preparers now both face a penalty if there is not

---

[9] Treas. Reg. § 1.6694-3.

[10] The regulations in effect in 2008 provide that a position will not be reckless or an intentional disregard of the rules if the position has a realistic possibility of success. In light of the change in § 6694 to the substantial authority standard, it is likely that such a standard will be required even if the regulations are not modified.

substantial authority for a position (and the position leads to an understatement of tax).

The substantial authority standard is a standard higher than the realistic possibility of success standard and lower than the MLTN standard. It is generally believed that a practitioner must have around a 40% chance of success on the merits to satisfy the substantial authority standard.

Notice that a practitioner is not subject to the penalty if the item was properly disclosed by the taxpayer and there is reasonable basis for the position. Because it is the disclosure by the taxpayer that protects the preparer, we need to examine case law involving the validity of taxpayer disclosure. These cases appear in the context of penalties imposed on taxpayers under old § 6661 [now § 6662]. Section 6662 provides a penalty when there is an understatement of tax on a return and the taxpayer did not have substantial authority for the position, or did not disclose the position and have a reasonable basis.

## (b) Disclosure

# DOLPHUS E. & MARY J. SCHIRMER
## v.
# COMMISSIONER OF INTERNAL REVENUE
### 89 T.C. 277 (1987)

FAY, JUDGE:
* * *

After concessions, the issues are (1) whether petitioners' activity with respect to a farm is an activity engaged in for profit, [and] (2) whether petitioner Dolphus E. Schirmer is liable for the addition to tax under § 6661(a) [now § 6662]. * * *[11]

FINDINGS OF FACT

[This case involves a farm activity and whether the activity was conducted for profit. Taxpayers owned 554 acres of land. They did not live on the farm, nor did the keep separate books or checking accounts for the farm. Taxpayers reported losses from farm activity of approximately $10,000 a year for the years 1978-1983. These

---

[11] Although both taxpayers were petitioners in this case, the § 6661(a) issue involved only Dolphus Schirmer.

losses were mainly attributable to depreciation deductions on two buildings located on the farm. Taxpayers only income from the farm activity was proceeds from the sale of some timber, and proceeds from a lawsuit alleging that another farmer improperly grazed cattle on their property without permission. The Tax Court determined that the activity was not engaged in for profit.] * * *

We now turn to the addition to tax determined by respondent under § 6661(a) [now § 6662]. Section 6661(a) imposes an addition to tax if there is a substantial understatement of income tax. * * * Where an item is not attributable to a tax shelter, the understatement may be reduced by such item, and the addition to tax accordingly reduced if the taxpayer's treatment of the item was based on substantial authority, § 6661(a)(2)(B)(i), or if the taxpayer had adequately disclosed on the return or in a statement attached to the return the relevant facts affecting such item's tax treatment, § 6661(b)(2)(B)(ii) [now § 6662(d)(2)(B)(ii)].

* * *

Petitioner also argues that he adequately disclosed the relevant facts affecting the treatment of the deductions relating to his farming activity. Petitioner argues that by completing Schedule F for farm income and expenses and Form 4562 for depreciation and amortization, he had made adequate disclosure under § 6661(b)(2)(B)(ii). Petitioner did not make specific references to § 6661 on his returns.

The statute does not set forth what constitutes 'adequate disclosure' of 'relevant facts' Under generally applicable regulatory authority, respondent may prescribe the form of such disclosure. H. Rept. 97-760 (Conf.) at 575-576 (1982), 1982-2 C.B. 600, 650. Respondent's Regulations provide two types of disclosure under § 6661(b)(2)(B)(ii): disclosure in statements attached to the return, § 1.6661-4(b), Income Tax Regs., and disclosure on the return, § 1.6661-4(c), Income Tax Regs. Petitioner has not attached a statement to his return; therefore, § 1.6661-4(b), Income Tax Regs., is not applicable here.

Section 1.6661-4(c), Income Tax Regs., provides that respondent may by revenue procedure prescribe the circumstances in which information provided on the return will be adequate disclosure for § 6661. Consistent therewith, respondent issued [revenue procedures]. These Revenue Procedures list categories of controversies and forms that constitute sufficient disclosure to each controversy. They do not list Schedule F or Form 4562 for the controversy at issue here. Accordingly, petitioner has not satisfied the requirements of the relevant Revenue Procedures issued pursuant to § 1.6661- 4(c), Income Tax Regs. Further, petitioner did not make specific reference to § 6661 on his returns.

Our inquiry does not end here, however. Where a taxpayer fails to comply with the Revenue Procedures issued in accordance with § 1.6661-4(c), Income Tax Regs., and fails to make specific reference to § 6661, the requirements of adequate disclosure on the return can nonetheless be satisfied by providing on the return sufficient information to enable respondent to identify the potential controversy involved. S. Rep. 97-494 at 274 (1982). In this regard, petitioner merely listed on Schedule F and Form 4562 the amount of farm income and expenses and the depreciation and amortization he claimed. Such information, without more, was insufficient to enable respondent to identify the potential controversy involved here, that is, whether petitioner engaged in the activity for profit. We hold that petitioners have failed to adequately disclose the relevant facts relating to the farming activity deductions.* * *

NOTE:   Treasury Regulation § 1.6662-4(e),(f) now provides the rules for adequate disclosure. The regulation indicates that disclosure must be made on Form 8275 (disclosure statement), Form 8275-R (disclosure when position contrary to regulation) or on the return in accordance with Revenue Procedures issued by the Commissioner.

## Questions and Comments:

1. The court in *Schirmer* notes that disclosure may in some cases be made on the actual income tax return. The IRS periodically issues a Revenue Procedure indicating the disclosures that may properly be made on an income tax return. The most recent such Revenue Procedure is Revenue Procedure 2008-14. Some examples of items that Taxpayers may disclose on their returns include:
1) medical expenses, 2) taxes, 3) interest expenses and 4) moving expenses.

2. In Accardo v. Commissioner, 95 T.C. 484 (1990), another case considering "adequate disclosure" in the context of a penalty for a substantial underpayment of taxes, the court determined that a mere declaration of a deduction falls short of the disclosure of relevant facts required. Accardo stated on his return that the

deduction at issue was for "Legal fees re conversation [sic] of property held for production of income." In rejecting the notion that this was sufficient disclosure, the court also noted that "[p]articularly where taxpayer lacked substantial authority for his position and where he appeared to think that his deduction presented novel legal issues, the mere declaration of a deduction does not entitle taxpayer to a reduced penalty." *Id.* at 453.

3. In making the disclosure either on Forms 8275, 8275-R, or on the return, the basic requirement is that the disclosure provide the IRS with sufficient notice and information to recognize the tax problem at issue. *Schirmer* and other cases indicate that vague disclosure will not protect a taxpayer or a practitioner from penalties.

## 4. SUMMARY OF STANDARDS

This chapter discusses a range of standards that apply to tax professionals advising a taxpayer on a return position. The standards range from not-frivolous at the low end, to more likely than not on the high end. Various cases, rules and pronouncements have interpreted what each standard means. The following graphic provides a basic percentage *estimate* for each standard. The percentage requirements for the MLTN and realistic possibility of success standards have been set by statute or regulation. The other standards are gleaned from different sources.

| | |
|---|---|
| MLTN | Greater than 50% chance of success |
| Substantial authority | Approx. 40% chance of success |
| Realistic possibility | Above 33% chance of success |
| Reasonable basis | Between 10% to 20% |
| Nonfrivolous | Something above 0% chance and below 10% to 15% |

Throughout this chapter, we have provided an analysis of the different standards for tax preparers. What standard do you think should apply? Just between 2007 and 2008, three standards applied to tax preparers – the realistic possibility of success, substantial authority, and more-likely-than-not standard. In general, tax preparers argued that too high a standard would significantly increase the cost of tax preparation because tax lawyers would have to prepare tax opinions on a host of issues. Is this a sufficient justification for allowing tax attorneys to recommend a position when they believe there is a greater chance that they are wrong than that they are right?

## TAX ADVICE BEFORE THE RETURN: THE CASE FOR RAISING STANDARDS AND DENYING EVIDENTIARY PRIVILEGES
### 25 Va. Tax Rev. 583 (2006)
### Linda M. Beale[*]

* * *

III. Policy Solutions

My thesis is that professionalism as it is currently practiced cannot adequately counter the pressures that encourage tax advisors' aggressive interpretations. Tax returns are treated confidentially, and tax opinions written in support of structured transactions are generally privileged and accessible only to the client and her attorney. Even the work product doctrine may reach back to protect pre-adversarial tax planning advice, due to the statutory requirement that tax advice assess possibility of success on the merits, which implies an ultimate judicial review. Because of the Service's limited enforcement resources, the audit lottery remains a manageable risk for many sophisticated taxpayers. As a result, numerous transactions that the government would consider abusive likely remain obscured within a complex layer of business transactions and are never exposed to litigation. Even if litigated, privilege may protect crucial information about participants' business purposes from the Service. Something further is necessary to discourage literalist interpretations as tax-avoidance mechanisms and the no-holds-barred tax minimization norm.

* * *

---

[*] Reprinted with permission. © University of Virginia Tax Review (2006).

## A. Institute a More Likely Than Not Standard

Strengthening the standard for taking positions on a return is particularly appropriate in the context of the recent revisions to the statutory penalty provisions and Circular 230. Those amendments reflect a growing concern in Congress and at Treasury about tax-motivated transactions that disregard the underlying purpose of statutory and regulatory provisions. There is a tension between strengthening standards and stiffening penalties for reportable transactions and retaining a lower standard in other contexts, even for SPTs [significant purpose transactions].[12] When combined with the possibility of winning the audit lottery, the reasonable possibility standard may encourage practitioners and taxpayers to incorrectly treat an aggressive transaction that should be subject to the higher "shelter" standard as an ordinary transaction. It would be reasonable to establish a standard for taxpayers and advisors that requires them to report and advise, respectively, only positions that they believe in good faith more likely than not to reflect proper application of the tax laws based on substantial authority, whether in the context of a super-aggressive tax transaction or one which is borderline or even ordinary.

## 1. Rationale for Heightened Standard

The first and most important supporting rationale is the effect the higher standard should have on tax compliance norms. If tax lawyers' duty to uphold the law is comparable to their duty towards their clients, then they should be permitted to advise a position at the pre-return stage only if they believe the position is correct and will prevail if litigated. This approach forces practitioners to adopt coherence-reinforcing interpretations rather than literalist interpretations that break the connection between language and underlying purpose. Tax practitioners' own statements support this argument that raising standards changes norms: they complain that the 2004 Jobs Act penalty provisions and Circular 230 opinion requirements require a radical shift in perspective, especially if significant purpose transactions are interpreted to encompass a broad range of tax planning advice.

---

[12] A significant purpose transaction is one in which a significant purpose of the transaction is to avoid tax. We will discuss the rules regarding these transactions in the chapter on tax shelters. See Cir. 230, § 10.35.

The current standard still results in a mixed message, even for significant purpose transactions. Although taxpayer penalty protection for many SPTs and other "shelter" transactions is only available under more exacting conditions, advisors' ability to provide oral advice generally, and written opinions at a level lower than MLTN (even though they cannot be relied upon for penalty protection in respect of many significant-purpose transactions), invites exploitation of loopholes. So long as advisors can advise taxpayers to take return positions that they do not expect to prevail on the merits, taxpayers will continue to adopt aggressive positions that might succeed depending on the luck of the draw in the audit lottery and forum selection process.

In contrast, adoption of a MLTN standard supported by substantial authority that is applicable to taxpayers and advisors in respect of all tax positions reported on a return would mandate a new approach to tax planning that appropriately encourages taxpayers and advisors to find the most likely correct answer. Aggressive loophole exploitation relying solely on literalist interpretations should be curtailed, as those applications would lack authority other than the bare language of the purportedly applicable Code provisions.

------

The ABA Tax Section, however, opposed the use of the MLTN standard in § 6694, and sent the following to Congress:

## Legislative Changes Impacting Standards for Imposition of Penalties[*]
ABA Tax Section
November 2007

\* \* \*

A. The Recent Amendment to Section 6694 Is Difficult to Apply and Will Increase Burdens on Taxpayers, Return Preparers and the Service.

---

[*] "Legislative Changes Impacting Standards for Imposition of Penalties," published by the American Bar Association Section of Taxation, 2007. Copyright © 2007 by the American Bar Association. Reprinted with permission. All rights reserved. This information or any or portion thereof may not be copied or disseminated in any form or by any means or stored in an electronic database or retrieval system without the express written consent of the American Bar Association.

The tax law is exceedingly complex and the correct interpretation of a position on a tax return is often ambiguous and uncertain. As a result, the law traditionally did not penalize taxpayers and return preparers for taking a good faith reasonable position on a tax return even when they were not sure that the position was correct. * * *

Under current law, a taxpayer will be subject to a penalty on any substantial understatement arising from a position attributable to a "tax shelter" unless there is both substantial authority for the position and the taxpayer reasonably believed that the position was more likely than not proper. A tax shelter is defined broadly to include any entity, plan or arrangement that has a significant purpose of avoiding (*i.e.*, reducing) taxes.

We believe that the reasonable belief/more likely than not standard is an appropriate standard to be applied to tax-motivated transactions because such transactions deserve more scrutiny and justify higher transaction costs. However, the majority of positions asserted on tax returns for which the law is unclear arise from transactions that are not tax-motivated. Accordingly, we believe the benefits to be derived from raising the penalty standard with respect to regular non-tax shelter transactions do not outweigh the resulting costs and problems in the administration of the tax system.

1.  The New Standard Is Difficult to Apply

Because the tax law is complex and ambiguous, it is often difficult to quantify the likelihood of success on the merits of a particular position, particularly when factual issues are involved. This is one of the reasons why Congress originally chose "substantial authority" as the applicable taxpayer penalty standard in section 6662(d). The substantial authority standard is a reasonably high standard of conduct and recognizes that many *bona fide* tax return positions do not benefit from settled law. In contrast, the more likely than not standard is a very specific standard that requires a positive determination regarding the likelihood of success of return positions. It will not always be possible to make such precise determinations in situations involving complicated legal and factual issues. Even relatively simple determinations, such as whether an expenditure should be expensed or capitalized, may not be susceptible to a precise quantification regarding the likelihood of success.

The difficulty in determining whether a return position satisfies the more likely than not standard is exacerbated by the regular amendment of the Code, and the lack of regulations providing clear guidance to taxpayers on the operation of many complex rules. When the statute is ambiguous, and the Treasury Department has not filled in the gaps through regulations or other interpretive rules, taxpayers and return preparers are left to reason their way to an appropriate return position. Likewise, the Service is likely to have significant difficulty applying a more likely than not standard to situations where the law is not completely clear. When a statute is clear on its face, these determinations obviously can be made much more easily than where the taxpayer, return preparer, or revenue agent instead is faced with the difficult task of sorting through varying shades of gray.

Further, the more likely than not standard is the same standard that the Service and courts use in determining whether a tax return position should be upheld. When the standard for imposition of a penalty is the same as the standard used to determine whether a position is, in fact, correct, there will be almost a presumption, imposed with the benefit of hindsight, that any position resulting in an understatement should also be subject to a penalty. Given the complexity and ambiguity of the tax law, it is not appropriate to presume that taxpayers and return preparers should be subject to a penalty simply because the taxpayer's or preparer's interpretation of those complex or ambiguous rules turns out not to be upheld by the Service (or a court).

2. The New Standard Will Increase the Cost of Tax Return Preparation

By requiring a positive determination regarding the accuracy of a return position, the new standard will require a significant amount of research and diligence to ensure compliance with the law. More taxpayers likely will be required to hire a professional return preparer to help them review their return positions. Further, the only way taxpayers can avoid a penalty for a return position that ultimately is not upheld by the Service (or a court) is to prove that they reasonably believed that the position was correct. The best way for taxpayers to prove that they believed that a return position was correct is to hire and rely on a return preparer to make that determination for them. Indeed, hiring a tax return preparer will provide almost automatic insurance against a penalty in cases were there is an understatement on a tax return.

As a result, we believe the new standard will cause more taxpayers to hire tax return preparers and return preparers will spend more time analyzing the positions taken on the returns. * * * This will dramatically increase the cost of return preparation for taxpayers. * * *

3.   The New Standard Will Result In Over-Disclosures

Under prior law, taxpayers and return preparers evaluating a non-tax shelter item would consider the objective strength of the return position and evaluate whether penalties were likely if the position was disallowed. In light of the recent amendment to section 6694, there will be close to a presumption that penalties will be imposed in every case in which a return position is disallowed by the Service or a court. This means that return preparers likely will err on the side of attaching a Form 8275 disclosure statement to every return they prepare that contains a position that potentially could be disallowed. We are concerned that such over disclosure will result in the Service being flooded with so many disclosure statements that the statements will become practically meaningless.

## Questions and Comments:

1. You have learned a lot about standards for tax preparers. What do you think the proper standard should be?

2. Under the MLTN standard, a preparer is not subject to a penalty if the position is disclosed.  What is the problem with requiring a lawyer to believe he is more likely right than wrong when preparing a return?

## Problem 1.1

Your client invested in solar panels for his business expecting that the equipment would be depreciable over a 2-year period under a new depreciation schedule designed to increase the use of alternative energy sources.  The next year, Congress decides the solar energy is not a realistic option and passes statutory language that says that solar panels are subject to a 10-year depreciation schedule.   The language also clearly indicates that it applies to property already placed in service. You believe that the change is grossly unfair to your client. The client wants to depreciate the asset over 2-years.  Do you have a realistic possibility of success? Do you have substantial authority?

## Problem 1.2

Your client invests in residential real estate (he rents houses to students). Congress passes a statute that says that real estate held for rental to others is not entitled to a depreciation deduction. The Committee Report, however, indicates that the provision does not apply to residential real estate rented to others and that residential real estate rented to others is still entitled to a depreciation deduction. You decide to advise the client that he can rely on the language in the Committee Report. Have you done anything wrong?

## Problem 1.3

Your client rents residential real estate to students. Since students love hot tubs, he puts a hot tub on the deck of every apartment. The client wants to depreciate the hot tub over 5 years. The hot tub, however, may be part of the real estate and thus subject to depreciation over 27.5 years. When you research the subject, you find a case in state court dealing with this exact issue for state income tax purposes. It indicates that the hot tub is separate from the real estate and can be depreciated over 5 years. You go to the senior partner and indicate that the position has a realistic possibility of success. Do you get a raise or more time in the library?

## Problem 1.4

Section 527 of the Code defines "exempt function" as the function of "influencing or attempting to influence . . . the nomination [or] election . . . of any individual to any Federal . . . office . . . ." Your client is an issue organization that opposes genetically modified food. Your client does not want to be classified as a 527 organization, so it wants to avoid engaging in exempt function activities. An election is coming up and the organization wants to run a series of negative ads against candidates that support genetically modified foods. The ads say "genetically modified foods are bad for you. Senator Jones supports genetically modified foods. Call Senator Jones and tell him what you think."

You are researching whether you can meet the realistic possibility of success standard in arguing that your client is not engaged in exempt function activities. You find similar language in the Federal Election Campaign Act, which has been interpreted favorably towards your position. For purposes of that act, "influencing an election" usually requires the use of specific "magic words," like vote for, or vote against the candidate. Under this standard, your client is not engaged in "influencing or attempting to influence."

Is this research sufficient to establish that you have a realistic possibility of success? Do you have substantial authority for your position?

## Scenario 1.1

John is a very smart and able tax lawyer. He never litigates before the IRS and never prepares or signs tax returns. He does, however, advise taxpayers on a regular basis on how to set up their affairs to avoid tax.

One of John's specialties is advising same-sex and non-married partners on their tax returns. He encourages them to set up business arrangements to mimic the benefits of marriage. For couples with one wealthy and one not-so-wealthy partner, John creates a small business and has the business hire the not-so-wealthy partner at a very high rate. This allows the wealthy partner to transfer some income to the not-so-wealthy partner, thus avoiding some potential gift tax problems.

John notes that the IRS almost never questions these arrangements. John recognizes that his chances of winning the case if it goes to court are very low. He believes, however, that his position can be justified on the merits, and on moral grounds and that the position is not frivolous.

Has John violated either his ethical obligations under the ABA rules, or the rules set out in Circular 230?

## Scenario 1.2

Peter was the sole proprietor of an antique store that carried a wide array of merchandise. Lower-cost merchandise turned over on a regular basis. For example, a medium priced baseball card, magazine, or coin would probably sit on the shelf for a month or two. Peter included these items on his tax return as ordinary income and paid tax at his ordinary income rate of 35%.

More expensive merchandise would often not sell for a year or two. For example, Peter purchased a painting for $1,000. Two years later, he sold the painting for $3,000. Because the painting was a collectable, Peter claimed the painting as a long-term capital gain subject to the special 28% capital gains rate for collectables. Peter disclosed on his return that he was selling a collectable and indicated it was a painting.

Peter also sold a beautiful dinning room table. The table took up room in his store for over a year, but it was worth it. He bought the table for $50 and sold it for $2,000. This did not meet the definition of collectable under the Code, so Peter reported this item as long-term capital gains and paid tax on the gain at the 15% long-term capital gains rate. Peter disclosed the sale of the table on his return.

Lawyer regularly prepared the return for Peter's antique business. He knew that Peter did not regularly invest in art and noticed that Peter had sold a significant number of items for which he claimed capital treatment. Lawyer was told that Peter sold a painting and a table that he held for over a year. Lawyer then signed the return.

The IRS Office of Professional Responsibility is investigating Peter's lawyer. Did Peter's lawyer violate either the ABA Model Rules or Circular 230?

## Scenario 1.3

John, a farmer and current client, comes to Lawyer for advice. Lawyer has been John's tax attorney and has prepared his returns for the last 30 years. John is tired of farming and wants to retire. He wants to lease the farm to his son, Max. Max is an experienced farmer and John is confident that Max can keep the farm profitable. The bank, however, is less sure.

Max needs a business loan in order to have the revolving credit necessary to deal with the cash flow swings that naturally occur in farming. John has agreed to sign as guarantor on the loan up to $300,000. The loan was secured by personal property related to the farm including farm equipment, crops, and livestock. The farm itself was owned by John and was not collateral on the loan.

Lawyer indicates that there are no real tax consequences to the arrangement except that John will owe tax on the rental income he receives from his son. Lawyer claims that Max will not have income due to the guarantee because nothing has been expended on his behalf. John leaves lawyer's office happy and goes forward with the deal.

Four years later John is in Lawyer's office once again. Due to severe hardships, Max was unable to turn a profit in the farming activity, and has an outstanding loan balance of $150,000 that he cannot pay. John has paid the bank $150,000 as guarantor on the loan. Lawyer advises John that all is not lost and that he can take the loss as a non-business bad debt. Lawyer fills out John's return and claims a bad debt deduction for the amount paid on the guarantee. On his return John indicated that the bad debt deduction involved the guarantee of a farm loan.

The IRS audits John's return and questions the bad debt deduction. Treas. Reg. § 1.166-9(e) provides that a taxpayer's payment to discharge a debt as guarantor will only be considered a worthless debt if the taxpayer received reasonable consideration for entering into the agreement. The IRS seeks penalties against John and Lawyer.

Lawyer argues that the lease payment from Max was consideration for the guarantee of the loan. He further argues that he is not subject to the preparer penalty because there was substantial authority for the position. Finally, Lawyer argues that even if there was not substantial authority, he is not subject to penalty or discipline because the position was disclosed.

1. You work for the Office of Professional Responsibility. Should the office take any action against Lawyer?

2. If John and Lawyer contest the penalties in court, will the court likely uphold the IRS's determination that a penalty against John is appropriate under § 6662 and preparer penalties are proper against Lawyer under § 6694.

# B.  Who is a Preparer?

Section 6694 only applies to tax return preparers for position that are taken on a return. The definition of preparer is far broader than one might think, and the specter of sanctions, both economic and professional, make it very important for a lawyer to know whether she will be deemed a "preparer" for purposes of § 6694.

An income tax preparer is anyone who prepares a substantial portion of an income tax return, or a person who provides advice about "the existence, characterization or amount" of any entry on a return, if the entry constitutes a substantial portion of the return. (See § 7701(a)(36)).  Furthermore, in order to be a "preparer" the person preparing the return or providing advice must be compensated in some way for her services.  The regulations also make clear that providing tax-planning advice about a future activity does not make a tax advisor a preparer. (See Treas. Reg. § 301.7701-15(a)(2)).

There are two types of preparers – a signing preparer and a nonsigning preparer.  As is no surprise, a signing preparer is a tax return preparer who signs a tax return.  Current regulations define a nonsigning preparer as "any preparer who is not a signing preparer." Maybe recognizing that this is unhelpful, the regulations provide that "examples of nonsigning preparers are preparers who provide advice (written or oral) to a taxpayer or to a preparer who is not associated with the same firm as the preparer who provides the advice."

The Service recently issued new regulations to both § 6694 and § 7701 further defining the term preparer (see Treas. Reg § 1.6694-1 through § 1.6694-4) . Under the regulations, a nonsigning preparer is a preparer who did not sign the return, but "who prepares all or a substantial portion of a return or claim for refund." (see Treas. Reg. § 301.7701-15)  There is an exception for lawyers who primarily assist clients in planning a transaction.  If an attorney provides tax preparation advice that is only 5% of the total amount of time advising the taxpayer on a transaction, the attorney will not be considered a preparer.  There is an anti-abuse provision under Treasury Regulation § 301.7701-15(b)(2)(i) that indicates that time spent before a transaction takes place will be considered if: 1) position giving rise to the understatement is primarily attributable to that advice, the advice was  primarily given before to avoid preparer status, and advice given before was confirmed after the events for the purpose of preparing the return.

This provision is designed to allow attorneys to provide some preparation advice without having to become a preparer. Advice a lawyer gives prior to a transaction taking place does not make the lawyer a preparer under the Code. Thus a lawyer can give advice about a transaction before it happens without being considered a preparer. It is inefficient, however, for the attorney who knows the most about the transaction not to be involved in giving the return preparation advice. The regulations recognize this by providing that the attorney can provide 5% of the total time expended on the issue to aid in preparing the return and the attorney will not be considered a preparer.

The regulations also provide different obligations for signing and nonsigning preparers with regard to disclosure. In short, a nonsigning preparer must make the disclosures to the client so it is clear that the client knows of any problems. The non-signing preparer does not need to determine whether the taxpayer actually makes the disclosure on the return. A signing preparer, is subject to penalty unless the position is actually disclosed on the return. It does not matter that the attorney advised the taxpayer to disclose, and the taxpayer chose not to do so.

Finally, the regulations change the "one preparer rule." Under the current regulations, there could only be one preparer per firm. The proposed regulations modify that rule and provide that if there are individuals in the firm besides the signing preparer who were primarily responsible for the position that gave rise to the understatement, those attorneys could also be considered preparers.

# RANDALL S. GOULDING
## v.
## UNITED STATES
957 F.2d 1420 (1992)

RIPPLE, CIRCUIT JUDGE.

Randall Goulding was retained to act as the attorney for several limited partnerships. Mr. Goulding prepared the partnership returns and the Schedules K-1 for each partnership. Under Treasury Regulation § 301.7701-15(b)(3), the IRS deemed Mr. Goulding the preparer of the returns of the limited partners and assessed penalties against Mr. Goulding under 26 U.S.C. § 6694 for the negligent preparation of those returns. Mr. Goulding challenged the penalties in the district court, and the district court upheld them. For the reasons set forth in this opinion, we affirm the judgment of the district court.

I

BACKGROUND

* * * In 1979, Mr. Goulding took an active part in the formation and operation of three limited partnerships * * *.
Mr. Goulding helped set up the partnerships, helped draft offering memoranda and reviewed final drafts, acted as legal counsel, helped decide how to invest the partnerships' capital, and negotiated and drafted purchase agreements and other agreements for the partnerships. He also prepared the partnerships' informational tax returns, which he signed as "paid preparer." For acting as legal counsel, Mr. Goulding received compensation from the partnerships-$90,000 in 1979, $80,000 in 1980, and $86,250 in 1981.

[The court then explain the formation and purpose of each partnership]

For the years 1979 through 1981, Mr. Goulding prepared each partnership's 1065 form, reporting gains and losses, the Schedule K for each partnership, computing the partnership profits and losses, and Schedules K-1, allocating to each limited partner his share of the partnership's profits and losses. The general partner provided each limited partner with a copy of the Schedule K-1, and the limited partners (or their tax return preparers) used the numbers on it in filling out their returns. Mr. Goulding had no contact with the limited partners other than through his preparation of the partnership tax returns and the Schedules K-1. He gave them no advice regarding the use of the information on the Schedules K-1, and he did not prepare their individual returns.

In preparing the partnership tax returns, Mr. Goulding listed what the district court later found to be non-deductible start-up costs as expenses/losses and depreciated the entire purchase price of the technologies, including the contingent portion. In computing the basis of each limited partner in his partnership interest, Mr. Goulding used the debt guaranteed by each to increase his basis and thus increase the allowable deductions.

The IRS, asserting that Mr. Goulding was the preparer of the limited partners' returns, assessed penalties against him under § 6694(a), which penalizes tax preparers for understatements of tax on negligently prepared returns. Mr. Goulding paid fifteen percent of the penalty and brought suit for refund in the district court under 26 U.S.C. § 6694(c). In a bifurcated proceeding, the district court first determined that the Treasury regulation under which Mr. Goulding was deemed preparer of the limited partnerss' returns was valid and that, under the terms of that regulation, Mr. Goulding could properly be considered the preparer of those returns. In a second trial, the district court determined that Mr. Goulding's negligence had resulted in substantial understatements of tax liability on the returns of the limited partners and upheld the penalties assessed by the IRS.

## II

## ANALYSIS

Mr. Goulding challenges both the validity of the Regulation under which he was deemed the preparer of the partners' returns, and the district court's determination that he was negligent in preparing those returns.

* * *

### A. Statutory and Regulatory Scheme

### 1. Statute

Section 6694 of the Internal Revenue Code penalizes income tax return preparers for understatements of taxpayer's liability which result from negligent disregard of rules and regulations by the return preparer or from willful attempts by the return preparer to understate the tax due.  * * *  These provisions were enacted in response to abuses by tax return preparers. * * *

Along with the penalty provisions, the 1976 Act provided a statutory definition of "income tax return preparer." The definition was intended to limit application of the penalty provisions to professional and commercial preparers, and to exclude those preparing returns for employers, friends and relatives. Another purpose of the definition was to ensure that the person who makes the decisions and calculations involved in preparing a particular return will be considered the preparer of that return, even if that person "does not actually place the figures on the lines of the taxpayer's final tax return." H.R.Rep. No. 658, 94th Cong., 2d Sess. 275, reprinted in 1976 U.S.C.C.A.N. 3171. Thus, furnishing of advice can make one a preparer, while mechanical assistance in preparing the return does not.

2. Regulation

Pursuant to his statutory authority, see 26 U.S.C. § 7805, the Commissioner promulgated a regulation elucidating the definition of "income tax return preparer." This regulation, Treasury Regulation §1.301.7701-15, was adopted in 1977 and thus is a "substantially contemporaneous construction of the statute," which was passed in 1976. Subparagraph (b)(3) of the regulation defines the circumstances in which the preparer of one return may be deemed the preparer of another which directly reflects an entry (or entries) of the return actually prepared:

A preparer of a return is not considered a preparer of another return merely because an entry or entries reported on the return may affect an entry reported on the other return, unless the entry or entries reported on the prepared return are directly reflected on the other return and constitute a substantial portion of the other return.

The subparagraph gives the example of the preparer of a partnership return:

For example, the sole preparer of a partnership return of income or a small business corporation income tax return is considered a preparer of a partner's or a shareholder's return if the entry or entries on the partnership or small business corporation return reportable on the partner's or shareholder's return constitutes a substantial portion of the partner's or shareholder's return.

Both the regulation quoted above and the statutory definition of preparer state that a person is not the preparer of a return unless one is responsible for a "substantial portion" of it. Treasury Regulation 301.7701-15(b)(1) sets forth what constitutes substantial preparation:

(b) Substantial preparation.-(1) Only a person (or persons acting in concert) who prepares all or a substantial portion of a return or claim for refund shall be considered to be a preparer (or preparers) of the return or claim for refund.  A person who renders advice which is directly relevant to the determination of the existence, characterization, or amount of an entry on a return or claim for refund, will be regarded as having prepared that entry.  Whether a schedule, entry, or other portion of a return or claim for refund is a substantial portion is determined by comparing the length and complexity of, and the tax liability or refund involved in, that portion to the length and complexity of, and tax liability or refund involved in, the return or claim for refund as a whole.

\* \* \*

B. Application of Statutory and Regulatory Scheme to the Case

1. Contentions of the parties

Mr. Goulding challenges the validity of Treasury Regulation §301.7701-15(b)(3), in accordance with which he was deemed the preparer of the partners' returns and penalized for the understatements in them.  As the sole preparer of the partnership return, Mr. Goulding provided copies of the partnership K-1 forms to the individual partners, who then entered (or whose own return preparers then entered) a single number (a deduction) on their own tax returns.  Mr. Goulding argues that he cannot have "prepared" returns he never saw or touched, that he did not give advice to partners he never met or spoke with, and that in any case, he cannot be considered as having prepared a "substantial portion" of returns on which he is responsible for a single entry.  Mr. Goulding also argues that he was not "compensated" by the partners, as required by the statutory definition of preparer.

Mr. Goulding contends that in deeming him the preparer of the partner returns, the regulation is contrary to the statutory definition of preparer, to the Commissioner's own regulation defining "substantial portion," and to the intent of Congress as revealed in the legislative history.  Under the statutory definition of preparer, Mr. Goulding cannot be the preparer of these returns unless he prepared a "substantial portion" of the returns.  According to Mr. Goulding, the single entry on the partnership returns cannot constitute a "substantial portion."   He argues that in promulgating a regulation which transforms a single entry into a "substantial portion," the Commissioner has exceeded his authority.  * * *

As noted above, the regulation defining substantial preparation also directs that length and complexity be taken into consideration. Mr. Goulding maintains that the single entry on a partner's return which reflects information from the partnership return cannot be considered a substantial portion of the partner's return under the "length and complexity" standard.

* * *

The government argues that the legislative history makes clear that a person who supplies substantive information and advice relating to specific entries on a return may be treated as a preparer of that return even though someone else fills it out.   See H.R.Rep. No. 658, 94th Cong., 2d Sess. 275, reprinted in 1976 U.S.C.C.A.N. 3171. The Regulations "apply that principle to a person in appellant's position, treating the preparer of a partnership return as the preparer of a partner's return if the information on the partnership return is directly reflected on, and constitutes a substantial portion of, the partner's return."   The objective of the statutory scheme is to impose the penalty on the person who is responsible as a substantive matter for the way in which a return is prepared.   Because the partnership pays no taxes itself, the purpose of the partnership tax  return and the Schedules K-1 is to figure out the deductions or income that  each partner may state on his return. * * *

2. Analysis

* * *

Here the government's position reflects both the congressional intent and the realities of the limited partnership relationship.  * * *

As the partnership is both entity and aggregate, the tax preparer's relationship to the partnership is necessarily dual-he is dealing with the partnership both as entity and as aggregate of partners. Appellant was retained to analyze the partnership operation; however, the analysis of the partnership operation was a making of decisions and calculations for all the individual partners, to whom the tax liability or deductions would flow through the partnership. These decisions and calculations were directly reflected on the returns of the partners; all the individual partners depended upon Mr. Goulding's analysis. Thus while appellant was retained by the partnership and compensated by the partnership, in reality his work was for all the partners.

True, Mr. Goulding's work boiled down to one entry on each partner's return, but it represented a far more complicated analysis of partnership earnings-an analysis upon which the limited partners necessarily relied. Thus, Mr. Goulding's comparison of the Schedules K-1 to other informational forms is unconvincing. * * * [B]ecause of the often complicated nature of a partnership return and partnership transactions, a partner cannot readily verify the information and calculations on the partnership return. Moreover, the Internal Revenue Code requires, as a general rule, that tax treatment of partnership items be determined at the partnership level, see 26 U.S.C. § 6221, and that an individual partner, on his own return, treat a partnership item in a manner which is consistent with the treatment of the item on the partnership return. See 26 U.S.C. § 6222.

Because appellant's analysis of the partnership's financial operations was in essence an analysis of income directly taxable to the partners and losses directly deductible by them, the regulation making him the preparer of their returns reflects the real relationship between Mr. Goulding and the partners.* * *

## Questions and Comments:

1. What are the justifications for changing the one-preparer rule? Are you convinced that some like Mr. Goulding should be considered a preparer?

2. Assume that you advise a taxpayer on a transaction and the tax ramifications from that transaction, but you do not advise the taxpayer with regard to filing his tax return. Are you a preparer subject to Circular 230?

# Chapter 2

## Ethical Obligations of Tax Lawyers

———

Although tax lawyers may have special legal and ethical obligations that apply in the tax context, the ethical responsibilities and requirements facing tax lawyers are mainly derived from general ethical constraints facing lawyers. This chapter examines the ethical dilemmas that face tax lawyers in tax practice and the ways in which the ABA Model Rules and Circular 230 guide a lawyer's decisions in this area. For example, what are a lawyer's responsibilities regarding honesty in dealings with the Service? May the lawyer be silent in the face of mistakes by the Service? May the lawyer go forward with a case if she knows the client has lied in filings with the Service? What does a tax lawyer do if she knows a client has made a mistake? The general requirement in Rule 4.1 that a lawyer deal truthfully and honestly with regard to material facts still obviously applies in the tax context, but here we explore the application of Rule 4.1 and other model Rules to questions that often occur in tax practice.

Throughout this chapter we will see a significant interplay between various provisions in the Model Rules. For example, Rule 1.2 provides that a lawyer shall not assist a client in criminal or fraudulent conduct. Rule 1.6 places an obligation on an attorney to maintain client confidences. Rule 4.1 prohibits a lawyer from making false statements of material fact or law to a third party, and rule 8.4 prohibits an attorney from engaging in dishonest conduct, fraud or deceit. Each of these rules seems fairly simple on its face, but the interplay of these rules often causes trouble for lawyers. This chapter is designed to help students and lawyers work their way through the difficult questions that arise in tax practice.

## A. Mistake

What is an attorney's duty when she realizes that the client has made an honest or not so honest mistake? For example, a client comes to you to resolve a tax issue and you realize that the client has made a mistake on a prior year's return. Does the client have an obligation to amend the return? What if you made the mistake, what are your obligations? What happens if the Service makes a computational error in your client's favor; can you sit in silence? What do you think the right answer should be? What do you think the right answer is under the Model Rules and Circular 230? How do the obligations in the Model Rules with regard to fairness to other parties and truthfulness in statements to others play out in the tax context? We explore these questions in the next section.

## 1.    MISTAKE CORRECTION

# STANDARDS OF TAX PRACTICE STATEMENT 1999-1[*]

Tax Section, American Bar Association[13]

Issue Presented

This Statement addresses the issue of counsel's responsibilities upon discovering a computational error made by the Service in the client's favor that is unrelated to any affirmative representation or omission of either the client or counsel.

\* \* \*

An error in calculating the correct tax liability can be computational, such as an arithmetic mistake, or clerical, such as a typographical mistake. Computational errors can also be conceptual,

---

[*] Standards of Tax Practice 1999-1, published by the American Bar Association of Taxation. Copyright © 1991 by the American Bar Association. Reprinted with permission. All rights reserved. This information or any or portion thereof may not be copied or disseminated in any form or by any means or stored in an electronic database or retrieval system without the express written consent of the American Bar Association.

[13] The statement includes the following explanation: "The following Standards of Tax Practice Statement is issued for the guidance of tax practitioners. It was prepared by the Committee on Standards of Tax Practice of the Section of Taxation of the American Bar Association. The Statement was reviewed before issuance by the Council of the Section of Taxation. The Statement has not been approved by the Section or by the American Bar Association and should not be construed as policy of those entities. The ABA Standing Committee on Ethics and Professional Responsibility has indicated that it has no objection to the issuance of the Statement. The Reporter for this Statement was Donald P. Lan, Jr. of Dallas, Texas. The Chair of the Committee on Standards of Tax Practice was Leslie S. Shapiro of Washington, D. C.; the Vice Chair was Linda Galler of Hempstead, New York; and the Chair of its Subcommittee on Standards of Tax Practice Statements was Charles Pulaski of Phoenix, Arizona.

such as where the calculation depends on the application or interpretation of a particular Code section. The computational error need not relate to the tax liability, but can occur with respect to penalties or interest. Courts generally have not been reluctant to correct clerical errors. An arithmetic error, rather than a conceptual error, can be corrected by the Service without the need for a statutory notice of deficiency. An arithmetic error generally is not subject to dispute. This is not necessarily the case with conceptual errors, where the courts are more reluctant to permit correction. In Stamm International Corp. v. Commissioner, 90 T.C. 315 (1988), for example, the Tax Court refused to allow the Service to withdraw a stipulated settlement upon discovering its unilateral mistake of not considering the application of a Code provision in calculating the settlement amount. The Tax Court held that silence by the taxpayer's counsel, although misleading, was not the equivalent of a misrepresentation in that case.

\* \* \*

Discussion

When counsel learns that the Service has made a computational error of tax, penalty, or interest in the client's favor, the information gained is a client confidence under Rule 1.6(a), which generally may not be disclosed without the client's consent unless otherwise provided in the Rules or by other law. Confidentiality applies to all information obtained about the client relating to the representation and not just communications from the client. But Rule 8.4(c) provides that a lawyer may not engage in conduct that is dishonest.

The lawyer's ethical obligations will depend on the circumstances; thus, this Statement recognizes that different conclusions should be reached in different factual situations. There is nonetheless a common theme. A client should not profit from a clear unilateral arithmetic or clerical error made by the Service and a lawyer may not knowingly assist the client in doing so. This is not the case, however, if the computational error is conceptual, such that a reasonable dispute still exists concerning the calculation.

Docketed Case

If the parties in a docketed case are required to document the amount of the client's tax liability or overpayment, such as in a decision document filed in Tax Court or in a judgment entered on a counterclaim in the U. S. District Court or the U. S. Court of Federal Claims, counsel must disclose an error to the court. Model Rule 3.3(a)(1). Because counsel knows that the deficiency is understated, or refund overstated, counsel cannot file a document with the court that contains an incorrect deficiency or overpayment without making a false statement to a tribunal. Disclosure of the error may be made in this situation without the consent of, or consultation with, the client. Rule 3.3(b) specifically requires disclosure not-withstanding that the error is a client confidence under Rule 1.6.

Where the parties need not document the amount of the tax liability or refund, as is generally the case in the U.S. District Courts or the U. S. Court of Federal Claims, the dismissal document generally does not contain the false statement of material fact. Nonetheless, under Rule 3.3, counsel owes a greater duty to a tribunal than is owed to an opposing party, and the rules of conduct should not vary depending on the particular forum. Disclosure is required and may be made without consulting the client.

Settlement of Non-Docketed Case

A lawyer must disclose a clear arithmetic or clerical calculation error (but not a conceptual error), the amount of which is not de minimis to the Service, if there exists express or implied authority from the client to make the disclosure. Whether implied authority exists is a question of fact. Implied authority will generally exist where the terms of a settlement have been reached and the Service then commits a unilateral arithmetic or clerical error in the computation of the tax, penalty or interest owed, or refund due. Implied authority generally will not exist if the calculation error is conceptual; that is, for example, it depends on the application or interpretation of a Code section for which a reasonable dispute could exist.

In refund situations, the cashing of an erroneous refund check can constitute a criminal violation for converting government property. A lawyer who knows that a miscalculation will result in an erroneous refund cannot become an instrumentality in creating the erroneous refund. However, the potential crime is a client confidence that generally cannot be disclosed, unless express or implied authority to do so exists.

Therefore, in non-docketed cases involving refunds or deficiencies, if the client refuses to consent where there is no implied authorization, counsel must withdraw from the engagement because the failure to act would constitute a violation of Rule 8.4(c) and Rule 1.2(d).    Counsel need not withdraw if express consent is withheld and the error is conceptual.

## Questions and Comments:

1.  Does this opinion make sense to you?  Does an attorney have implied authority from her client to correct these types of mistakes? How would you argue against such implied authority?

2.  This is a Standard of Tax Practice published by the Tax Section of the American Bar Association.  How binding is it?

3.  The Standard of Tax Practice notes that a lawyer must disclose a mistake to the court so that when a court document indicates a number that is wrong, the lawyer is obligated to disclose the mistake.  Why would a similar obligation exist in district court or the U.S. Court of Federal Claims when no such document exists? Are you convinced by the Statement's argument?

4.  The statement provides that a client should not profit from a clerical error and that a lawyer may not assist a client in doing so. What ethical rule provides this constraint on a lawyer?

## Problem 2.1

You are negotiating with the IRS over the amount of an ordinary and necessary business deduction under IRC § 162. Negotiations have been positive and you have not filed suit in court. You reach an agreement with the IRS that 40% of the business deduction will be allowed. You receive the settlement papers from the IRS, and the IRS has erroneously disallowed 40% of the deduction, thus allowing 60%. What actions do you take and why?

## Problem 2.2

You reach an agreement with the Service regarding the tax treatment of an asset that is subject to depreciation.  You told the client that the settlement would result in $25,000 of additional tax liability.  You receive the Service's calculations claiming that the taxpayer owes $50,000.  You check the calculations and realize that the Service has made an error, but you also realize that the correct amount is $75,000, not $25,000.  What actions do you take and why?

**Problem 2.3**

Your client has a beach front rental property in Miami, Florida and has deducted depreciation and other expenses from the rental. You recognize that there is a strong argument that some of the expenses are not deductible because the property was used for personal purposes. You have an argument, however, that the taxpayer was making repairs to the property while he was there and that the use was therefore not personal. The personal use issue was not raised by the Service and the settlement agreement treats the entire amount as deductible. What actions do you take and why?

## 2.    MISTAKE AND THE DUTY TO AMEND A RETURN

Lawyers, accountants, tax preparers, the Service, and clients all make mistakes. Those mistakes may be clerical as those discussed above; they may be factual; or they may be legal. What is the duty of a lawyer and a taxpayer upon realizing that a mistake has been made on a prior year's return? What ethical duties guide lawyers in deciding what to do when a mistake has been found? This article grapples with some of these difficult issues.

# ON REQUIRING THE CORRECTION OF ERROR UNDER THE FEDERAL TAX LAW*
Kenneth L. Harris
42 Tax Law. 515

## III. CURRENT LAW: THE LAWYER'S OBLIGATION ON DISCOVERY OF THE TAXPAYER'S PRIOR ERROR

Lawyers often make it a practice to review prior years' returns when engaged to plan a transaction or prepare a current year's return. In the process of reviewing the client's prior return, the attorney may discover that the client made an unintentional error on the earlier return. As discussed above, it is fairly well established that under current law the taxpayer is not obligated to file an amended return to correct the error. This absence of a legal

---

* "On Requiring the Correction of Error under the Federal Tax Law," by Kenneth Harris, 1988, *Tax Lawyer 42:3*, 515-576. Copyright © 1988 by the American Bar Association. Reprinted with permission. All rights reserved. This information or any or portion thereof may not be copied or disseminated in any form or by any means or stored in an electronic database or retrieval system without the express written consent of the American Bar Association.

obligation of the taxpayer does not, however, automatically resolve the legal and ethical issues faced by the attorney on discovery of the taxpayer's error. The attorney must consider not only the traditional duties of loyalty, confidentiality, and competence that run to the client: Because the relationship between the tax attorney and the federal government is not wholly adversarial (at least at the stage of return preparation and advice), the attorney must also consider obligations owing to the federal government. In particular, the attorney has an obligation to the federal government to see that the 'citizen's report to the government of his or her relevant activities for the year' serves the necessary 'disclosure, reporting, and self-assessment function. This section addresses the extent and nature of the attorney's obligations, both to the client and to the federal government, on discovery of the taxpayer's error.

A. *Obligation On Discovery*

As a general rule, the current standards governing the attorney's conduct require that on discovery of the taxpayer's error the attorney advise the client of the existence of the error, and with a possible exception in the case of an intentional error, the attorney advise the client that the error should be corrected.

Treasury Circular 230, which governs practice before the Service in general, states that the practitioner 'shall' advise the client of the fact of an error in or omission from the client's return. It does not, however, require that the practitioner advise the client that an amended return should be filed.[14]

The American Bar Association, in Opinion 314, provides in relatively straight-forward terms that the lawyer must not only advise the client of the existence of the error, but must advise that the error should be corrected. ABA Opinion 314 does not, however, explicitly address the problem of whether the attorney is required to advise correction even when the error is an intentional error which, if discovered, could result in criminal prosecution of the taxpayer.

The ethical standards governing the conduct of the certified public accountant (CPA), as stated in the American Institute of Certified Public Accountants' (AICPA) 'Statement of Responsibility in Tax Practice,' provide that the CPA shall advise the client

---

[14] [Ed. Note] The current version of Circular 230 (Rev. 4-2008) requires practitioners to advise the client of the error, and "must advise the client of the consequences as provided under the Code and regulations of such noncompliance, error or omission."

immediately upon the discovery of an error on the client's return. As in the case of Treasury Circular 230, while the accountant is directed to advise the client of the existence of an error, there is no explicit requirement that he or she advise the client that the error should be corrected. The accompanying explanation explicitly provides that 'it is the client's responsibility to decide whether to correct the error.'

In view of the above discussion, must a lawyer advise his client to file an amended return when the error was intentional and disclosure may subject the client to criminal prosecution? As noted, the directive in ABA Opinion 314 that the attorney advise the client to correct a prior error does not contain a stated exception in the case of an intentional, as opposed to an innocent, error. The silence of Treasury Circular 230 and the AICPA Standards on this point suggests, however, that when disclosure would operate to incriminate the client, the lawyer should not automatically advise disclosure. The ABA Tax Section's Guidelines to Tax Practice appears to adopt this position in recommending that in any situation involving potential fraud charges, the lawyer 'should carefully explain to the taxpayer the benefits and hazards of the various options available, including any constitutional right not to cooperate with the Service.'[15]

* * *

B. *Obligations When Client Refuses to Correct*

If the client refuses to heed his or her attorney's general moral directive (the client will naturally ask the attorney not what should be done, but what the law requires to be done), may the attorney continue to represent the client? What if the representation involves the subject matter of the prior error? Should it matter if the representation involves proceedings before the Service? May the attorney, in any event, disclose the error without the client's consent? Should it matter that the attorney prepared the prior return? Finally, may the error be corrected by including an overstatement of income in the current year?

At the threshold, when the client refuses to correct a prior error, the attorney is faced with the issue of whether he or she may, or indeed must, disclose the error to the Service. This decision may be particularly troublesome when the attorney was directly involved

---

[15] Report of Comm. On Standards of Tax Practice, Guidelines to Tax Practice, 31 Tax Law. 551, 553-54 (1978)

in the preparation of the return and is, therefore, concerned that if the unintentional error is discovered, the government may view the failure to disclose as concealment by the attorney of a prior wrongdoing.

ABA Opinion 314 suggests that the duty not to mislead does not imply that the attorney has a duty to disclose the error to the Service, except when the facts indicate beyond a reasonable doubt that a crime will be committed. Indeed, rule 1.6 of the Model Rules of Professional Conduct provides that a lawyer generally may not reveal confidential client information except when the disclosure is believed by the lawyer to be necessary (1) to prevent the commission of a crime likely to result in death or serious bodily harm, or (2) to establish a claim of defense of the lawyer.[16] Moreover, the lawyer's duty of truthfulness in Model Rule 4.1, requiring the disclosure of material facts to third persons when necessary to avoid assisting in a crime or fraudulent act, is limited when 'disclosure is prohibited by rule 1.6.' Thus, except for the possible situation in which the attorney would be required to disclose the error to claim a defense, it is difficult to imagine a situation under which the exceptions to Model Rule 1.6 would apply to permit disclosure in the case of a discovered error. In short, under the current ethical standards governing attorney conduct in general, and the tax attorney in particular, an attorney is generally neither required nor permitted to disclose a prior error to the Service when the client refuses to confess the error. [17]

As to preparation of the current year's return, the practitioner's duties to exercise due diligence in the preparation and filing of returns and not to participate in any way in the giving of false or misleading information prohibit the attorney from preparing the current year's return in a manner incorporating the prior error.

---

[16] [Ed. Note] As amended, Rule 1.6(b)(2) provides that an attorney may disclose information to the extent the lawyer believes it is necessary to prevent a client from committing a crime or fraud that will cause a substantial injury. Rule 1.6(b)(3) allows disclosure to "prevent, mitigate or rectify substantial injury" to financial interests that is reasonable certain to result from fraud when the client has used the lawyer's services to commit the fraud. These provisions are written as "may" provisions not "shall" provisions, so disclosure is not required. In addition, it is unclear whether this applies when the Government is a party and how large the amount at issue would have to be for it to constitute a substantial injury to the Government.

[17] [Ed. Note] This statement was written before ABA Formal Opinion 92-366. Keep this statement in mind when you read Opinion 92-366.

Model Rules 4.1(a), requiring that the 'lawyer shall not knowingly make a false statement of material fact or law to a third person,' and 8.4(c), prohibiting the lawyer from engaging in fraudulent or dishonest conduct, confirm the conclusion that the lawyer may not complete the return when doing so would further the error.

\* \* \*

If the current year's return does not incorporate the prior error, the lawyer is generally not required to withdraw. Certain commentators have argued, however, that the attorney should consider withdrawing in this situation because (1) a lawyer should not represent a client who fails to satisfy his legal obligations (*i.e.*, a tax due-whether discovered by the government or not-is a legal debt that is owing), and (2) it is imprudent for a lawyer to place himself at risk of building on a prior year's error.

Before considering this view, it is useful to examine first the issue of withdrawal in the context of an ongoing IRS audit.

In an ongoing audit, a prior error of the taxpayer may or may not be involved directly. When the error is directly involved in the proceedings, it is fairly well established under the above standards that the attorney should withdraw from representation, unless to do so would cause undue prejudice to the taxpayer. Otherwise, the attorney's services are being directly used by the taxpayer to create a misrepresentation. This misuse is prohibited whether the Service is viewed solely as an 'impartial arbiter' or as part adversary.

When the error is not directly involved, existing ethical standards appear also to point the attorney in the direction of withdrawal. Again, the attorney is clearly *not* required, nor generally permitted, to disclose the error. However, as noted, Treasury Circular 230 and Model Rules 4.1(a) and 8.4 prevent the attorney from giving false or misleading information or making false statements to the Service. Because an ongoing audit involves resolution of the taxpayer's liability for the entire tax year, an attorney aware of a prior error who does not (perhaps cannot) disclose the error, and yet continues to represent the taxpayer before the Service, is corroborating the taxpayer's statement as to the liability for the year (excluding the error) and, thus, is misleading the Service. Since the attorney is not permitted to disclose the error, the attorney should therefore generally be required to withdraw, provided that the act of withdrawal would not cause 'undue prejudice' to the taxpayer.[18]   ABA Opinion 314 appears to confirm this result by providing that while the question of withdrawal is a 'facts and circumstances' question, '[f]undamentally . . . the lawyer may have the duty to withdraw from the matter,' when the Service is relying on the attorney as corroborating statements of the client, which he or she knows to be false.

\* \* \*

**Question and Comments:**

1.  Harris wrote the above article before the publication of Standards of Practice 1999-1.  He also wrote the article before the formal opinions discussed below.  The article, however, provides a great insight into the interplay between the obligations created by the model rules.

2.  Chart out the various scenarios discussed by Harris and the lawyers obligations in each scenario.  Keep the chart handy when you read Form. Op. 92-366 in the following section.  What if any changes would you make to Harris's analysis in light of the formal opinion?

3.  Does the amendment to Model Rule 1.6 change your analyses regarding whether a lawyer may withdraw?

## B.  False Statements and Fraud

We all recognize that lawyers should not lie or commit fraud, but the situation gets much more complicated when trying to figure out whether something is in fact a lie. We generally think we know a lie when we see one, but application in the real world is often tricky.

Professor Tobin retells this story from his childhood.  A friend came over after school.  The friend and Professor Tobin proceeded to eat all the cookies in the cupboard.  When Professor Tobin's father arrived home, he went to get a cookie and they were all gone.  The father then asked, "Donald, did you eat all the cookies?"  As you can probably guess, Professor Tobin said "no."

---

[18] [Ed. Note] Harris notes that the comments to Rule 1.16 indicate that a lawyer may withdraw "if the lawyer's services were misused in the past even if that would materially prejudice the client."

After all, his friend ate some, and he knew his father had some yesterday. Professor Tobin's father did not like the answer, and indicated it was a lie. But would that answer be a lie if it were provided by a lawyer to the Service? What obligations do lawyers have to provide the truth and the whole truth? Several ABA Formal Opinions shed light on this topic.

## ABA FORMAL OPINION 92-366*
### Withdrawal When A Lawyer's Services Will Otherwise Be Used To Perpetrate A Fraud
### August 8, 1992

A lawyer who knows or with reason believes that her services or work product are being used or are intended to be used by a client to perpetrate a fraud must withdraw from further representation of the client, and may disaffirm documents prepared in the course of the representation that are being, or will be, used in furtherance of the fraud, even though such a "noisy" withdrawal may have the collateral effect of inferentially revealing client confidences.

When a lawyer's services have been used in the past by a client to perpetrate a fraud, but the fraud has ceased, the lawyer may but is not required to withdraw from further representation of the client; in these circumstances, a "noisy" withdrawal is not permitted.

The Committee has been asked its views on what the ABA Model Rules of Professional Conduct (1983, amended 1992) require, and what the Rules permit a lawyer to do when she learns that her client has used her work product to perpetrate a fraud, is continuing so to use it, or plans so to use it in the future. The answers to these questions require a somewhat difficult reconciliation of the text and commentary of three Rules: Rule 1.6, imposing a broad requirement of confidentiality; 1.2(d), prohibiting a lawyer from assisting client crime or fraud; and Rule 1.16(a)(1), requiring withdrawal from a representation where continued representation would result in a violation of the Rules.

As more fully explained below, the Committee's conclusions are these:

First, the lawyer must withdraw from any representation of the client that, directly or indirectly, would have the effect of assisting the client's continuing or intended future fraud.

Second, the lawyer may withdraw from all representation of the client, and must withdraw from all representation if the fact of such representation is likely to be known to and relied upon by third persons to whom the continuing fraud is directed, and the representation is therefore likely to assist in the fraud.

Third, the lawyer may disavow any of her work product to prevent its use in the client's continuing or intended future fraud, even though this may have the collateral effect of disclosing inferentially client confidences obtained during the representation. In some circumstances, such a disavowal of work product (commonly referred to as a "noisy" withdrawal) may be necessary in order to effectuate the lawyer's withdrawal from representation of the client.

Fourth and finally, if the fraud is completed, and the lawyer does not know or reasonably believe that the client intends to continue the fraud or commit a future fraud by use of the lawyer's services or work product, the lawyer may withdraw from representation of the client but may not disavow any work product.

\* \* \*

[The facts at issue involved an opinion letter prepared by a lawyer for a corporation involved in a loan transaction. The lender, as part of its agreeing to make the loan, relied upon the opinion letter by the lawyer and audited financial statements. The opinion letter, among other things, asserted that the installation contracts upon which the value of the corporation were based, were enforceable. A year after the loan transaction occurred, the lawyer learned that officers of the corporation had fraudulently invented the contracts. The lawyer recognized that her opinion letter was false, and that it might be used by the client to obtain or at least maintain existing loans.]

Thus it is that the lawyer knows that so much of her opinion as certifies to the enforceability of the installation contracts is false and its use by the client has been fraudulent. The lawyer also knows, by virtue of the client's representations to her, that the client intends further use of her opinion to defraud the bank and/or other third parties. The lawyer recognizes that in these circumstances, even if the client had not proposed to replace her as counsel, she would be required by Rule 1.16(a)(1) to withdraw from further representation of the client in matters directly involving her opinion, the fraudulent contracts to which her opinion referred, or the false financial statements that rest upon the fraudulent contracts. She believes that she would also be required to withdraw from representation of the client in any matters involving a continuing relationship with the bank from which the $5 million loan was fraudulently obtained, since her very presence as a representative of the client could lull the bank into a continuing reliance on its erroneous view of the company's financial condition, as reflected in her false opinion that the installment contracts were enforceable obligations. In either case she believes she would be put in the position of assisting the client's continuing fraudulent course of conduct in violation of Rule 1.2(d). * * *

The Committee agrees that Rule 1.16(a)(1) compels the lawyer to "withdraw from the representation" of the company in any matters involving her opinion, the fraudulent contracts, the erroneous financial statements or the bank, since continued representation would constitute assisting the client in a course of conduct known to be fraudulent in violation of Rule 1.2(d).

It is not clear from the facts presented to the Committee whether severance of the entire relationship is ethically compelled in this case, as the lawyer apparently believes, or whether she is ethically required to withdraw from representation of the client only in matters relating to the fraud. We do not believe that knowledge of a client's ongoing fraud necessarily requires the lawyer's withdrawal from representation wholly unrelated to the fraud, even if the fraud involves the lawyer's past services or work product. On the other hand, complete severance may be the preferred course in these circumstances, in order to avoid any possibility of the lawyer's continued association with the client's fraud. We would simply point out, however, that withdrawal from matters totally unrelated to the fraud is more likely to be permissive, and governed by Rule 1.16(b), than mandatory under Rule 1.16(a)(1).

The question then arises, what if anything may or must the lawyer do, beyond the simple silent act of ceasing further activity on behalf of the client, if she is obliged to withdraw under Rules 1.16(a)(1) and 1.2(d)? Specifically, may she withdraw or disaffirm opinions or other documents that she has issued in the course of her representation?

The lawyer is subject to the general prohibition of Rule 1.6 against disclosing information relating to her representation of the company, and the text of this Rule itself contains no exception that would permit her to reveal the fraud . . . Nor is disclosure explicitly authorized by any other ethical rule. Therefore, the lawyer may not, as a general matter, reveal the client's fraud          . . . The question we address is whether the lawyer may nonetheless in the circumstances here in question accompany her withdrawal from the representation with disaffirmance of the formal opinion on which the bank relied in making the loan, and which she now knows to be based upon false information provided her by the client, in order to avoid providing assistance in violation of Rule 1.2(d). Such a "noisy" withdrawal is, of course, likely to have the collateral consequence of disclosing, inferentially, information relating to the representation that is otherwise protected as a client confidence under Rule 1.6.

For reasons discussed below, we believe that Rule 1.6 should not necessarily and in every case "trump" other ethical rules with which it collides, at least to the extent that a lawyer should be allowed (if indeed she should not be required) to withdraw assistance that has unknowingly been provided to a continuing or future fraudulent project in order to comply fully with her obligation to "withdraw" so as to avoid "assisting" client fraud under Rules 1.16(a)(1) and 1.2(d).

Such a "noisy" withdrawal, with its potential for indirectly signaling the client's past wrongdoing, notwithstanding the strict obligation of confidentiality otherwise imposed by the black letter text of Rule 1.6, is clearly contemplated in the following Comment to that Rule:

Withdrawal

> If the lawyer's services will be used by the client in materially furthering a course of criminal or fraudulent conduct, the lawyer must withdraw, as stated in Rule 1.16(a)(1).

After withdrawal the lawyer is required to refrain from making disclosure of the client's confidence, except as otherwise provided in Rule 1.6. Neither this rule nor Rule 1.8(b) nor Rule 1.16(d) prevents the lawyer from giving notice of the fact of withdrawal, and the lawyer may also withdraw or disaffirm any opinion, document, affirmation, or the like.

\* \* \*

The questions presented by the Comment are, first, in just what circumstances it contemplates a "noisy" withdrawal; and second, whether the Comment correctly interprets the confidentiality requirements of Rule 1.6 in stating that a "noisy" withdrawal is permissible in any circumstances.

As to the first question, we think it clear that the Comment would allow disaffirmance only in circumstances where the lawyer's withdrawal is ethically required because of the client's intention of using the lawyer's services (absent effective withdrawal) in a continuing or future fraud. The first of the three paragraphs of the Comment addresses the situation in which "the lawyer's services will be used by the client in materially furthering a course of criminal or fraudulent conduct," a situation in which the lawyer "must withdraw, as stated in Rule 1.16(a)(1)." The third paragraph concerns the lawyer's doubt as to the client's intention to carry out "contemplated conduct," plainly a reference to the "criminal or fraudulent conduct" referred to in the first paragraph. It would strain common rules of construction to conclude that the middle of three related paragraphs of text, containing the disaffirmance provision, was intended to address broader circumstances than those to which the first and third paragraph are limited: viz., the situation in which withdrawal is mandatory. Disaffirmance is, thus, not contemplated by the Comment where the lawyer's withdrawal from representation is only optional, under Rule 1.16(b). It follows that disaffirmance is not allowed where the fraud is completed, and the client does not, so far as the lawyer knows or reasonably believes, intend to make further fraudulent use of the lawyer's services.

The question before us is, at heart, whether the "Withdrawal" Comment is appropriately to be given meaning--i.e., viewed as legitimate interpretation of the Rules--or instead simply ignored. We think the former: that the Comment correctly reflects the need to interpret Rule 1.6's requirement of confidentiality in light of what Rules 1.2(d) and 1.16(a)(1) require of a lawyer in a situation where continued representation of the client will entail the lawyer's assisting in the client's continuing or future fraud and withdrawal is therefore mandatory.

We note that neither Rule 1.16(a)(1) nor Rule 1.2(d) is qualified, as are other possibly relevant provisions of the Rules, by a caveat that compliance is subject to the obligation to protect client confidences contained in Rule 1.6. While it is also true that neither Rule contains language explicitly overriding the confidentiality requirement of Rule 1.6 (as do Rule 3.3 and, of course, Rule 1.6 itself), the absence from their text of a preemption clause does not seem to us necessarily determinative of the proper course of conduct in a situation where compliance with Rules 1.16(a)(1) and 1.2(d) appears to require conduct that may have the collateral consequence of disclosing client confidences. In the absence of a clear textual indication of how such a conflict should be resolved, the Committee believes that the confidentiality requirement of Rule 1.6 should not be interpreted so rigidly as to prevent the lawyer from undertaking to the limited extent necessary that which is required to avoid a violation of Rules 1.2(d) and 1.16(a)(1).

* * *

This reading of Rule 1.6 finds ample support in the text of Rules 1.16(a)(1) and 1.2(d). Under the mandate of Rule 1.16(a)(1) that a lawyer shall withdraw if the "representation will result in a violation," the term "representation" must be read to include a lawyer's permitting the client's continued use of the lawyer's pre-existing work product. Similarly, under the injunction in Rule 1.2(d) that a lawyer shall not "assist a client in conduct the lawyer knows is criminal or fraudulent," the term "assist" must be reasonably construed to cover a failure to repudiate or otherwise disassociate herself from prior work product the lawyer knows or has reason to believe is furthering the client's continuing or future criminal or fraudulent conduct. It would follow from such a construction of these key terms in Rules 1.16(a)(1) and 1.2(d) that a lawyer's disavowal of work product would be an essential accompaniment to the lawyer's withdrawal from representation. Indeed, it would also follow that such a disaffirmance might be necessary in order to make the withdrawal effective; that is, the lawyer may be required to do more than simply decline to perform further services in order to fully effectuate a "withdrawal" from representation under Rule 1.16(a)(1) and to avoid "assistance" under Rule 1.2(d). In this view, where the client avowedly intends to continue to use the lawyer's work product, this amounts to a de facto continuation of the representation even if the lawyer has ceased to perform any additional work. The representation is not completed, any more than the fraud itself is completed. In order to fully effectuate the withdrawal mandated by Rule 1.16(a)(1), and to avoid assisting client fraud as mandated by Rule 1.2(d), the lawyer may have to repudiate her preexisting work product in addition to refusing to perform any further work for the client.

\* \* \*

Two consequences flow from this interpretation of these key terms in Rules 1.16(a)(1) and 1.2(d). First, it provides a rationale for limiting a "noisy" withdrawal to circumstances where the withdrawal is mandatory. Absent imperatives imposed by these other two Rules, that a lawyer disassociate herself from a client's ongoing wrongdoing in order to avoid assisting it, it is neither necessary nor appropriate to permit disavowal of work product and possible consequent revelation of client confidences.

The second conclusion logically to be drawn from this construction of the Rules is that the lawyer's ability to disaffirm work product, and thus attempt to disassociate herself from further client fraud based upon that work product, cannot depend upon whether the client or the lawyer is the first to act in discontinuing the representation. The possibility of a noisy withdrawal cannot be preempted by a swift dismissal of the lawyer by the client. Whenever circumstances exist that would otherwise require a lawyer to withdraw, disaffirmance may be in order even if the client fires her before she has a chance to do so.

Applying Rule 1.6, so construed, we conclude that the instant inquiry presents a situation in which a "noisy" withdrawal would be proper since the client has declared itself determined to engage in further fraudulent conduct that will implicate the lawyer's past services, and the lawyer knows it. Withdrawal from further representation of the client is therefore mandated by Rule 1.16(a)(1). And, if the lawyer reasonably believes that her withdrawal in silence will be ineffective to prevent the client from using the lawyer's work product to accomplish its unlawful purpose, in order to avoid violating Rule 1.2(d), she may take the additional step of disaffirming her work product, with the hope and expectation that this will prevent reliance on that work product by future victims of the client's continuing fraud. Indeed, disavowal of her opinion may be the only way of making her withdrawal effective.

But disaffirmance should be a last resort, and should in any event go no further than necessary to accomplish its purpose of avoiding the lawyer's assisting the client's fraud. Before taking this drastic step, the lawyer should determine whether the circumstances are such that disaffirmance is necessary to disassociate herself from the client's fraud, or whether measures short of disaffirmance will suffice. We can envision situations in which the lawyer's simple silent withdrawal from representation would be sufficient to accomplish this end. We can also envision situations in which the lawyer's intention to disaffirm, announced to the client, would accomplish the same result as actual disaffirmance. And even where disaffirmance is necessary, it may be enough to take measures short of notifying the bank. For example, it may be sufficient for the lawyer to notify the client's new lawyers that she can no longer stand behind the opinion she gave at the loan closing about the enforceability of the installation contracts. Finally, if the bank must be notified, in disaffirming her work product the lawyer should take only such steps as are reasonably necessary to accomplish the intended purpose of preventing use of her work product in the client's fraud. The lawyer may and indeed must decline to discuss or otherwise reveal anything about the disaffirmed work product beyond the simple fact that she no longer stands behind it.

## Questions and Comments:

1. There was a dissent to ABA Formal Opinion 92-366. The dissent argued that there was no evidence that the fraudulent work product would be used by the client in the future, thus there was no requirement that the attorney withdraw from the representation. It further questioned the majority's reading of the interplay between Rule 1.2 and Rule 1.16.

Specifically, Rule 1.16 requires a lawyer to withdraw if the representation will result in a violation of the rules of professional conduct or other law, and Rule 1.2 provides that a lawyer shall not assist a client in conduct that the lawyer knows is criminal or fraudulent. The dissent argues that the attorney had not assisted the client in engaging in criminal or fraudulent conduct. How does the majority reach the opposite result?

2. Obviously if the attorney had prepared the document above knowing of the falsehood then the attorney would have violated Rule 1.2, but what is the violation here? Assume the attorney prepared a document based on fraudulent information and the client never used the document again, would the attorney have a duty to withdraw from representation?

3. Another question at issue was whether the attorney could continue to represent the client on other matters? If the attorney is representing a client in a separate matter, how does that assist the client in fraudulent conduct? The majority seems to say that the mere presence of the attorney in any transaction would make the bank believe that the original documents were accurate. Does this make sense to you?

4. The dissent is very disturbed by the majority's conclusion that a noisy withdrawal is appropriate. Nothing in the language of Rule 1.6 makes a noisy withdrawal mandatory. The Comments to Rule 1.6 indicate that a lawyer "may also withdraw or disaffirm any opinion, document, affirmation, or the like." If the comment says may, why does the opinion indicate that a lawyer must withdraw?

**Problem 2.4**

You are hired by a corporation to represent it in a tax controversy. The corporation was involved in a complicated sale and leaseback transaction that the IRS believed was entered into solely for tax purposes. The client presents you with corporate minutes from a meeting where the board of the corporation discussed the plan. The minutes indicate significant discussion of the business purpose of the transaction. You provide the minutes to the IRS agent. The case goes to trial and the minutes are entered into evidence as part of the stipulation of facts. During the trial, you meet up with an old friend who is on the board of the corporation and who had recommended you to the President of the corporation. In the conversation, your friend mentions that he has been at every board meeting and that he never heard about the transaction at issue. He said he was surprised that the President went and did this on his own, but hoped you could help them through this controversy. What do you do and why? Would your answer be different if this was during an audit instead of in court?

**Problem 2.5**

You prepare taxpayer's 2005 tax return. You receive a letter from the Service asking about an issue on the taxpayer's return. Upon examination, you realize that there is a material error on the client's tax return and notify the client of the opportunity to file an amended return. The client decides not to do so? What action must you or may you take? How do you respond to an audit letter from the service?

**Problem 2.6**

Same facts as problem 2.5. You decide that you do not want to continue to represent the client and withdraw from representation. The client goes to another tax firm for representation. A partner in the successor firm calls you to ask why the representation was terminated. How should you respond and why? What rules apply?

**Problem 2.7**

Your client maintained a dog breading operation. The Service has disallowed the losses from this operation claiming that the activity is a hobby. You and your client claim that the activity was primarily engaged in for profit. You know you have a tough case, but believe your position is correct. The client will agree to pay the full deficiency if the Service waives the penalties. The client urges you to try to get a better deal than that, and gives you authorization to settle the case within those parameters. As part of the negotiations, the Service agrees to waive penalties if the taxpayer will pay the deficiency. You reject the offer saying, "my client will never settle for that amount. He wants to be able to deduct half the losses on the operation." You ultimately agree to a settlement whereby taxpayer agrees to pay 80% of the deficiency and penalties are waived. Has the attorney violated any ethical rules?

## 1.    FALSE STATEMENT/FRAUD BY CLIENT

# ABA FORMAL OPINION 93-375[*]
The Lawyer's Obligation to Disclose Information Adverse to the
Client in the Context of a Bank Examination
August 6, 1993

\* \* \*

The Committee has been asked its views on a lawyer's obligations under the Model Rules of Professional Conduct (1983, amended 1993) to disclose facts adverse to a client bank in the course of an examination of the client by a bank regulatory agency. This inquiry requires us once again to consider the interplay between a lawyer's duties to her client, including her obligation to preserve client confidences under Rule 1.6, and her duty under Rule 1.2(d).

\* \* \*

It is the Committee's conclusion that in representing a client in a bank examination, a lawyer may not under any circumstances lie to or mislead agency officials, either by affirmative misstatement or by omitting a material fact necessary to assure that statements made are not false and misleading. However, she is under no duty to disclose weaknesses in her client's case or otherwise to reveal confidential information that would be protected under Rule 1.6. At the same time, a lawyer may not be a party to fraud on the part of the client, and must take all steps necessary to avoid assisting the client in a course of action she reasonably believes to be fraudulent, including, if necessary, withdrawing from the representation.

These general conclusions may be elucidated by reference to the following hypothetical situation.[19] A lawyer is outside counsel to a bank that is undergoing a routine examination by the banking agency that regulates it. In the course of the examination, an examiner from the agency identifies eight

---

[*] "Formal Opinion 93-375" 1993. Copyright © 1993 by the American Bar Association. Reprinted with permission. Copies of ABA Formal Ethics Opinions are available from Service Center, American Bar Association, 321 North Clark Street, Chicago, IL 60654, 1-800-285-2221. All rights reserved. This information or any or portion thereof may not be copied or disseminated in any form or by any means or stored in an electronic database or retrieval system without the express written consent of the American Bar Association.

[19] The hypothetical is taken from the Report by the ABA Working Group on Lawyers' Representation of Regulated Clients (Discussion Draft, January 1993) at 169-175.

loans that he believes should be aggregated under the loan-to-one-borrower (LTOB) rules governing the bank. See 12 U.S.C. § 84(a)(1). If the eight loans in question are aggregated, the total loans to one person will exceed the 15 percent statutory limit and the bank will be in violation of the LTOB rules. An officer of the client bank believes that the bank has a powerful argument that one of the eight loans identified by the examiner ("Loan 8") should not be combined with the others, in which case the LTOB rules would not be violated. The officer asks the lawyer (who has not heretofore been involved in the bank examination) to review the bank's records and consider the issue before the officer meets with the examiner. The lawyer does so, and agrees that a substantial legal argument can be made that Loan 8 should not be aggregated. In the course of her review of the bank's records, however, the lawyer discovers another loan ("Loan 9") about which the examiner has not made any particular inquiry, that arguably should be aggregated with Loans 1 through 7, in which case also the LTOB rules would be violated. What are the lawyer's obligations under these circumstances? Do they change when the lawyer's role changes from that of a background advisor to that of a front-line representative of the client, articulating a position in behalf of the client or otherwise communicating and dealing directly with the bank examiner?

\* \* \*

In the hypothetical situation here, however, we are assuming that the lawyer's involvement in the bank examination is indirect and attenuated; she is functioning solely as an advisor to the client, and her role is limited to reviewing facts and conclusions that cannot fairly be considered her own work product. The lawyer's duties thus derive not from any obligation that the client may have under applicable regulations to respond fully to the bank examiners' inquiries; rather, they derive from her obligations under ethics rules applicable generally to the legal profession. The duty to respond to the agency remains that of the client; the lawyer's sole ethical obligation is not to mislead the agency, and there is no duty to respond to the agency's inquiries to the client unless the lawyer has put herself in the position of offering, or vouching for, the client's responses.

Three provisions of the Model Rules of Professional Conduct define a lawyer's ethical duties where facts adverse to a client come to her attention in the course of a representation: Rule 3.3 ("Candor Toward the Tribunal"), Rule 3.9 ("Advocate in Nonadjudicative Proceedings"); and Rule 4.1 ("Truthfulness in Statements to Others"). Under all three of these provisions, it is clear that a lawyer may not tell a lie, whether or not it might be considered necessary to protect client confidences. See Rule 3.3(a)(1) and Rule 4.1(a) (a lawyer "shall not knowingly . . . make a false statement of material fact or law . . ."). See also Rule 3.9 (a lawyer "shall conform to the provisions of Rule 3.3(a) through (c)   . . ."). This obligation of truthfulness is unqualified, applies on all occasions, and contains no exceptions.

Once past outright falsehood, however, it is somewhat less clear whether and to what extent a lawyer in a regulatory proceeding has an ethical obligation to be forthcoming. We do believe that a "false statement of material fact" includes a statement that the lawyer knows is misleading, whether or not it is intended to mislead. A more difficult question is whether and to what extent a lawyer representing a client in a bank examination by a government regulatory agency has an affirmative obligation to come forward with information that is material to the purposes of the examination, the disclosure of which would be against the client's interests or otherwise violate her duty of confidentiality.

While Rules 3.3, 3.9 and 4.1 all impose a duty on a lawyer to disclose material facts when such disclosure is "necessary to avoid assisting a criminal or fraudulent act by a client," this duty overrides the duty to protect client confidences only under Rules 3.3 and 3.9. * * *

The question then arises whether a bank examination should be regarded as falling under either Rule 3.3 or Rule 3.9 for purposes of determining whether disclosure may be required. We believe that it should not. While the Model Rules contain no definition of a "tribunal," the Committee is of the view that a bank regulatory agency should not, at least as such agencies are constituted at this time, be so regarded. Nor should a routine bank examination be considered an "adjudicative proceeding" so as to bring into play the lawyer's duty of candor under Rule 3.3(b). The terms "tribunal" and "adjudicative proceeding" plainly refer to a trial-type proceeding in which evidence is presented to a fact-finder by the parties, witnesses are examined, and a decision by a neutral decision-maker is reached on the basis of evidence and argument developed in the proceeding. While there is no relevant authority under the Model Rules, precedent under the Model Code supports this conclusion. See ABA Formal Opinion No. 314 (1965) (Internal Revenue Service is "neither a true tribunal, nor even a quasi-judicial institution," and "does not purport to be unprejudiced and unbiased in the judicial sense"). See also Wolfram, Modern Legal Ethics @ 12.6.5 at 673 (1986) (application to the Patent Office for a patent is "a substantially nonadjudicatory proceeding").

\* \* \*

While a regulatory examination does not fit precisely into the category "negotiation or other bilateral transaction," it is more clearly suggested by these terms than it is by the terms "rule-making or policy-making." Accordingly, we conclude that the duty of disclosure applicable in the context of a bank examination is the qualified duty to "third parties" in Rule 4.1, and not the unqualified duty of disclosure in Rules 3.3 and 3.9. Because of the importance the profession places on protecting client confidences, we also believe that the prohibition on disclosure of client confidences expressly stated in Rule 4.1 must be given effect in this context, even if the result is to allow the client to engage in fraud.

\* \* \*

## Questions and Comments:

1. The ABA Formal Opinion concludes that a bank examination is not a judicial opinion and that Rules 3.3 and 3.9 do not apply. Is the logic of the opinion convincing?

2. What implications does Formal Opinion 93-375 have for practice before the IRS?

## ABA FORMAL OPINION 93-375
The Lawyer's Obligation to Disclose Information Adverse to the Client in the Context of a Bank Examination
August 6, 1993
(Continued)

II. False Statement By Client In Presence Of Lawyer

Let us suppose the lawyer has concluded that Loan 9 must be aggregated, that failure to report it to the examiners would be unlawful, and that she has so advised the client. And the client, against the lawyer's advice and in the lawyer's presence, makes an unequivocal representation to the bank examiners that there are no loans beyond those already known to them that even arguably should be aggregated. In the face of this clear misrepresentation by the client, and the client's apparent decision to commit a fraud in the lawyer's presence, the lawyer must act to disassociate herself from the client's intended course of action. She is undoubtedly obliged at the first private opportunity to urge the client to correct the falsehood and to consider the possible courses of action identified in Model Rule 1.13.

However, unless the lawyer knew in advance that the client intended to make such a misrepresentation, she herself to this point cannot be said to be a party to it and has violated no ethical duty. We therefore see no reason, in this context, why the lawyer should be required to do anything that would signal to the bank examiners her disapproval of the client's course of conduct. She is not required to jump to her feet and leave the premises upon hearing the client's false statement. Because she cannot yet be charged with knowledge that her services are being used by the client to assist the fraud, she is not required to terminate the representation on the spot or otherwise make a "noisy withdrawal" that would effectively disaffirm her involvement to date. And it is to everyone's benefit that she make a final effort to counsel the client, and take the opportunity to consider climbing the corporate ladder to persuade the bank to correct the falsehood.

On the other hand, if the client refuses to correct his lie to the examiners about the existence of Loan 9, the lawyer may be required to consider whether or not to terminate the representation. See Rule 1.16(b)(1). In any event, she should not come to any subsequent meetings with the examiners if she knows the client intends to persist in the deception, since even her silent presence could make her a party to the client's fraud by conveying the impression that she believes the client's statements, now made a second time in her presence, are correct.

* * *

**Questions and Comments:**

1. The Formal Opinion is balancing the lawyer's duty to the client and the lawyer's duty of truthfulness. Do you think it balances those priorities correctly? Should the bank examiners be able to rely on the fact that an attorney is present as some type of

seal of approval for what the bank is doing? Do you think they do? Is there any example outside of law where a professional's participation is seen as such a seal?

2. Under this opinion, a bank regulatory agency is not a tribunal for purposes of the Model Rules. When the IRS is involved in an audit, should that be seen as a tribunal for purposes of the model rules? Cir. 230, §10.51(a)(4) provides that an attorney may not "give false or misleading information to the Department of Treasury in connection with any tax matter." This rule appears to cover the same one as Rule 4.1 but its language is a little stronger.

### Scenario 2.1

Taxpayer runs a local business in Baltimore, Maryland painting parking lots. You have done his taxes for years and have advised him on business matters. He has a very successful local business and he is looking to expand. You know that the taxpayer is originally from Columbus, Ohio and that his family lives in Ohio. You also know he is a huge Buckeye football fan.

Taxpayer takes a trip to Columbus, Ohio right before Ohio State plays Michigan. Taxpayer loves going to the Ohio State-Michigan game and does so whenever he can. In the two days prior to the game, the taxpayer calls on shopping malls in Columbus and solicits business painting their parking lots. Despite the fact that Maryland is seven hours away, it makes economic sense for the taxpayer to try to obtain business in Ohio. Taxpayer spent approximately 10 hours making business calls, approximately 8 hours at the Ohio State-Michigan game, approximately 8 hours visiting friends and family, and approximately 14 hours driving to and from Ohio.

The taxpayer seeks to deduct as ordinary and necessary business expenses the travel to and from Ohio, his hotel expenses, and his meals (as allowed by section 24). In discussions prior to filling out the return the taxpayer tells you that the primary reason for the travel was business but that it was nice that he could see his family and go to the game.

You fill out the return and claim the expenses as ordinary and necessary business expenses. You include the expenses for the hotel the night before the game because taxpayer made a business call late that day and you felt that it was reasonable for taxpayer to stay overnight.

The taxpayer's return is audited. During the audit, the agent asks about the trip and the client tells him that he went to Ohio to drum up business. The auditor does not know about taxpayer's passion for the Buckeyes or the fact that the taxpayer has family in Ohio. The auditor asks the taxpayer if the purpose of the trip was 100% business. The taxpayer replied that "the purpose of the trip was 100% business." The auditor then asked the taxpayer what he did on the trip. The taxpayer recounted the business elements of the trip but not the personal ones. Assume you are the lawyer for the taxpayer; do you have an ethical obligation to tell the IRS that the taxpayer has relatives in Columbus or that the taxpayer went to the Ohio State-Michigan game? Would your position be different if you were the Director of the IRS Office of Professional Responsibility?

## 2.    FALSE STATEMENT THROUGH SILENCE OR DIRECT MISREPRESENTATION

Return to the bank examiner hypothetical in Formal Opinion 93-375. What if instead of merely sitting back and letting the client talk, the lawyer was actively involved in discussions with the bank examiners and also made less than frank representations? Formal Opinion 93-375 provides some guidance.

# ABA FORMAL OPINION 93-375
The Lawyer's Obligation to Disclose Information Adverse to the
Client in the Context of a Bank Examination
August 6, 1993
(Continued)

\* \* \*

III. False Statement by Lawyer

If the lawyer concludes that Loan 9 was made to the same borrower as Loans 1 through 8, and she herself represents to the bank examiners that the client has made no other loans to that borrower, the lawyer has violated the clear prohibition in Rule 4.1(a) against making false or misleading statements to third parties. It does not matter whether the false statement was volunteered by the lawyer, or whether the client directed her to offer it. Nor does it matter whether she made the statement in response to a specific question from the regulators. She may not in any circumstances herself make a statement that she knows to be false and misleading. This may, of course, lead to some awkwardness where the client is adamant in his refusal to allow the lawyer to disclose the existence of Loan 9, and if the question is put directly to the lawyer by the bank examiner: in such a circumstance, the lawyer has no permissible option but to decline to respond, regardless of the inference that the examiner may draw. If the lawyer believes there is significant risk that she will be asked a question that she cannot ethically answer consistently with her client's instructions, she should so inform the client and give the client the choice whether she should attend before the meeting takes place.

## IV. True Statement by Lawyer but Omission of Other Material Information

Our conclusions respecting false statements by the lawyer extend to circumstances in which the lawyer omits mention of Loan 9, if the context is such that she knows the omission is likely to mislead the bank examiners. An omission may in a particular context be tantamount to an affirmative false statement. For example, if the lawyer knows that the examiners are unaware of Loan 9 and/or its implications for the LTOB rule, and if what she says to them affirmatively leads them to conclude that there is no such loan, or that it need not be aggregated, the lawyer may have violated her ethical obligation under Rule 4.1(a) not to mislead a third party. On the other hand, if the lawyer limits her statements to the question whether Loan 8 should be aggregated, and says nothing at all about any other loans, she cannot be faulted for failing to volunteer information about Loan 9 even if the examiners themselves make statements in the lawyer's presence to the effect that there are no other loans that need be aggregated. If Loan 9 has escaped the examiners' notice through no fault of the lawyer, the lawyer has no ethical obligation to dispel their erroneous impression that no such loan exists, and indeed is precluded from doing so by Rule 1.6.

We stress that a lawyer's ethical obligation to disclose in this context depends upon the role she has herself played in creating any misimpression. As noted earlier, if the client does all of the talking during the examination, and the lawyer does not continue her participation in successive meetings with the examiners on these matters, she has no obligation to come forward to divulge the existence of Loan 9. However, as the lawyer's role expands, so does her responsibility for making certain the examiners are not misled. If she is speaking for the client, then her ethical obligations are substantially greater than if she is merely present when the client himself is speaking to the examiners.

\* \* \*

## Question and Comments:

Take a look at the Harris article, Standards of Tax Practice 1999-1, and Formal Opinion 92-366. What does your chart look like now regarding what a lawyer must do when there is a client mistake? Work through the next group of problems to see if your chart leads you to the right results.

### Problem 2.8

John is a writer who writes children's books. He has hired a lawyer in the past to review some contracts. John asks the lawyer to file his income tax returns. He hands the lawyer approximately $400 worth of restaurant bills. He tells the lawyer that the receipts are for deductible business meals. The lawyer does not inquire further and files a return claiming the meals as ordinary and necessary business expense. The writer is audited and tells the Service that he thought the meals were deductible because he worked on his book in the restaurant while he was eating the meals. The Office of Professional Responsibility calls the lawyer and asks him to explain his actions. Is the lawyer in trouble?

### Problem 2.9

You prepared Tom Travelingman's income tax return for the year 2008, which included numerous schedules and attachments. Tom received a notice from the IRS that his 2008 return would be audited. Tom asked you to handle the audit, and you asked Tom to send you all of the supporting documents. In looking through the supporting documents and records, you become aware that Tom omitted reporting a transaction resulting in a capital gain of $250,000.00. You investigate the transaction further and conclude that the omission was not intentional, but the result of carelessness. While you were investigating, the audit proceeded and the IRS narrowed the audit to Tom's ordinary and necessary business deductions for approximately half of the expenses Tom took on the return. The agent is unaware of and is unlikely to find the omitted transaction that gave rise to the capital gain. What do you do? Why? What disciplinary rules apply? Would the answer be different if you did not prepare the 2000 return?

## Problem 2.10

Gerry Generous reports that he has received a notice from the IRS that his personal return for 2008 is to be audited with respect to charitable contributions. He tells you that a major part of the contribution deductions claimed was due to his practice of making out checks to charities in relatively small amounts, such as $25, and then when the check was returned to him, writing "1" or "2" in front of the amount, and then claiming a deduction for $125 or $225. What action would you take if Gerry Generous were a new client who came to you with this matter? Why? What disciplinary rules apply? What action would you take if you had prepared the 2008 return for Gerry Generous using his phony numbers? Why? What disciplinary rules apply?

## Problem 2.11

John works for a landscaping company that purchases large amounts of gardening supplies. A large gardening supplier invites John out to its headquarters to get more information about the company. The gardening supplier gives John a new chainsaw as a gift saying "this is a little gift for you, we enjoyed having you out." John tells you, his lawyer, about the gift and asserts that they gave it to him with detached and disinterested generosity and that he does not have to include the item in income. John does not use you to prepare the return. A year later, John tells you he is being audited and asks you to represent him. The Service does not know about the chainsaw. Are you obligated to tell the Service about the chainsaw during the audit? Can you represent John?

## Scenario 2.2

You have a long-term attorney-client relationship with Client A. Client A owns a local Restaurant in town as a sole proprietorship. You represent Client A in most of his business and tax matters and have had a close relationship with Client A for some time. In addition, you have represented Client A in another matter involving a debt client A owes on some business assets. Client A has requested that the creditor discharge  a portion of the loan, and you have provided Client A's tax return to the creditor as proof of the client's income stream. You also provide an affidavit to the creditor indicating that you have prepared Client A's tax return and that it accurately reflects Client A's income. The client is hoping that the creditor will agree to accept eighty cents on the dollar with regard to the note.

You decide to take a vacation cruise to Alaska and bump into Client A on the cruise. You are surprised to see Client A because of Client A's financial troubles. Client A then tells you. "Wow. One of the great things about owning a restaurant is that there are a lot of cash transactions. Not claiming cash receipts on my taxes allows me to travel to Alaska in style and still claim poverty."

You are now sick to your stomach and your vacation has been ruined. You tell the client you need to meet with him as soon as the vacation is over. You recognize that you have signed off on past returns and have represented to the creditor that Client A's income tax returns accurately reflect Client A's income.

You meet with Client A and Client A admits to failing to tell you about all the cash receipts. Client A does not want to file an amended tax return and does not want to correct the filing with the creditor. He doesn't want to put you in an uncomfortable position and tells you he will use lawyer B in the future for his tax transactions and for the current negotiations with the creditor. He wants you to continue to handle his other business issues.

What are your ethical obligations upon leaving the meeting with Client A? Can you continue to represent the client? Must you tell someone of his error? For help see Model Rules 1.2, 1.6, 8.4, 1.16, Cir. 230 §§10.21, 10.22.

## 3.    CANDOR TOWARD TRIBUNAL

As discussed in the Formal Opinion 93–375, lawyers have an obligation to act honestly and to tell the truth. A lawyer can also violate ethical obligations when she does not tell the truth and the whole truth. But as an advocate, an attorney does have a right and an obligation to put on her best case. This fact causes some tension in legal practice. One thing, however, is clear. When you are in court, do not play games with the judge.

Model Rule 3.3 requires candor towards a tribunal. This means that you cannot make a false statement of fact or law to the tribunal.    Rule 3.3 also requires attorneys to correct a "false statement of material fact or law previously made to the tribunal by the lawyer.    As discussed earlier, you may not introduce false evidence and must take reasonable remedial measures if you realize false evidence has been introduced.

You also have an obligation under Rule 3.3 to disclose to the tribunal legal authority *"in the controlling jurisdiction known to the lawyer to be **directly** adverse to the position of the client and not disclosed by opposing counsel."* (emphasis and italics added).    To some it seems strange that in an adversarial process the lawyer should have an obligation to help the other side.  Here, however, you are in a sense making sure that you act truthfully to the tribunal.  If you are making a legal argument, but leaving out a case in your jurisdiction that is directly adverse to your position, you are not being completely frank with the tribunal.  Another way to look at it is that you are not just an advocate for your client, but also a member of the bar.  Your membership in the bar lets the court know that you will aid the court, even as an advocate, in reaching its decision.

The reporting of directly adverse authority also helps ensure optimal operation of the adversarial system.  The system depends on competent representation on both sides ensuring that the court has the right information to reach a proper result.  The reporting of adverse authority helps maintain correct decisions and reduces the likelihood of incorrect decisions.

In real life, most attorneys want to disclose contrary cases so they can distinguish them or explain to the court why they should be overturned.  It is not usually good strategy to hide the ball from a judge since the judge will likely find the case anyway.  Strategy aside, however, it is unethical for you to fail to disclose adverse cases in the jurisdiction.  Note, if the case is in another jurisdiction or is not directly adverse, you have no obligation to disclose the case.

## Problem 2.12

Your client is being audited by the Service.  The Service asks you to supply the agent with the case citations relevant to your client's position.  You supply cases that support your position, but you purposely omit adverse controlling cases.  Have you violated any ethical rules or standards?

# C. Professional Conduct

This section examines the rules that guide the conduct of attorneys in their dealings with their clients and each other. For example, attorneys have a duty to exercise due diligence. They should not engage in contemptuous conduct, and they should conduct themselves in an appropriate manner when dealing with other attorneys. But what does that really mean? What actions are expected of attorneys when dealing with others? How does an attorney exercise due diligence?

## 1. DUE DILIGENCE

Lawyers often get in trouble when they are rushed and are not as careful as they should be. The Model Rules and Circular 230 require that an attorney exercise due diligence in the practice of law. Under the Model Rules, a lawyer has an obligation to provide competent representation (Rule 1.1) and to act with reasonable diligence and promptness in representing a client (Rule 1.3). Circular 230, §10.22(a), is the Service's means of enforcing this obligation. Section 10.22 requires that a lawyer exercise due diligence in preparing material relating to Revenue Service matters and in her communications with her client. The Service has used this provision to reprimand and suspend attorneys who are not careful in their advice and preparation.

# PROPOSED RULES, DEPARTMENT OF TREASURY
# OFFICE OF THE SECRETARY
### 31 CFR Part 10
### 51 FR 29113

This Notice proposes modification of the regulations governing practice before the Internal Revenue Service (31 CFR Part 10) by clarifying the regulations in two respects. The first is a proposed requirement that tax practitioners exercise due diligence in giving advice regarding positions to be taken on Federal tax returns and other documents relation to our tax systems. * * *

Due Diligence

The regulations in Circular 230 impose at section 10.22, a "due diligence" requirement on practitioners concerning oral and written representations made to clients and the IRS relative to tax matters. Such requirement addresses both advice on positions to be taken on tax returns and tax return preparation itself. While this discussion addresses the area of tax returns, it generally has equal applicability to all advice and documents impacting on tax matters.

The proposed amendments include a requirement that a practitioner exercise due diligence with respect to advice given concerning positions on tax returns. While this may be considered to be mandated already by Circular 230, we wish to punctuate the link between a practitioner's responsibility to exercise due diligence and his or her responsibility to adhere to the compliance provisions of the Internal Revenue Code.

The term "due diligence" is subject to varying interpretations and, as a result, affords elasticity in its application. The Treasury Department takes the position that, as a standard of professional responsibility in the area of tax return preparation, due diligence requires the practitioner to be assured that any reporting position is in compliance with and supportable by the revenue laws. Unless the position is reasonable, meritorious and made in good faith, a practitioner has not exercised the necessary diligence imposed upon his or her [sic.]. The due diligence standard cannot be met by a position advanced principally to exploit the audit selection process, a position that serve as a mere "arguing" position advanced solely to obtain leverage in the bargaining process of settlement negotiation within the IRS, a position that would serve merely to avert a successful charge that the return is false or fraudulent, or a position that has no practical and realistic possibility of being sustained in the courts.

## Questions and Comments:

The Service indicates that due diligence is subject to varying interpretation and affords "elasticity" in its application. What does that mean? How is a practitioner supposed to know if they have met the due diligence standard? The following problems explore the standard and are based on actual enforcement cases by the Office of Professional Responsibility.

**Problem 2.13**

A taxpayer hires an attorney to prepare the taxpayers Federal income tax return. The attorney does not file the return by the due date but does file an extension. Despite efforts by the taxpayer to obtain a final return, the attorney does not file a return by the new due date. The taxpayer then requests that his records be returned. The attorney does not return the records, and the taxpayer hires an attorney to obtain the records. Obviously the attorney's behavior was not appropriate, but did it violate the due diligence standard? If it did, what sanction do you think would be appropriate?

**Problem 2.14**

A practitioner files returns for multiple taxpayers claiming charitable deductions to a mail order ministry. The Service determines the deductions are inappropriate. The practitioner claims that he did not have knowledge regarding the mail order ministry, but the evidence indicates that he was not only aware of meetings discussing the ministry but that the ministry referred members to the attorney for tax return preparation. Did the attorney exercise due diligence? If not, what is the appropriate sanction?

**Problem 2.15**

A practitioner prepared a return for a professional corporation. The practitioner had a long standing relationship with the client and had prepared the client's returns in the past. The return included significant deductions for country club dues and magazine subscriptions, which upon audit were found to be substantial overstatements. The practitioner reports that he informed the client that the client would need substantiation for the deductions and was assured by the client that it existed. Did the practitioner exercise due diligence? If not, what is the appropriate sanction?

**Problem 2.16**

Practitioner prepared a return claiming taxpayer's brother as a dependent. The return also indicated that the brother lived with the taxpayer for the entire year. The brother, however, lived in Mexico. The practitioner claimed that the taxpayer had provided receipts showing that the taxpayer provided sufficient support to claim his brother as a dependent. The practitioner further claimed that the form was filled out by a secretary, and he did not notice that it indicated that the dependent resided with taxpayer for the full year. Did the practitioner exercise due diligence? If not, what is the appropriate sanction?

## Problem 2.17

Taxpayer owned 50% of a farm operation. The practitioner erroneously deducted 100% of the losses from the operation. He also used the Accelerated Cost Recovery System (a method of depreciation) when the method was not available as a matter of law. Did the practitioner exercise due diligence? If not, what is the appropriate sanction?

## 2.    CONTEMPTUOUS CONDUCT

Although there is no specific model rule dealing with contemptuous conduct, it is generally recognized that lawyers have a responsibility to conduct themselves in a honorable way. Rule 8.4(d) provides that a lawyer shall not "engage in conduct that is prejudicial to the administration of justice," and Rule 3.5(d) prohibits a lawyer from engaging in conduct intended to disrupt a tribunal. Just how outrageous a lawyer's behavior has to get before it is "prejudicial" is unclear, but there is some level of conduct that is required of a lawyer as a professional. Circular 230 places a more stringent requirement on attorneys subject to its rules. Circular 230 provides a sanction for "incompetence and disreputable conduct." Disreputable conduct includes, among other things, making false statements, improperly soliciting clients, willfully failing to file tax returns, and counseling people to violate federal tax law.[20] Disreputable conduct also includes "contemptuous conduct in connection with practice before the Internal Revenue Service, including the use of abusive language, making false accusations or statements, knowing them to be false, or circulating or publishing malicious or libelous matter."

---

[20] The model Rules also prohibit the making of false statements, improper of class and encouraging people to violate the law. CF 4.1, 4.4.

# BADGES OF PRACTITIONER ABUSE
Internal Revenue Manual
5.1.1.7.6.1 (05-20-2005)

Practitioners may be subject to discipline under Circular 230 if they exhibit a pattern of attempting to influence the case disposition or a Service employee to obtain the desired results in several collection investigations by:

Using abusive language

Threatening claims of misconduct (e.g. Section 1203)

Making false claims of misconduct

Making false accusations

Verbal/Physical threats or assaults

Making a bribe (e.g. offering gifts or other things of value)

\* \* \*

A second badge of practitioner misconduct is a pattern of delay by the practitioner in performing one or more of the following actions (Circular No. 230 Section 10.20) during the course of several collection cases:

Missing appointments

Canceling appointments at the last moment with no good cause provided

Agreeing to provide requested documentation and/or information and then refusing to do so, thereby hindering the Service's efforts to continue its investigation

Providing partial information requiring repeated call backs and correspondence causing delays

\* \* \*

## THE FLORIDA BAR
### v.
## MARTOCCI
791 So. 2d 1074 (Fla. 2001)

PER CURIAM:

We have for review a referee's report regarding alleged ethical breaches by respondent Henry John Martocci (Martocci). For the reasons stated herein, we affirm the referee's findings of fact, conclusions of guilt, and recommended discipline.

\* \* \*

Regarding count one, the referee found that, in December 1996, Martocci called Ms. Berger a "nut case." After a deposition on May 5, 1998, Martocci referred to Ms. Berger as a "crazy" and a "nut case." During another deposition on May 5, 1998, Martocci made demeaning facial gestures and stuck out his tongue at Ms. Berger and Ms. Figueroa. After a hearing on June 24, 1998, upon exiting an elevator, Martocci told Ms. Figueroa that she was a "stupid idiot" and that she should "go back to Puerto Rico." In another incident, on June 19, 1998, during an intermission of a deposition, Ms. Figueroa telephoned the office of Judge Edward J. Richardson and reached Pamela Walker, a judicial assistant. After Ms. Figueroa spoke to Ms. Walker, Martocci took the telephone and yelled the word "bitch." Martocci admitted that because the phone was dead when he received it from Ms. Figueroa, he said "son of a bitch" as a frustrated response to missing the opportunity to speak to Ms. Walker. Martocci claims that he did not say these words to anyone in particular. The referee also found that throughout the Berger proceedings Martocci repeatedly told Ms. Figueroa that she did not know the law or the rules of procedure and that she needed to go back to school.

As to the second count, the referee found that on May 8, 1998, during a recess to a hearing in the Berger proceedings, when Mr. Paton entered the courtroom, Martocci said "here comes the father of the nut case." Mr. Paton responded by approaching respondent and saying, "If you have something to say to me, say it to my face, not in front of everyone here in the courtroom." Thereafter, in open court and for all to see, Martocci closely approached Mr. Paton and threatened to beat him. Upon Ms. Figueroa's attempt to intervene,

Martocci told her to "go back to Puerto Rico." This confrontation only ended when a bailiff entered the courtroom.

On the basis of such misconduct, the referee recommended the imposition against Martocci of a public reprimand and a two-year period of probation with conditions including an evaluation by Florida Lawyers Assistance for possible anger management or mental health assistance or both. In recommending discipline, the referee noted that the underlying Berger proceedings were difficult cases which caused frustration to all the parties involved, including the presiding judges. The referee also noted that Martocci had a good reputation for representing his clients and had no prior disciplinary convictions. In aggravation, the referee recognized that, despite Martocci's substantial experience in the practice of law, Martocci engaged in a pattern of unethical misconduct and refused to acknowledge the wrongful nature of his conduct.

\* \* \*

Martocci's second claim is that, even if the referee's findings of fact are correct, Martocci's conduct was not prejudicial to the administration of justice as it did not rise to a level that violated rule 4-8.4(d). In support of this proposition, Martocci argues that Florida Bar v. Martocci, 699 So.2d 1357 (Fla.1997), established a distinction between unprofessional conduct and unethical conduct violating rule 4-8.4(d). In that case, we upheld the referee's conclusion that the Bar did not clearly and convincingly prove that Martocci violated rules 4-8.4(c) and (d), although Martocci used profanity against the opposing attorney and threatened the court reporter. However, we find Martocci to be distinguishable from the case before us today.

In Martocci, we reasoned that, despite the contrary evidence in the record, there was competent, substantial evidence to support the referee's resolution of the debatable issues in respondent's favor. See Martocci, 699 So.2d at 1360. Likewise, in the present case, because there is competent, substantial evidence supporting the referee's conclusion of guilt, we will not substitute our judgement for that of the referee. Such misconduct clearly prejudiced the administration of justice by further exacerbating relationships between respondent, opposing counsel, and the various judges involved in the already difficult underlying Berger cases. See Florida Bar v. Wasserman, 675 So.2d 103 (Fla.1996) (attorney was disciplined under rule 4-8.4(a), violating Rules of Professional Conduct, for swearing at a judicial assistant over telephone after receiving unfavorable response to question posed to judge presiding over his case); Florida Bar v. Uhrig, 666 So.2d 887 (Fla.1996) (attorney violated rule 4-8.4(d) by mailing insulting letter to opposing party who was a member of a minority group).

We previously have admonished members of the Bar to refrain from offensive conduct.. Martocci's disrespectful and abusive comments cross the line from that of zealous advocacy to unethical misconduct. Such unethical conduct shall not be tolerated.

DISCIPLINE

We disagree with Martocci's claim that the referee's recommended discipline is excessive and only warranting of a private reprimand. Martocci disrupted the already difficult Berger cases by engaging in a pattern of unethical conduct against the opposing litigant, her family, and her counsel. In addition, several cases support the referee's conclusion that a public reprimand is the appropriate sanction for Martocci's misconduct. First, in Martocci, where this Court affirmed the referee's not-guilty finding, we found that:

[W]e find the conduct of the lawyers involved in the incident giving rise to these proceedings to be patently unprofessional***. We should be and are embarrassed and ashamed for all bar members that such childish and demeaning conduct takes place in the justice system. It is our hope that by publishing this opinion and thereby making public the offending and demeaning exchanges between these particular attorneys, that the entire bar will benefit and realize an attorney's obligation to adhere to the highest professional standards of conduct no matter the location or circumstances in which an attorney's services are being rendered.

* * * Second, in Buckle and in Uhrig, this Court publicly reprimanded the attorneys for violating rule 4-8.4(d) by sending the opposing party letters deemed to be discriminatory, disparaging, or frightening. See Buckle, 771 So.2d at 1133; Uhrig, 666 So.2d at 887. In the case before us, Martocci's behavior is more egregious than that in Buckle or Uhrig because Martocci engaged in a consistent pattern of unethical misconduct. Finally, the referee's report reflects that the aggravators and mitigators that were considered and the recommended sanctions serve the purposes of lawyer discipline * * *.

## Questions and Comments:

The adversarial process can get very adversarial. It is very important that as lawyers we remain professionals throughout the process. There may be times where your patience is tested, but it is very clear that inappropriate behavior can lead to significant disciplinary consequences. In addition, aggressive advocacy is not an excuse for abhorrent behavior. For a much longer and detailed case involving inappropriate behavior *see* In re Fletcher, 424 F.3d 783 (8th Cir. 2005)(upholding sanction of attorney who used profanity to opposing counsel, selectively quoted and mischaracterized deposition testimony, and used racially charged language to intimidate opponents).; See also In re Golden, 496 S.E.2d 619 (S.C.1998)(attorney was publicly reprimanded for making insulting and degrading comments during a deposition).

The following problems are based on actual cases published by the Service.

### Problem 2.18

Practitioner and the Service were meeting about a taxpayer's return and the meeting "deteriorated into acrimony." The meeting ended, and the practitioner "grasped a revenue officer by the shoulder and urged her to continue the meeting." The officer refused the request. The practitioner continued to hold the officer and made the request again. The revenue officer once again refused and left. Is this contemptuous conduct?

### Problem 2.19

You are an IRS lawyer involved in negotiations with a taxpayer's attorney. During the negotiations, the attorney uses profane language and calls you names. He also raises his voice and indicates that he is going to complain to higher ups about your behavior. In a previous meeting, the practitioner refused to leave your office when he was asked to do so. Is this sufficient to warrant a finding of "contemptuous conduct?" Would you report this to the OPR?

### Problem 2.20

You are a supervisor at the IRS. A Practitioner calls and complains that an agent was improperly seeking penalties against practitioner's client.  The practitioner stated that if this treatment continued he would call the district director and his Congressman and try to get you and the auditor fired.  Is this conduct sufficient to warrant referral to OPR?  Why or why not?

**Problem 2.21**

The following, with some modifications, is from an actual deposition.

Mr. Rose: If you're going to hand the complaint to him to coach him we are going to see the Judge.

Mr. Will: Just get your foul odious body on the other side.

Mr. Rose: Then don't show the witness anymore-

Mr. Will: I'm giving the witness the Complaint-

Mr. Rose: You're not entitled to coach the witness any further, you're not entitled to-

Mr. Will: Don't use your little [ethnic slur] tricks on me.

Mr. Rose: Off the record-

Mr. Will: No, on the record.

Mr. Rose: You son of a bitch.

Third party: Let's call a recess.

Mr. Rose: Tell the Judge I called him a rotten son of a bitch for calling me a [ethnic slur] and I want to go see the Judge right now.

Do you think either Mr. Will or Mr. Rose should be sanctioned?  If so, what punishment would you recommend?

## 3.   COMMUNICATION

As technology becomes more sophisticated and there are more options for communicating with clients, significant questions have arisen regarding client communication.  For example, should an attorney be allowed to communicate with a client by e-mail or fax? What do you do if you improperly receive communication from an opposing attorney? For example, you hit reply all on your e-mail and send the client communication to all the parties to the case.

In addition, issues arise regarding with whom you may communicate. When may you contact the client directly? When, if you are representing a taxpayer, may you go over the IRS attorney's head, or try to negotiate independently with the Department of Justice?

### (a) Unintended Communication

The bar has struggled with the appropriate remedy when an attorney receives unintended privileged communication from a third party. The ABA originally issued two opinions on the subject. One which indicated that if an attorney was unintentionally sent a privileged document, the attorney had an ethical obligation to avoid reading the document, to notify opposing counsel regarding its receipt, and to deal with the document in accordance with opposing counsel's wishes. See Form. Op. 92-368 (withdrawn). If an attorney received a document from a third party, the attorney still had an obligation to notify counsel of its receipt and to follow instructions from opposing counsel regarding the treatment of the document (unless the document was inappropriately held back from discovery). See Form. Op. 94-382 (withdrawn).

The model rules were revised in 2002, and now contain a specific provision indicating that "[a] lawyer who receives a document relating to the representation of the lawyer's client and knows or reasonably should know that the document was inadvertently sent shall promptly notify the sender." See Rule 4.4(b). There is therefore a clear obligation to notify the sender but nothing prohibiting the lawyer from reading the document and benefiting from the information obtained. Comment 2 to Rule 4.4 states "[w]hether the lawyer is required to take additional steps, such as returning the original document, is a matter of law beyond the scope of these rules..."

The ABA's basic position is that this is not an ethical issue but is instead an evidentiary one. The question is whether the attorney-client privilege has been waived by the disclosure of the document. If it has been waived, the opposing counsel may use the document. If it has not been waived, then use is prohibited. Some states, however, have either developed case law based on the old rule or have adopted a rule similar to the one originally interpreted in Formal Opinion 92-368.

For example, Arizona Rule of Professional Conduct 4.4(b) provides that the recipient of unintended communication must "preserve the status quo for a reasonable period of time in order to permit the sender to take protective measures" and Louisiana Rule of Professional Conduct 4.4(b) provides "[a] lawyer who receives a writing that, on its face, appears to be subject to the attorney-client privilege or otherwise confidential, under circumstances where it is clear that the writing was not intended for the receiving lawyer, shall refrain from examining the writing, promptly notify the sending lawyer, and return the writing." See also N.J. Rule of Prof'l Conduct 4.4(b).

Other jurisdictions have followed the new rule and see the consequences of the inadvertent disclosure as a question of "substantive law, not ethics." See Pa. Ethics Op. 2005-22. The following case from Maryland provides an analysis on the substantive law issue. What do you think is the best way of resolving this issue? What type of rule would you like to live under as a practitioner?

# ELKTON CARE CENTER ASSOCIATES LIMITED PARTNERSHIP t/a Medpointe
## v.
# QUALITY CARE MANAGEMENT, INC.
Court of Special Appeals of Maryland.
805 A.2d 1177 (2002)

MURPHY, C.J.

In the Circuit Court for Cecil County, a jury (the Honorable Dexter M. Thompson, Jr., presiding) found that Elkton Care Center Associates Limited Partnership t/a Medpointe (Medpointe), appellant, breached its contract with Quality Care Management, Inc. (QCM), appellee. Appellant argues that it is entitled to a new trial [because the court inappropriately allowed documents protected by the attorney-client privilege and the work product doctrine into evidence]

Factual Background

Appellant constructed a nursing home in Elkton, Maryland and on June 27, 1994, entered into a Nursing Center Management Agreement with appellee.  * * *

In November of 1996, appellant terminated its agreement with appellee pursuant to Paragraph 11(7) of the Nursing Center Management Agreement. In April of 1998, appellee sued appellant for "wrongful termination" of the agreement.

Procedural History

During the discovery phase of this case, pursuant to a request for document production, a lawyer in the firm that was then representing appellant produced a box that contained a number of documents. It was agreed that (1) appellee's counsel would examine the documents in the box and identify which documents they wanted copied, and (2) appellant's counsel would make, and deliver to appellee's counsel, a copy of each document that had been "tabbed" by appellee's counsel. Included among these documents was a memorandum from a lawyer to Mr. Willits, the president of Medpointe, who had retained that lawyer's firm to determine what defenses would be available to appellant if appellee filed a wrongful termination action. This memorandum was expressly designated as "ATTORNEY/CLIENT PRIVILEGE ATTORNEY WORK PRODUCT PREPARED IN ANTICIPATION OF LITIGATION." The memorandum was tabbed by appellee's counsel, and a copy was later forwarded to appellee's counsel along with copies of other tabbed documents.

At trial, appellant's trial counsel called Mr. Willits, who testified as follows during his direct examination:

Q. And what I'd like to do is to cut right to the chaff [sic], if I could. I'd like you to point the ladies and gentleman of the jury to the section of the contract that Medpointe relies upon in terminating its management contract with OCM.

* * *

Q. What portions of that section of the contract does Medpointe rely upon in saying that it had the unequivocal right to terminate the agreement?

The following transpired during Mr. Willits' cross-examination:

[APPELLEE'S COUNSEL]: Isn't it true that it wasn't until after March of 1997 when [the] lawyer [retained by MedPointe's principal owner] told you that you had breached the contract by improperly terminating it, that you first came up with the excuse that you testified to today?

[APPELLANT'S COUNSEL]: Your Honor, I object to that.

THE COURT: Approach the bench.

*  *  *

THE COURT:  Have you all discussed this yet? Has everybody knew this was coming?

[APPELLANT'S COUNSEL]: No, no, judge.

THE COURT: Where did it come from?

[APPELLEE'S COUNSEL]: They produced it in their documents. We tabbed it. They copied it. They sent it to us. I intend to use it.
[APPELLANT'S COUNSEL]: I have no idea. I am not calling him a liar. I just have no idea.

THE COURT: You better get together and discuss this *** you might have a waiver.

A luncheon recess occurred at this point. The following transpired when the proceedings resumed:

THE COURT: * * * How did you get this, by requesting documents?

 [APPELLEE'S CO-COUNSEL]: Your Honor, there was a-we got about a half full box, bankers box of documents that the other side produced.

THE COURT: From whom?

[APPELLEE'S CO-COUNSEL]: From the law firm representing the [appellant], and I tabbed the documents. I did not tab every document. I tabbed the documents I wanted. This was among them. We received documents in a-just a manila envelope from the-with a white first class sticker on it. * * *

[Appellant's counsel then objected to the use of the document throughout the questioning]

* * *

As stated above, the jury concluded that appellant had breached the contract.

The Consequences of Inadvertent Disclosure

Appellant argues that the attorney-client privilege and/or work product privilege was not waived by the inadvertent disclosure that occurred during document production in the case at bar. The attorney-client privilege and the work product doctrine are separate and distinct. E.I. du Pont de Nemours & Co. v. Forma-Pack, Inc., 351 Md. 396, 406, 718 A.2d 1129 (1998). For purposes of this appeal, however, whether inadvertent disclosure constituted a waiver does not depend upon which privilege is asserted. "When the disclosure is made to the adverse party, . . . the distinction between waiver of attorney client privilege and of work product immunity disappears." Hartford Fire Insurance v. Garvey, 109 F.R.D. 323, 328 (N.D.Cal.1985).

Neither the Court of Appeals nor this Court has decided the issue of whether the attorney-client privilege is waived by the inadvertent disclosure of a document protected by that privilege. Dean Wigmore took the position that any disclosure causes a loss of protection. See 8 Wigmore, Evidence § 2325 at 633 (McNaughton rev.1961). Following Wigmore, some courts have adopted the "strict test" or "waiver" test, under which an inadvertent disclosure constitutes a waiver of the privilege. Some courts have adopted the "lenient" or "no waiver" test, under which the attorney's negligence cannot waive the privilege because the client, and not the attorney, is the holder of the privilege. Professors Mueller and Kirkpatrick have criticized these inflexible positions:

Courts are divided on whether the attorney-client privilege is lost by accidental or inadvertent disclosure. Usually inadvertent or accidental disclosure happens when a privileged document is released during discovery, and in this setting there are three primary views on the question whether privilege protection continues. Modern courts generally reject Wigmore's wooden and mechanical view that any unprivileged disclosure waives the privilege, but some modern courts take a pretty strict position on this point. They hold that the privilege is waived by any unprivileged disclosure that is voluntary, even though made inadvertently and without intent to waive. A second view is very nearly at the opposite end of the spectrum, and it holds that the privilege is waived only where the disclosing party actually intended to waive it.

A third intermediate view sensibly holds that the question whether disclosure during discovery results in loss of privilege protection depends very much on the circumstances and the issue should be resolved by looking mostly to three factors: First is the degree of care apparently exercised by the claimant. Second is the presence of extenuating circumstances, the most obvious being the press of massive discovery going forward under the pressure of deadlines, where even caution in producing documents is likely to generate occasional mistakes. Third is the behavior of the privilege claimant in taking remedial steps after disclosing material.

We agree with Professors Mueller and Kirkpatrick, and with those courts that have adopted an "intermediate" (or "middle") test, under which the court makes a fact specific case-by-case analysis to determine whether the privilege has been waived. The courts that use this approach examine the following factors: "(1) the reasonableness of the precautions taken to prevent inadvertent disclosure in view of the extent of the document production; (2) the number of inadvertent disclosures; (3) the extent of the disclosure; (4) any delay and measures taken to rectify the disclosure; and (5) whether the overriding interests of justice would or would not be served by relieving a party of its error." See Sampson Fire Sales v. Oaks, 201 F.R.D., 351, 360 (M.D.Pa.2001). We are persuaded that neither the lenient test nor the strict test is as fair as the intermediate test, and that the intermediate test is consistent with Court of Appeals' precedent.

The attorney-client privilege is not absolute and "is not an inviolable seal upon the attorney's lips." Pitney-Bowes, Inc. v. Mestre, 86 F.R.D. 444, 446 (S.D.Fl.1980)(citing Laughner v. U.S., 373 F.2d 326, 327 (5th Cir.1967)). Invocation of the privilege can create evidentiary inequities between parties during discovery and the absence of fact and truth at trial. "Because the application of the attorney-client privilege withholds relevant information from the fact finder, the privilege contains some limitations and should be narrowly construed." E.I. du Pont de Nemours & Co., 351 Md. at 415, 718 A.2d 1129. Only the client has the power to waive the attorney-client privilege. See City of College Park v. Cotter, 309 Md. 573, 591, 525 A.2d 1059 (1987). Nonetheless, express and implied waivers of the privilege are universally recognized limitations on client power to hold the privilege. Applying the intermediate test to the facts of this case, in which the inadvertent disclosure occurred during pre-trial discovery, but was not brought to Judge Thompson's attention until (in the words of appellant's brief) "the penultimate day of trial," we conclude that the inadvertent disclosure constituted a waiver.

In most inadvertent disclosure cases, at least one factor is closely related to another factor. The case at bar is no exception. Factors one, two and three- the reasonableness of precautions taken to prevent inadvertent disclosure, the number of inadvertent disclosures, and the extent of the disclosure-all strongly favor waiver. Here, the privileged document was inadvertently included in a half-full box of documents produced by a lawyer who was then representing appellant. Appellee's counsel tabbed that document, along with others, and returned all of the tabbed documents to the lawyer then representing appellant, who arranged to have the tabbed documents copied and delivered to appellee's counsel. Thus, on two occasions during the pretrial discovery phase of this case, counsel then representing appellant had the opportunity to assert the attorney-client privilege with respect to the memorandum at issue. This is not a case in which hundreds of boxes and/or thousands of documents were produced.

Factor four, any delay and measures taken to rectify the disclosure, also strongly favors waiver. Had this issue been brought to Judge Thompson's attention prior to trial, (1) Judge Thompson could have entered an in limine order that would have prohibited appellee's counsel from making any use of the memorandum unless and until appellant introduced evidence that "opened the door" to its use, and (2) appellant's defense would have focused on its right to terminate the contract rather than on its reasons for doing so. In light of Mr. Willits' direct examination, factor five, whether the overriding interests of justice would or would not be served by relieving the party of its error, also strongly favors waiver. The inadvertent disclosure in the case at bar constitutes a waiver of the attorney-client and attorney work product privileges.

**Questions and Comments:**

1.  The original ABA Opinion (92-368) now adopted in many states provides that a lawyer must not benefit from materials protected by privilege and inadvertently sent by opposing counsel. Does this rule make sense to you? Is it realistic to expect that lawyers will not look at documents they receive from opposing counsel? Is there some benefit to the rule even if we recognize that at least some attorneys will read the document at issue?

2.  The ABA originally determined that if a lawyer received information from a third party that was protected by the Attorney-Client privilege the lawyer needed to notify opposing counsel and could not use the privileged information.  Since Rule 4.4(b) was modified the ABA withdrew its opinion. What should the rule be in the case of information received from third parties? Should it matter how the information was obtained?

3.  The ABA Opinion indicates that an attorney might be able to use the document if it should have been turned over during discovery. In other words, if the other attorney acted unethically in not turning over a document, then the third party was in a sense curing that error. The attorney, however, must read at least part of the document to recognize whether it should have been turned over in discovery. How much may the attorney read?

4.  The now withdrawn Formal Opinion mentions that client communication is now sent by e-mail and fax and that one might expect some mistakes regarding transmission. Is there an argument that lawyers should not be sending privileged material by unencrypted e-mail? Formal Opinion 99-413 provides that a lawyer has an expectation of privacy in unencrypted e-mail and that transmission by e-mail is acceptable. Although it may be ethical, it may be bad business practice. The problem is not the security of the e-mail. It is the human error in sending an e-mail. Also remember that electronic documents often imbed deleted text within a document so the text can be restored. That text can also be restored by an opposing party.

**Problem 2.23**

You are a lawyer for the United State Senate Finance Committee. You receive testimony from an administration witness who opposes a measure that your boss supports. When you open an electronic copy of the document and hit "track changes" you see all the edits that the Office of Management and Budget added to the testimony. As an attorney, may you ethically read the edits? Assume instead that you are a very sophisticated computer user and you check to see if there are undeleted documents on the disc. You notice several documents that you think would be damaging to the witness. May you undelete the documents and read them?

**Problem 2.24**

Assume instead you are in the midst of litigation, and opposing counsel provides you with a disc that contains his opposition to your motion for summary judgment. Your technology people have the capacity to run a scan on the disc to determine whether there is any other information on the disc. May you ethically instruct them to do so?

**Problem 2.25**

Instead, you are a lawyer working for the IRS. The opposing party sends you a disc with scanned copies of its exhibits. You realize that in addition to the scanned exhibits, the disc contains the taxpayer's return and other financial information that is available to you. You do not have it easily at your disposal, but the IRS has the information. May you look at and use the documents? What if instead the disc contained information that should have been turned over but was not?

## (b) Communication with Represented Party

Model Rule 4.2 provides that "a lawyer shall not communicate about the subject of the representation with a party the lawyer knows to be represented by another lawyer in the matter, unless the lawyer has the consent of the other lawyer or is authorized by law to do so." The general rule is that when someone is represented by an attorney, the attorney for the other side should communicate with the attorney, not the client.

This rule, however, gets a little more complicated when the Government is involved. If you have a case pending before the Department of Justice, can you try to negotiate with the IRS? Can you call your Congressman to complain? Despite Rule 4.2's prohibition, the First Amendment provides citizens with the right to petition the Government for a redress of grievances. Thus Rule 4.2's limitation is interpreted not to apply when a citizen is attempting to seek redress on policy grounds. Model Rule 4.2, Comment 5. While it would not be appropriate to contact the IRS to seek settlement of your case, it might be appropriate to contact the IRS to urge them to reconsider a policy stance that they were taking with regard to an issue (even if that issue was pending in court).

# LOBATO V. FORD
### 2007 WL 3342598 (D.Colo.2007)

SHAFFER, MAGISTRATE JUDGE:

The facts underlying the instant action were summarized in detail in this court's Order on Pending Motions to Strike, Lobato v. Ford, 2007 WL 2593458 (D.Colo.2007), and do not bear repeating here. Suffice to say, Plaintiffs have alleged various constitutional violations arising out of the fatal shooting of Frank Lobato on July 11, 2004 by Denver police officer Ranjan Ford.* * *

Plaintiffs have separately moved to disqualify counsel for the City Defendants, arguing that Ms. Pierce improperly initiated an investigation of Plaintiffs' counsel by the Attorney Regulation Counsel for the State of Colorado based upon Mr. Padilla's contacts with officials of the City and County of Denver. Plaintiffs contend that Ms. Pierce took these actions to gain an advantage in violation of Rule 4.5(a) of the Colorado rules of Professional Conduct.

Some relevant facts are not in dispute. It appears that Mr. Padilla spoke to Denver City Councilman Rick Garcia while attending as an honoree a banquet organized by the Colorado Hispanic Bar Association on January 20, 2007. After learning of this conversation from Councilman Garcia, Ms. Pierce sent a letter to Mr. Padilla on February 9, 2007, in which she referenced Rule 4.2 of the Colorado Rules of Professional Conduct and enclosed a copy of Ethics Opinion 93, Ex Parte Communications with Government Officials, a Formal Opinion written by the Ethics Committee of the Colorado Bar Association. In her letter, Ms. Pierce wrote:

> I cannot fathom how you could have possibly thought it was permissible for you to communicate directly with Councilman Garcia about settlement in this case. Your communication with him is no less ethical than if I called one of the Lobato children directly and told them that you were being obstinate in settlement negotiations and not looking after their best interests.

Ms. Pierce closed by stating that she would not "tolerate" Mr. Padilla's *ex parte* communications with her clients. It is also undisputed that on March 29, 2007, Mr. Padilla spoke by telephone with Alvin LaCabe, an attorney and the City of Denver's Manager of Safety. On March 30, 2007, Ms. Pierce again wrote to Mr. Padilla complaining of his recent *ex parte* communication with Mr. LaCabe. Ms. Pierce closed this letter by telling Mr. Padilla that he "may expect that I will be taking appropriate action in regard to this incident, as well as your prior inappropriate *ex parte* contacts with Councilman Rick Garcia."On April 4, 2007, Ms. Pierce wrote to the Office of the Attorney Regulation Counsel stating that she wished to file a complaint against Mr. Padilla.

Mr. Padilla contends that his banquet conversation with Councilman Garcia lasted less than a minute, and that he merely expressed his belief that taxpayer funds should be directed to resolving this litigation rather than "defending this indefensible shooting and killing of an innocent man" and "exacerbating the conflict through litigation." Councilman Garcia represents Mr. Padilla's district and they have known each other for years through their involvement in Denver politics. According to Mr. Padilla, "City Councilman Garcia had in fact called Mr. Padilla to inquire about the status of the Lobato case and to seek his opinion prior to [Councilman] Garcia's taking a position on the request for a grand jury investigation of Denver Police Officer Ford in the Lobato killing." As for his March 29 conversation with Mr. LaCabe, Plaintiffs' counsel contends that he called to inquire about the administrative appeal involving James Turney, a Denver Police officer who had shot and killed a developmentally disabled minor, Paul Childs, on July 5, 2003, and the status of disciplinary action against Denver Police officer Joseph Bini, who allegedly had filed a false affidavit in a separate incident involving the death of Ismael Mena on September 23, 1999. According to Mr. Padilla, Mr. LaCabe stated that the Turney administrative appeal was pending before the Civil Service Commission. Mr. Padilla insists that he has known Mr. LaCabe in a professional capacity for a number of years and that he and Mr. LaCabe did not discuss the Lobato shooting during their March 29th conversation. Mr. Padilla also contends that all the information he sought in the conversation with Mr. LaCabe was publically available. *Id.* at 3.

Ms. Pierce claims that she received a telephone call from Councilman Garcia on February 8, 2007, relating his conversation with Mr. Padilla. According Ms. Pierce, Councilman Garcia recounted how Mr. Padilla had expressed his displeasure "about the City's stance on mediation and his belief that settlement of his case would be in the best interests of the City." (citation omitted) In a subsequent letter to Ms. Culberson-Smith on May 29, 2007, Ms. Pierce elaborated on her conversation with Councilman Garcia.

> When Councilman Garcia contacted me to report his interaction with Mr. Padilla, he specifically related Mr. Padilla's expressed concerns that attorneys for the City and for the other defendants in the *Lobato* case were being unreasonable both about the conditions under which they would agree to private mediation and in their stance on settlement to date. In fact, his call to me had two expressed purposes: to report the conversation, which would not have been necessary had it not related directly to the case; and to ask me why the parties had not yet been successful settling the case or agreeing on terms for mediation, something Councilman Garcia would not have been aware of unless Mr. Padilla told him.

> As for Mr. Padilla's conversation with Mr. LaCabe, Ms. Pierce claims she was told by Mr. LaCabe that he cautioned [Mr. Padilla] up front that he could not discuss the *Lobato* case with [him] directly. [Mr. Padilla] agreed, but then proceeded to elicit information from Mr. LaCabe about prior police shooting cases, including the *Turney* discipline matter and the *Mena* case, specifically inquiring as to the status of the *Turney* case, what actions he had taken in regard to that case, and where [Mr. Padilla] could obtain documents pertaining to that case.

Mr. Padilla and Ms. Pierce both cite the Colorado Rules of Professional Conduct in attempting to justify their actions. Plaintiffs' Motion to Disqualify invokes Rule 4.5(a) of the Colorado rules of Professional Conduct, which provides that a lawyer "shall not threaten to present criminal, administrative or disciplinary charges to obtain an advantage in a civil matter, nor shall a lawyer present or participate in presenting criminal, administrative or disciplinary charges solely to obtain an advantage in a civil matter."[21]   The Comment accompanying Rule 4.5(a) points out that

> The rule distinguishes between threats to bring criminal, administrative or disciplinary charges and the actual filing or presentation of such charges. Threats to file such charges are prohibited if a purpose is to obtain *any* advantage in a civil matter while the actual presentation of such charges is proscribed by this rule only if the *sole* purpose for presenting the charges is to obtain an advantage in a civil matter.

Mr. Padilla contends that a grievance was filed with the OARC in an effort to chill his efforts to seek redress from government officials who "publicly promised to compensate Plaintiffs for their injuries in the wrongful death of their father," and to stigmatize Mr. Padilla. Counsel insists that Ms. Pierce's actions have infringed upon his First Amendment rights and the First Amendment rights of his clients.

\* \* \*

Ms. Pierce insists that her contacts with the OARC were prompted solely by Mr. Padilla's repeated failure to comply with Rule 4.2 of the Colorado rules of Professional Conduct, which states that in representing a client, a lawyer shall not communicate about the subject of the representation with a party the lawyer knows to be represented by another lawyer in the matter, unless the lawyer has the consent of the other lawyer or is authorized by law to do so.

Rule 4.2 is designed "to prevent situations in which a represented party may be taken advantage of by adverse counsel; the presence of the party's attorney theoretically neutralizes" any undue influence.

In the context of this case, Councilman Garcia and Manager of Safety LaCabe fall within the expansive definition of "party" contemplated by Rule 4.2. See Chancellor v. Boeing Co., 678 F.Supp. 250, 253 (D.Kan.1988) (holding that for purposes of Rule 4.2, a

---

[21] Ms. Pierce's letters of February 9 and March 30, 2007 did not violate Rule 4.5, which permits an attorney to notify another person that "the lawyer reasonably believes that the other's conduct may violate criminal, administrative or disciplinary rules." *See* Rule 4.5(b), Colorado Rules of Professional Conduct.

current employee is a "party" if he or she has managerial responsibilities, his or her acts or omissions in connection with the matter may be imputed to the organization, or if his or her statements may be admissions on the part of the organization). * * * Yet, Mr. Padilla contends that his *ex parte* contacts with these individuals fall within the Rule 4.2 exception for communications "authorized by law."

Courts have reached decidedly different results in applying Rule 4.2 to governmental entities. Compare Frey v. Department of Health and Human Services, 106 F.R.D. 32, 35 (E.D.N.Y.1985) (precluding *ex parte* contacts with government employees having managerial authority) and Camden v. State of Maryland, 910 F.Supp. 1115, 1118 n. 8 (D.Md.1996) (observing that "Rule 4.2 has been uniformly interpreted to be inapplicable" where a governmental organization is a party). * * * Another court has suggested that counsel may ethically engage in *ex parte* communications with government employees who have

> "authority to take or recommend action in the matter;" when the sole purpose of the communication is to address a policy issue, including settling the controversy; and when the lawyer for the party gives government counsel reasonable advance notice of the intent to communicate with the official.

Hammond v. City of junction City, Kansas, 2002 WL 169370, (D.Kan.2002) (citing ABA Committee on Ethics and Professional Responsibility, Formal Op. 97- 408 (1997)).

Ultimately, the disposition of Plaintiffs' Motion to Disqualify does not require this court to decide whether Mr. Padilla or Ms. Pierce violated any Rule of Professional Conduct. [The court went on to examine whether the alleged violation was grounds for Ms. Pierce's disqualification as counsel. The court easily determined that it was not.]

### Scenario 2.3

Assume you are counsel for Mr. Padilla in a disciplinary hearing. What arguments would you make on behalf of your client? What arguments would you make if you were disciplinary counsel?

## Question and Comments:

1. Do you have any recourse if opposing counsel is a government attorney, and you do not believe counsel is acting appropriately? In almost all cases, it is ethical to contact that attorney's supervisor. If your problem is with a Department of Justice attorney, you may ethically call that attorney's supervisor, assuming that person is a lawyer. In addition, the prohibition applies to you, not your client. The client may continue to contact the IRS if she chooses to do so.

2. What if the IRS wants to call the client to get routine information like a copy of the taxpayer's tax return? Once the taxpayer has an attorney, Rule 4.2 applies and the attorney representing the IRS cannot contact the taxpayer seeking information. It is less clear, however, whether a non-attorney at the IRS may contact the taxpayer seeking information. If the non-attorney IRS employee is just seeking documents or routine information it is probably permissible. The agent, however, cannot be seeking the information as an agent for the lawyer.

# Chapter 3

## Conflict of Interest

Conflict of interest issues can be very complicated and often cause ethical dilemmas for legal practitioners. In general, under Model Rule 1.7 a lawyer cannot represent a client if "the representation of one client will be directly adverse to another client" or if "there is a significant risk that representation of one client will be materially limited by the lawyer's responsibilities to another client, a former client or a third person or by a personal interest of the lawyer." Comment 8 to Rule 1.7 provides that there is a material limitation if "there is a significant risk that a lawyer's ability to consider, recommend or carry out an appropriate course of action for the client will be materially limited as a result of the lawyers other responsibilities or interests." In addition, under Rule 1.10 an individual attorney's conflicts are imputed to other lawyers associated with the attorney.

A lawyer may represent a client even if there is a conflict if the lawyer believes he can provide "competent and diligent" representation to both clients, and each client "gives informed consent" in writing. The representation also cannot be prohibited by law and it cannot involve a claim by one of the lawyer's clients against another. A similar obligation exists for those practicing before the IRS under Circular 230, § 10.29.

In addition, the conflict rules apply to both current and former clients. Rule 1.9 prohibits a lawyer from representing a new client in a substantially related matter if that new client's "interests are materially adverse to the interests of the former client" absent consent from the former client. This does not mean that a tax attorney could not argue for one position in Tax Court one year and a different position the next year.

Rule 1.8 also contains strict rules regarding conflicts of interests that may be caused by the attorney-client relationship. For example, Rule 1.8 restricts a lawyer's ability to enter into a business transaction with a client or to receive bequests under a will.

The conflict provisions come up often in the tax context and are very important. They may arise in both transactional and litigation work. In transactional work, tax lawyers are often involved in complicated business transactions with multiple parties and attorneys need to be careful that their firms have received a waiver of the conflict or are not representing in another matter any of the parties involved in the transaction.

In the litigation context, tax lawyers are usually less concerned about potential conflicts with their adversary because the adversary is almost always a government unit. Comment 24 to Rule 1.7 indicates that a "lawyer may take inconsistent legal positions in different tribunals at different times on behalf of different clients." A conflict exists only when there is "significant risk" that a position in litigation will "seriously weaken the position taken on behalf of the other client."

Despite the fact that government as an adversary poses less conflict problems, tax lawyers face significant conflict issues. It is often the person right in front of you or at least around the corner that causes the conflict. Tax lawyers are often asked to represent married couples, partners in a business venture, or both a corporation and its President. In some cases, this dual representation makes sense, and in other cases, the parties' interests are clearly not aligned and dual representation is not appropriate.

In addition, there are some situations where a lawyer's legal duties conflict with a taxpayer's legal duties. For example, a lawyer might not be able to take a position on the return unless the position is disclosed, while a taxpayer may find disclosure disadvantageous. How does a lawyer resolve this conflict? This has been more or less a problem over the years depending on the various standards and penalties that apply to taxpayers and lawyers. Our tax law has often had different standards for tax lawyers and individuals. When the lawyer's standards are higher than the taxpayer's standards, or the lawyer's standards require disclosure, the taxpayer has an incentive to move forward with a position and the attorney has an incentive to discourage the position or encourage disclosure. This was the case in 2007 when Congress amended the provisions for preparer penalties and required preparers to meet a more likely than not standard, while taxpayers only had to meet a substantial authority standard. Since the more likely than not standard is higher than the substantial authority standard, there was concern that lawyers could not ethically represent clients in those circumstances.

The concern was that the taxpayer would want to take a position that met the substantial authority standard but was less than the more likely than not standard without disclosure and the lawyer would be subject to a penalty under § 6694 if such a position was not disclosed. The client and lawyer were in positions that could be seen as adverse. The IRS issued regulations to soften this problem, and in 2008 Congress reduced the penalties for preparers to the same standard as taxpayers. Thus, as discussed in Chapter 1, lawyers and taxpayers must both have substantial authority for taking a position. If they do not have substantial authority and the position is not frivolous, they can avoid penalties if they disclose the position. As you will see, some small conflicts may still exist, but the major problem is now solved.

## A.    Internal Conflicts

These are conflicts that arise in the attorney-client relationship due to differing obligations on the attorney and the client. In 2008 the law was changed under § 6694 and the penalties for preparers now basically mirror the penalties for taxpayers. There are, however, still some situations where a conflict may exist.

**Problem 3.1**

Your client wants to take a return position that is not supported by the "rules and regulations" promulgated by the IRS, but also is not frivolous (assume the taxpayer has a 15% chance of success). What do you do? This situation might pose a conflict; what is the conflict?

**Problem 3.2**

Your client wants to take a return position that lacks substantial authority but satisfies the reasonable basis standard. The taxpayer is not subject to a substantial understatement penalty because the understatement is not substantial. The taxpayer is also not subject to a negligence penalty because there is reasonable basis. Does this pose a conflict?

## Questions and Comments:

If a conflict exists, what do you do?  Standards of Tax Practice Statement 2000-1 discusses situations like the above, where a conflict may exist. The statement was written before some of the standards changed, so be careful when reading it to make sure the underlying law is still the same. The section on what to do when a conflict exists, however, remains helpful. The statement provides:

> If the lawyer acts as a signing preparer of the return ... where a conflict exists between client and lawyer, the lawyer should advise the client fully concerning the penalty aspects of adopting the proposed return position and the fact that adequate disclosure will not benefit the taxpayer. The lawyer should advise the client that the client's decision regarding disclosure will affect the lawyer's ability to sign the return as preparer, as well as the reasons why that decision impacts the lawyer's ability to act in these capacities. However, the lawyer must make it clear to the taxpayer that disclosure will not advance the client's interest and may even be detrimental to those interests. The lawyer should advise the client that it may be in the client's best interest to seek independent legal counsel on the question whether to make adequate disclosure of the tax return position. (citation omitted) the lawyer may not advise the client to make adequate disclosure where the only purpose is to benefit the lawyer.

## B.    Representing Multiple Parties

In the tax context, it will often make sense for a lawyer to represent multiple parties. Clients may seek joint representation for return preparation and defense, for structuring a small business, or for estate planning purposes. A tax lawyer should not shy away from these situations merely because a potential conflict exists. In fact, there may be strong reasons relating to both expertise and costs for a lawyer to represent multiple parties. What is important, however, is that the attorney believes that the conflict will not adversely impact his representation and that the clients provide an informed waiver of the conflict.

### A v. B
#### 726 A.2d 924 (N.J. 1999)

In October 1997, the husband and wife retained Hill Wallack * * * to assist them with planning their estates. On the commencement of the joint representation, the husband and wife each signed a letter captioned "Waiver of Conflict of Interest." In explaining the possible conflicts of interest, the letter recited that the effect of a testamentary transfer by one spouse to the other would permit the transferee to dispose of the property as he or she desired. The firm's letter also explained that information provided by one spouse could become available to the other. Although the letter did not contain an express waiver of the confidentiality of any such information, each spouse consented to and waived any conflicts arising from the firm's joint representation.

Unfortunately, the clerk who opened the firm's estate planning file misspelled the clients' surname. The misspelled name was entered in the computer program that the firm uses to discover possible conflicts of interest. The firm then prepared reciprocal wills and related documents with the names of the husband and wife correctly spelled.

[It turns out Husband had an affair. The woman became pregnant and coincidentally retained Hill Wallack to pursue a paternity claim. Because of the error entering Husband's name, the firm did not learn of the conflict for some time. Husband, however, knew the firm was representing the mother because he received correspondence from the firm related to the case. Husband did not notify the firm. In the course of representing the mother in the paternity action, Hill Wallack learned of the conflict.]

* * * Hill Wallack promptly informed the mother that it unknowingly was representing both the husband and the wife in an unrelated matter.

Hill Wallack immediately withdrew from representing the mother in the paternity action. It also instructed the estate planning department not to disclose any information about the husband's assets to the member of the firm who had been representing the mother. The firm then wrote to the husband stating that it believed it had an ethical obligation to disclose to the wife the existence, but not the identity, of his illegitimate child. Additionally, the firm stated that it was obligated to inform the wife "that her current estate plan may devise a portion of her assets through her spouse to that child." The firm suggested that the husband so inform his wife and stated that if he did not do so, it would. Because of the restraints imposed by the Appellate Division, however, the firm has not disclosed the information to the wife.

II.

This appeal concerns the conflict between two fundamental obligations of lawyers: the duty of confidentiality, *Rules of Professional Conduct,* (RPC) 1.6(a), and the duty to inform clients of material facts, RPC 1.4(b). The conflict arises from a law firm's joint representation of two clients whose interests initially were, but no longer are, compatible.

Crucial to the attorney-client relationship is the attorney's obligation not to reveal confidential information learned in the course of representation. Thus, RPC 1.6(a) states that "[a] lawyer shall not reveal information relating to representation of a client unless the client consents after consultation, except for disclosures that are impliedly authorized in order to carry out the representation." Generally, "the principle of attorney-client confidentiality imposes a sacred trust on the attorney not to disclose the client's confidential communication." State v. Land, 73 N.J.24, 30, 372 A.2d 297 (1977).

A lawyer's obligation to communicate to one client all information needed to make an informed decision qualifies the firm's duty to maintain the confidentiality of a co-client's information. RPC 1.4(b), which reflects a lawyer's duty to keep clients informed, requires that "[a] lawyer shall explain a matter to the extent reasonably necessary to permit the client to make informed decisions regarding the representation." * * * In limited situations, moreover, an attorney is permitted or required to disclose confidential information. Hill Wallack argues that RPC 1.6 mandates, or at least permits, the firm to disclose to the wife the existence of the husband's illegitimate child. RPC 1.6(b) requires that a lawyer disclose "information relating to representation of a client" to the proper authorities if the lawyer "reasonably believes" that such disclosure is necessary to prevent the client "from committing a criminal, illegal or fraudulent act that the lawyer reasonably believes is likely to result in death or substantial bodily harm or substantial injury to the financial interest or property of another." RPC 1.6(b)(1). Despite Hill Wallack's claim that RPC 1.6(b) applies, the facts do not justify mandatory disclosure. The possible inheritance of the wife's estate by the husband's illegitimate child is too remote to constitute "substantial injury to the financial interest or property of another" within the meaning of RPC 1.6(b).

By comparison, in limited circumstances RPC 1.6(c) permits a lawyer to disclose a confidential communication. RPC 1.6(c) permits, but does not require, a lawyer to reveal confidential information to the extent the lawyer reasonably believes necessary "to rectify the consequences of a client's criminal, illegal or fraudulent act in furtherance of which the lawyer's services had been used." RPC 1.6(c).

\* \* \*

We likewise construe broadly the term "fraudulent act" within the meaning of RPC 1.6(c). So construed, the husband's deliberate omission of the existence of his illegitimate child constitutes a fraud on his wife. When discussing their respective estates with the firm, the husband and wife reasonably could expect that each would disclose information material to the distribution of their estates, including the existence of children who are contingent residuary beneficiaries. The husband breached that duty. Under the reciprocal wills, the existence of the husband's illegitimate child could affect the distribution of the wife's estate, if she predeceased him. \* \* \*

The New Jersey *RPC*s are based substantially on the American Bar Association Model Rules of Professional Conduct ("the Model Rules"). RPC 1.6, however, exceeds the Model Rules in authorizing the disclosure of confidential information.

Under RPC 1.6, the facts support disclosure to the wife. The law firm did not learn of the husband's illegitimate child in a confidential communication from him. Indeed, he concealed that information from both his wife and the firm. The law firm learned about the husband's child through its representation of the mother in her paternity action against the husband. Accordingly, the husband's expectation of nondisclosure of the information may be less than if he had communicated the information to the firm in confidence.

In addition, the husband and wife signed letters captioned "Waiver of Conflict of Interest." These letters acknowledge that information provided by one client could become available to the other. The letters, however, stop short of explicitly authorizing the firm to disclose one spouse's confidential information to the other. Even in the absence of any such explicit authorization, the spirit of the letters supports the firm's decision to disclose to the wife the existence of the husband's illegitimate child.

\* \* \*

In the absence of an agreement to share confidential information with co-clients, the Restatement [Restatement (Third) of the Law Governing Lawyers §112 comment l] reposes the resolution of the lawyer's competing duties within the lawyer's discretion:

> [T]he lawyer, after consideration of all relevant circumstances, has the ... discretion to inform the affected co-client of the specific communication if, in the lawyer's reasonable judgment, the immediacy and magnitude of the risk to the affected co-client outweigh the interest of the communicating client in continued secrecy.

Additionally, the *Restatement* advises that the lawyer, when withdrawing from representation of the co-clients, may inform the affected co-client that the attorney has learned of information adversely affecting that client's interests that the communicating co-client refuses to permit the lawyer to disclose.

In the context of estate planning, the *Restatement* also suggests that a lawyer's disclosure of confidential information communicated by one spouse is appropriate only if the other spouse's failure to learn of the information would be materially detrimental to that other spouse or frustrate the spouse's intended testamentary arrangement. *Id.* § 112 comment *l*, illustrations 2, 3. \* \* \*

The ACTEC [American College at Trust and Estate Counsel] reasons that if unsuccessful in persuading the client to disclose the information, the lawyer should consider several factors in deciding whether to reveal the confidential information to the co-client, including: (1) duties of impartiality and loyalty to the clients; (2) any express or implied agreement among the lawyer and the joint clients that information communicated by either client to the lawyer regarding the subject of the representation would be shared with the other client; (3) the reasonable expectations of the clients; and (4) the nature of the confidence and the harm that may result if the confidence is, or is not, disclosed.

\* \* \*

The Professional Ethics Committees of New York and Florida, however, have concluded that disclosure to a co-client is prohibited.

New York State Bar Ass'n Comm. on Professional Ethics, Op. 555 (1984); Florida State Bar Ass'n Comm. on Professional Ethics, Op. 95-4 (1997).

The New York opinion addressed the following situation:

> A and B formed a partnership and employed Lawyer L to represent them in connection with the partnership affairs. Subsequently, B, in a conversation with Lawyer L, advised Lawyer L that he was actively breaching the partnership agreement. B preceded this statement to Lawyer L with the statement that he proposed to tell Lawyer L something "in confidence." Lawyer L did not respond to that statement and did not understand that B intended to make a statement that would be of importance to A but that was to be kept confidential from A. Lawyer L had not, prior thereto, advised A or B that he could not receive from one communications regarding the subject of the joint representation that would be confidential from the other. B has subsequently declined to tell A what he has told Lawyer L.

In that situation, the New York Ethics Committee concluded that the lawyer may not disclose to the co-client the communicating client's statement. The Committee based its conclusion on the absence of prior consent by the clients to the sharing of all confidential communications and the fact that the client "specifically in advance designated his communication as confidential, and the lawyer did not demur."

The Florida Ethics Committee addressed a similar situation:

> Lawyer has represented Husband and Wife for many years in a range of personal matters, including estate planning. Husband and Wife have substantial individual assets, and they also own substantial jointly-held property. Recently, Lawyer prepared new updated wills that Husband and Wife signed. Like their previous wills, their new wills primarily benefit the survivor of them for his or her life, with beneficial disposition at the death of the survivor being made equally to their children.

\* \* \*

Several months after the execution of the new wills, Husband confers separately with Lawyer. Husband reveals to Lawyer that he has just executed a codicil (prepared by another law firm) that makes substantial beneficial disposition to a woman with whom Husband has been having an extra-marital relationship.

Reasoning that the lawyer's duty of confidentiality takes precedence over the duty to communicate all relevant information to a client, the Florida Ethics Committee concluded that the lawyer did not have discretion to reveal the information. In support of that conclusion, the Florida committee reasoned that joint clients do not necessarily expect that everything relating to the joint representation communicated by one co-client will be shared with the other co-client.

Because Hill Wallack wishes to make the disclosure, we need not reach the issue whether the lawyer's obligation to disclose is discretionary or mandatory. In conclusion, Hill Wallack may inform the wife of the existence of the husband's illegitimate child [but not the name].

\* \* \*

The law firm learned of the husband's paternity of the child through the mother's disclosure before the institution of the paternity suit. It does not seek to disclose the identity of the mother or the child. Given the wife's need for the information and the law firm's right to disclose it, the disclosure of the child's existence to the wife constitutes an exceptional case with "compelling reason clearly and convincingly shown."

The judgment of the Appellate Division is reversed and the matter is remanded to the Family Part.

## Questions and Comments:

1. The firm here seeks permission to tell B about A's illegitimate child. Does the firm need to take this action or could it resolve the conflict in another way? Why do you think the firm took this course of action?

2. Other states have prohibited the disclosure of confidential communications to a joint client. In those states, when a client communicates confidential information which the client wishes to remain confidential, the information may not be shared with a co-client. See N.Y. Op. 55 (1984)(regarding confidential information among partners); Fla. Op. 95-4 (lawyer who prepared joint wills could not disclose to wife that husband executed a codicil with provisions for his mistress).

3. Notice in A v. B that the clients agreed that information would be shared between them. The parties can execute an agreement that authorizes the lawyer to communicate all material information to each client. That communication, however, may also be revoked.

4. It is important to remember that in tax transactions involving related parties things can go wrong. There is a tendency, especially in family transactions, to assume everyone will get along and to create transactions that assume goodwill on the part of all parties. Unfortunately, this is not always the case. As an attorney it is important to prepare for what will happen if things do not go as planned.

## PARA TECHNOLOGIES TRUST
### v.
## COMMISSIONER OF INTERNAL REVENUE
T.C. Memo 1992-575

COHEN, JUDGE:

Each of these cases is before the Court for ruling on respondent's Motion to Compel Withdrawal of Petitioners' Counsel of Record for Conflict of Interest. The issue for decision is whether a conflict of interest exists that requires the disqualification of petitioners' counsel of record. * * *

* * *

*Background*

Nassau Life Insurance Company, Ltd. (Nassau Life), promoted the use of domestic and foreign entities to shelter United States business and investment income from United States Federal income taxation.\* \* \* From 1982 through 1988, Joe Alfred Izen, Jr. (Izen), was counsel to Nassau Life. In the course of that representation, among other services, he prepared and issued two opinion letters that related to the multiple-entity tax shelter promoted by Nassau Life. \* \* \*

Ferber is a songwriter with a high school education. Anderson completed the eighth grade. At the time of hearing on the pending motions, Ferber was 36 years old and Anderson was 30 years old.

Ferber and Anderson met in India in 1977 and became friends. In late 1984, Anderson began to engage in an electronics business, VideoLab, as a sole proprietor. Because of his limited education, Anderson wanted to adopt a structure for VideoLab that would minimize the amount of paperwork that was necessary to carry on the business. He discussed his plans with Ferber, who was then employed \*\*\* for Nassau Life. Ferber, relying at least partially on the 1983 opinion letter, advised Anderson, who also had access to the 1983 opinion letter, to structure his business as a trust such as those promoted by Nassau Life.

In January 1985, Anderson formed Para Tech as a common-law business trust. From its creation and thereafter, Para Tech conducted the business in which VideoLab had previously been engaged. Ferber was the trustee of Para Tech. The beneficial owner of Para Tech was another trust, Atram Investment Group (Atram), formed under the laws of the Turks and Caicos Islands, British West Indies. Anderson was one of the beneficiaries of Atram.

In a legal opinion letter prepared for Nassau Life dated June 20, 1985, Izen discussed the tax aspects of contractual trust companies (the 1985 opinion letter). Among other things, the letter concluded that the grantor trust provisions of the Internal Revenue Code did not apply to "contractual trust companies". Izen's letter failed to discuss decided cases contrary to the positions he was espousing. Anderson and Ferber gained access to the 1985 opinion letter.

Respondent determined deficiencies in petitioners' Federal income taxes for 1987 and 1988. Respondent determined that Para Tech was an association taxable as a corporation for Federal income tax purposes and disallowed its claimed distribution deductions. Respondent determined that Anderson and Ferber were each taxable on an amount equal to the taxable income of Para Tech. Respondent asserted three alternative theories in support of this determination. First, because Para Tech should be taxed as a corporation and because of their control over Para Tech and Atram, Anderson and Ferber were in constructive receipt of dividend income equal to the amounts transferred from Para Tech to Atram. Second, if Para Tech was a trust, it was a grantor trust owned by Anderson and Ferber, who were therefore taxable on Para Tech's income. Third, because both Para Tech and Atram were sham entities that should be disregarded for Federal income tax purposes, Anderson and Ferber are taxable on the income from Para Tech's business. Respondent also determined that all three petitioners are liable for additions to tax for fraud.

Para Tech, Anderson and Ferber filed petitions for redetermination with this Court. Izen is counsel of record for petitioners in these cases. Nassau Life is bankrupt. All legal fees are being paid by Para Tech. * * *

Respondent's counsel in these cases wrote letters to Izen dated September 19, 1991, and November 15, 1991, questioning Izen regarding possible conflicts of interest in his representation of petitioners. Izen did not respond to these letters. Respondent, therefore, moved the Court to compel withdrawal of Izen as petitioners' counsel.

*Discussion*

* * *

Model Rule 1.7(b) provides:

A lawyer shall not represent a client if the representation of that client may be materially limited by the lawyer's responsibilities to another client or to a third person, or by the lawyer's own interests, unless:

(1) the lawyer reasonably believes the representation will not be adversely affected; and

(2) the client consents after consultation. When representation of multiple clients in a single matter is undertaken, the consultation shall include explanation of the implications of the common representation and the advantages and risks involved.

Petitioners contend that Izen's representation of them does not violate Model Rule 1.7(b) because no potential conflict of interest exists among petitioners. Petitioners contend that each petitioner is contesting the deficiency and will argue that Para Tech should be recognized as a trust and that Para Tech's Federal income tax returns for 1987 and 1988 were correct.

Respondent contends that Izen's representation of each petitioner may be materially limited by his responsibilities to the other petitioners and by his own interests. Respondent states:

There are positions which can be advanced on behalf of each Petitioner which, if established, would enable that Petitioner to avoid liability for all or part of the deficiencies and additions to tax determined against that Petitioner, but which cannot be established without irreparably damaging some other Petitioner's case.

Izen and petitioners contend that petitioners have been informed of and waive Izen's conflict of interest. We are not persuaded, however, that the apparent consent of petitioners is informed and voluntary. They testified that they had no intention to sue either Nassau Life or Izen and that they understood that, if a dispute arose between Anderson and Ferber, Izen would have to withdraw. Neither Izen nor petitioners identified any disclosures of the potential adverse positions that might lead to a dispute between Anderson and Ferber. * * *

We are not persuaded that Izen made a full and fair disclosure or that petitioners understood the inherent potential conflicts between them. The backgrounds of the individuals suggest a lack of sophistication in assessing matters such as these, and they relied solely on the advice of Izen in deciding to waive the conflicts of interest. Compare Adams v. Commissioner, 85 T.C. at 372-374 (holding that taxpayers could not be relieved of a settlement agreement based on their attorney's conflict of interest because taxpayers were sophisticated, knew all of the relevant facts, and had been advised by independent counsel before employing the author of an opinion letter). It appears to us that the waiver is not based on informed consent but on the cost of employing independent and separate counsel and having such counsel become familiar with the underlying facts of the cases.

Izen admitted during the hearing on respondent's motion that he had not secured written consents or waivers from petitioners and that he had not contacted Nassau Life or other beneficiaries of the Para Tech trust. Under these circumstances, we conclude that it is "more important that unethical conduct be prevented than * * * [that petitioners] have an unfettered right to counsel of * * * [their] choice." Kevlik v. Goldstein, 724 F.2d 844, 849 (1st Cir. 1984). The potential for unfairness to petitioners and damage to the integrity of the judicial process is too serious to permit Izen's representation of petitioners to continue, even in the face of an apparent waiver. Figueroa-Olmo v. Westinghouse Elec. Corp., supra at 1451; Shadid v. Jackson, supra at 90; and Model Rules Rule 1.7 comment (1983) (stating that, "when a disinterested lawyer would conclude that the client should not agree to representation under the circumstances, the lawyer involved cannot * * * provide representation on the basis of the client's consent.")

Therefore, Izen must be disqualified from representing petitioners in these cases.

## Questions and Comments:

1. The court here upholds a motion by the IRS to disqualify opposing counsel for a conflict of interest even though the taxpayer wanted to be represented by that counsel. Why should the IRS be bringing this motion? Why does it matter to the IRS?

2. Doesn't it seem strange that taxpayers here do not have the opportunity to have the lawyer of their choice? Is that lack of sophistication an acceptable reason to deny taxpayers the attorney of their choice? If so, why? Sophisticated people get the attorney of their choice but less sophisticated people don not. What is really going on here?

3. The Court notes that the taxpayers might have a claim against the attorney. Is the court trying to protect taxpayers from the influence of this attorney?

4. This case appears to involve an abusive tax shelter. Does that impact the decision here?

5. If the taxpayers signed an informed waiver, should they have been able to keep Inez as counsel? Can you think of a strong argument why taxpayers would want to keep Inez?

### Problem 3.3

Daughter is a sophisticated business person and hires you to advise her on her business affairs. You also advise her on tax issues and have put together a complicated estate plan for her. She is very pleased with your work and asks you to prepare an estate plan for her father. She explains that her father is a little bit of a recluse and does not like to spend money on lawyers (despite the fact that he has a lot of money). She indicates that she will pay the fees associated with the plan. What do you do? May you represent her father? May she pay for the representation? See Rules 1.8(f), and 5.4(c).

### Problem 3.4

You are an attorney and have been engaged by Jim and Jane, a married couple, to represent them in an audit of their 2002 joint return. What steps must you take to ethically represent both Jim and Jane?

### Problem 3.5

During the audit, Jim and Jane get in a fight. Jane tells Jim that she can't take it anymore and wants a divorce. You ask that the audit be postponed for a week and the IRS agrees. You contact Jane and Jim and they tell you that they have been having marital problems for years and that they are filing for divorce. There will be no reconciliation. What do you do and what are your duties to Jane, Jim and the IRS. What disciplinary rules apply?

## Questions and Comments:

As a tax attorney you will often be asked to represent couples. Must a lawyer assume that there is always a possible conflict in relationships and therefore representing couples always presents a conflict? As a general matter, the answer to this question is usually no. See Mon. Op. 960731 (finding that the "marital relationship itself is not in most cases adversarial in nature and no conflict inherently exists in representing both parties); Fla. Op. 95-4 ("From the inception of the representation until Husband's communication to Lawyer of the information concerning the codicil and the extra-marital relationship (hereinafter the separate confidence), there was no objective indication that the interests of Husband and Wife diverged, nor did it objectively appear to Lawyer that any such divergence of interests was reasonably likely to arise. Such situations involving joint representation of Husband and Wife do not present a conflict of interest and, therefore, do not trigger the conflict of interest disclosure-and-consent requirements of Rules 4-1.7(a) and 4-1.7(b), Rules Regulating The Florida Bar.").

## Problem 3.6

You are a tax attorney and your practice involves tax and estate planning. Your brother comes to you and asks you to write an estate plan for his family. He has a wife and two children. You are not a beneficiary. May you devise an estate plan for your brother and his wife?

## Problem 3.7

You are a tax attorney for A, B, and C. Your firm represents Big Company in almost all its affairs. Big Company is working on a major merger and you have been assigned to handle the tax issues on the case. You love the work. While working on the case you meet lawyer B who works as a lawyer for Big Company and has been assigned oversight responsibility for parts of the merger. She is not involved in any of the tax issues. The two of you develop a deep friendship and both of you want to become more than friends. Lawyer B thinks you can enter into the relationship as long as you inform Big Company and A, B, and C. Is she right? Does this relationship pose any ethical concerns?

## Problem 3.8

You are a tax attorney for A, B, and C and your spouse is an executive with Big Company. Your spouse is not involved in the selection of outside counsel for Big Company and you are chosen by Big Company to assist Big Company in a major tax litigation case. Big Company is aware that your spouse works in its counsel's office and her involvement in the case is minimal. May you represent big company? Why or why not?

# C.   Personal Relationships

## FORMAL OPINION 92-364[*]
Sexual Relations with Clients
July 6, 1992

*A sexual relationship between lawyer and client may involve unfair exploitation of the lawyer's fiduciary position, and/or significantly impair a lawyer's ability to represent the client competently, and therefore may violate both the Model Rules of Professional Conduct and the Model Code of Professional Responsibility.*

The Committee has been asked whether a lawyer violates the ABA Model Rules of Professional Conduct (1983, amended 1991) or the ABA Model Code of Professional Responsibility (1969, amended 1980) by entering into a sexual relationship with a client during the course of representation.[22] In the opinion of the Committee, such a relationship may involve unfair exploitation of the lawyer's fiduciary position and presents a significant danger that the lawyer's ability to represent the client adequately may be impaired, and that as a consequence the lawyer may violate both the Model Rules and the Model Code. The roles of lover and lawyer are potentially conflicting ones as the emotional involvement that is fostered by a sexual relationship has the potential to undercut the objective detachment that is often demanded for adequate representation.

\* \* \*

The Committee recognizes that no provision in either the Rules or the Code specifically addresses, let alone prohibits, sexual relationships between lawyer and client. However, there are several provisions of the Model Rules that may be implicated by a sexual

---

[*] "Formal Opinion 92-364" 1992. Copyright © 1992 by the American Bar Association. Reprinted with permission. Copies of ABA Formal Ethics Opinions are available from Service Center, American Bar Association, 321 North Clark Street, Chicago, IL 60654, 1-800-285-2221. All rights reserved. This information or any or portion thereof may not be copied or disseminated in any form or by any means or stored in an electronic database or retrieval system without the express written consent of the American Bar Association.

[22] A sexual relationship predating the professional relationship could, in some circumstances, raise the same ethical problems as are here considered. Because the likelihood of this happening should be considerably less when the sexual relationship predates the professional one, this opinion focuses primarily on sexual relationships that develop after the formation of the professional relationship.

relationship, particularly one that arises after the formation of the attorney-client relationship. First, because of the dependence that so often characterizes the attorney-client relationship, there is a significant possibility that the sexual relationship will have resulted from exploitation of the lawyer's dominant position and influence and, thus, breached the lawyer's fiduciary obligations to the client. Second, a sexual relationship with a client may affect the independence of the lawyer's judgment. Third, the lawyer's engaging in a sexual relationship with a client may create a prohibited conflict between the interests of the lawyer and those of the client. Fourth, a non-professional, yet emotionally charged, relationship between attorney and client may result in confidences being imparted in circumstances where the attorney-client privilege is not available, yet would have been, absent the personal relationship.

The Lawyer Has Fiduciary Obligations to the Client that Require, *Inter Alia,* that the Lawyer not Take Advantage of His or Her Dominant Position or Exploit the Dependent and Vulnerable Position of the Client.

It is axiomatic that the attorney-client relationship is a fiduciary one in which the client places his or her trust and confidence in the lawyer in return for the lawyer's undertaking to place the interest of the client ahead of any self-interest of the lawyer. This fiduciary relationship imposes the highest standards of ethical conduct on the lawyer.

\* \* \*

A lawyer is bound to conduct himself as a fiduciary or trustee occupying the highest position of trust and confidence, so that, in all his relations with his client, it is his duty to exercise and maintain the utmost good faith, honesty, integrity, fairness and fidelity . . . This fiduciary or trust relationship precludes the attorney from personal interests antagonistic to those of the client or from obtaining personal advantage or profit out of the relationship. Halter v. Farkas, 498 F.2d 587 (C.A.N.Y. 1974)

\* \* \*

The fiduciary obligation inherent in the lawyer's role is heightened if the client is emotionally vulnerable in a way that affects the client's ability to make reasoned judgments about the future. Model Rule 1.14(a) provides that

[w]hen a client's ability to make adequately considered decisions in connection with the representation is impaired, whether because of minority, mental disability or for some other reason, the lawyer shall, as far as reasonably possible, maintain a normal client-lawyer relationship with the client.

\* \* \*

Thus, the more vulnerable the client, the heavier the obligation of the lawyer to avoid engaging in any relationship other than that of attorney-client. If the lawyer permits the otherwise benign and even recommended client reliance and trust to become the catalyst for a sexual relationship with a client, the lawyer may violate one of the most basic ethical obligations, i.e., not to use the trust of the client to the client's disadvantage.

\* \* \*

The same fundamental principle of fiduciary obligation that underlies the specific rules governing attorney-client financial dealings implies as well that a lawyer should not abuse the client's trust by taking sexual or emotional advantage of a client. Protecting a client's emotional and physical well-being is surely as important as protecting the client's financial well-being. The inherently unequal attorney-client relationship allows the unethical lawyer just as easily to exploit the client sexually as financially. The trust and confidence reposed in a lawyer can provide an opportunity for the lawyer to manipulate a client emotionally for the lawyer's sexual benefit. Moreover, the client may not feel free to rebuff unwanted sexual advances because of fear that such a rejection will either reduce the lawyer's ardor for the client's cause or, worse yet, require finding a new lawyer, causing the client to lose the time and money that has already been invested in the present representation and possibly damaging the client's legal position.

\* \* \*

Such an abuse of client trust, even though not explicitly prohibited by any ethical rule, would nonetheless be inconsistent with the fiduciary obligation reflected in both the Model Rules and the Model Code. Moreover, such a sexual relationship, whether or not resulting from an abuse of trust, poses a variety of risks to the attorney-client relationship.

* * *

While it may be argued that such a conflict only arises in the special situations presented, for example, by divorce proceedings, the fact is that these conflicting interests can arise even in seemingly benign settings. For instance, although it is generally thought that the ethical concerns raised by a sexual relationship are not present in the commercial corporate setting, a sexual relationship with a corporate client's representative can be just as problematic as in other contexts.

* * *

Conclusion

It is apparent that a sexual relationship during the course of representation can seriously harm the client's interests. Therefore, the Committee concludes that because of the danger of impairment to the lawyer's representation associated with a sexual relationship between lawyer and client, the lawyer would be well advised to refrain from such a relationship. If such a sexual relationship occurs and the impairment is not avoided, the lawyer will have violated ethical obligations to the client.

* * *

The client's consent to sexual relations alone will rarely be sufficient to eliminate this danger. In many cases, the client's ability to give meaningful consent is vitiated by the lawyer's potential undue influence and/or the emotional vulnerability of the client. The lawyer may, therefore, be called upon in a disciplinary or other proceeding to show that the client consented, that the consent was freely given based on full and reasonable disclosure of the risks involved, and that any ensuing sexual relationship did not in any way disadvantage the client in the representation; that is, the attorney's judgment remained independent, the representation proceeded free of conflicts, the privilege was not compromised and the other ethical obligations to the client were fulfilled.

# D. Waiver

As previously discussed, you may represent a client even if a conflict exists if you believe that no client will be adversely affected by the representation and the client consents. Questions have arisen whether a lawyer may seek a prospective waiver by a client as a condition of accepting representation.

Prospective waivers of conflict provisions are generally disfavored, but such waivers often make sense for tax professionals. Tax professionals are often called on to assist a client with a specific concrete tax issue. Law firms do not want to be barred from accepting other clients because of this work and will often seek a prospective waiver from these types of clients. Comment 22 to Rule 1.7 recognizes that consents to future conflicts may make sense in certain circumstances, especially when the client is sophisticated and is already represented by counsel (which happens often in tax transactions where a tax lawyer is called in to help with a particular part of a transaction).

ABA Formal Ethics Opinion 05-436 provides that the waiver of future conflicts of interest may be appropriate in certain circumstances. The opinion notes that "The Model Rules contemplate that a lawyer in appropriate circumstances may obtain the effective informed consent of a client to future conflicts of interest. General and open-ended consent is more likely to be effective when given by a client that is an experienced user of legal services, particularly if, for example, the client is independently represented by other counsel in giving consent and the consent is limited to future conflicts unrelated to the subject of the representation."

# WORLDSPAN, L.P. et al.
## v.
# THE SABRE GROUP HOLDINGS, INC. et al.
5 F. Supp. 2d 1356 (N.D. Ga. 1998)

MOYE, DISTRICT JUDGE.

\* \* \*

The law firm has served for several years, and currently is still serving, as counsel for plaintiffs in state tax matters in Georgia and Tennessee. This litigation as well as the tax matters all involve in different ways and to different degrees plaintiffs' computer airline reservations operation. The main computer located physically in Atlanta, Georgia, is the heart of plaintiff's entire business.

\* \* \*

The Georgia Code of Professional Responsibility provides (Ga. DR 5-105(A) and (C)):

> "(A) lawyer shall decline proffered employment if the exercise of his independent professional judgment in behalf of a client will be or is likely to be adversely affected by the acceptance of the proffered employment, except to the extent permitted under DR 5-105(C).

\* \* \*

> "(C) In the situation covered by DR5-105(A) and (B), a lawyer may represent multiple clients if it is obvious that he can adequately represent the interests of each and if each consents to the representation after full disclosure of the possible effect of such representation on the exercise of his independent professional Judgment on behalf of each."

\* \* \*

By its plain language, the Georgia State Bar Code of Professional Responsibility, and, by adoption, this Court require both a showing that adequate representation of both clients is probable, and also the informed consent of both clients. Glover v. Libman, 578 F.Supp. 748, 760 (N.D.Ga.1983.Forrester, D.J.):

> "If it is both 'obvious' to the lawyer that he can represent the interests of each client adequately, and agreeable by 'consent' to each client that the lawyer represent each client, however, multiple representation is permitted."

\* \* \*

\* \* \* the critical issue now before the court is whether plaintiffs have given their informed consent to the simultaneous, dual representation.

It is clear that when informed specifically that the law firm had undertaken to represent the defendants in this instant lawsuit brought by plaintiffs, the plaintiffs strenuously objected. The law firm, however, relies on its "standard" engagement letter sent to plaintiffs when their first representation was undertaken, September 16, 1992, to show that plaintiffs then prospectively gave the required consent to the present simultaneous, dual representation in this lawsuit commenced over five years subsequent to the claimed consent. While the significant lapse of time, and, indeed, an apparent on-again, off-again, series of representations in the interval, would seem to make it most difficult for a consent that may have been thoroughly informed in 1992 to be informed in 1998, in view of the pace of change in the world, and indeed in the airline and computer industries, it is not impossible, but, as one court has said, "such standing consent must by necessity be exceedingly explicit." Florida Ins. Guaranty Assn., Inc. v. Carey Canada, 749 F.Supp. 255, 260 (S.D.Fla.1990). The client-lawyer relationship is sui generis; it is based on mutual trust; it has important public implications beyond the mere relationship between the parties; it is not a mere contractual arrangement such that contract law relating to releases and waivers forms very persuasive precedent, nor does the court find such precedent helpful here. The requirements of this court's rules governing the conduct of lawyers practicing before it, and, of course, of the Georgia Code of Professional Responsibility, transcend mere contract law. The language of an engagement letter, while important to determine the nature and scope of any consent to representation of other clients, and to what extent such consent, if any, is "informed", does not definitively circumscribe the scope of the lawyer's professional responsibility under the circumstances. While not applicable here as experienced lawyers for plaintiffs were monitoring the engagement of the law firm, in the more normal situation, the lawyer, presumably possessing superior legal knowledge and experience, is presenting the prospective client with a document with legal implications prepared by the lawyer having possibly adverse effects on the client seeking his legal advice and to repose trust in him. It is the lawyer's duty to insure that each client has all the necessary information to make consent truly informed. The Court must determine whether the 1992 letter did in fact evidence an informed prospective consent to the precise simultaneous, dual representation undertaken in this case.

In this connection, it is necessary to refer to the language of that letter (Exhibit A to plaintiffs' motion to disqualify). Its relevant language follows:

"As we have discussed, because of the relatively large size of our firm and our representation of many other clients, it is possible that there may arise in the future a dispute between another client and WORLDSPAN, or a transaction in which WORLDSPAN's interests do not coincide with those of another client. In order to distinguish those instances in which WORLDSPAN consents to our representing such other clients from those instances in which such consent is not given, you have agreed, as a condition to our undertaking this engagement, that during the period of this engagement we will not be precluded from representing clients who may have interests adverse to WORLDSPAN so long as (1) such adverse matter is not substantially related to our work for WORLDSPAN, and (2) our representation of the other client does not involve the use, to the disadvantage of WORLDSPAN, of confidential information of WORLDSPAN we have obtained as a result of representing WORLDSPAN.

\* \* \*

"If any of the foregoing is not consistent with your understanding of the terms of our engagement, I would appreciate your advising me in writing as soon as possible so that we may resolve any misunderstanding. If you have any questions or wish to discuss any of these points, please give me a call."

The substance of the law firm's evidence with respect to the letter is that there was no response thereto by plaintiffs and the representation was thereupon commenced and continued without demur even though there were several periods of time in which no work was performed.

\* \* \*

Looking only at the original letter itself, the Court finds that its very language is ambiguous. The phrase "will not be precluded from representing clients who may have interests adverse to WORLDSPAN so long as (1) such adverse matter" does not necessarily or even impliedly foreshadow future directly adverse litigation. It is the opinion of this Court that future directly adverse litigation against one's present client is a matter of such an entirely different quality and exponentially greater magnitude, and so unusual given the position of trust existing between lawyer and client, that any document intended to grant standing consent for the lawyer to litigate against his own client must identify that possibility, if not in plain language, at least by irresistible inference including reference to specific parties, the circumstances under which such adverse representation would be undertaken, and all relevant like information. Cinema 5, Ltd. v. Cinerama, Inc., supra; Florida Ins. Guaranty Assn., Inc. v. Carey Canada, supra.

The Court believes the above point to carry added weight when, as here, the future conflict is caused by undertaking the representation of a client with whom the law firm has no present relationship. * * *

The Court now finds that the law firm's representation of defendants herein is in prohibited conflict with its ethical duties to and position of trust with plaintiffs, and orders it disqualified from further representation of defendants. As the result of this disqualification, it shall be necessary for the defendants to secure new local counsel (L.R. 83.1.B and E.4).

## ORDER ON RECONSIDERATION

Rule 1.7 was modified since the above opinion was issued and the Georgia's rule was based on the old Rule 1.7. What do you think the result would be under the new rules. Comment 22 to Rule 1.7 provides:

Whether a lawyer may properly request a client to waive conflicts that might arise in the future is subject to the test of paragraph (b). The effectiveness of such waivers is generally determined by the extent to which the client reasonably understands the material risks that the waiver entails. The more comprehensive the explanation of the types of future representations that might arise and the actual and reasonably foreseeable adverse consequences of those representations, the greater the likelihood that the client will have the requisite understanding. Thus, if the client agrees to consent to a particular type of conflict with which the client is already familiar, then the consent ordinarily will be effective with regard to that type of conflict. If the consent is general and open-ended, then the consent ordinarily will be ineffective, because it is not reasonably likely that the client will have understood the material risks involved. On the other hand, if the client is an experienced user of the legal services involved and is reasonably informed regarding the risk that a conflict may arise, such consent is more likely to be effective, particularly if, e.g., the client is independently represented by other counsel in giving consent and the consent is limited to future conflicts unrelated to the subject of the representation. In any case, advance consent cannot be effective if the circumstances that materialize in the future are such as would make the conflict nonconsentable under paragraph (b).

## Problem 3.9

ABC law firm represents Company A. Company A is a big company and is a major client of ABC. ABC will not take cases if they pose a conflict with Company A. Company B approaches ABC and asks them to represent them in a patent action (not involving Company A). Since Company A and B do business with each other, ABC law firm said it could not represent Company B absent a waiver. No conflict existed at the time but ABC law firm insisted that Company B agree to let ABC represent Company A in "any future disputes including litigation that may arise between Company A and B." After Company B agreed to the waiver, ABC law firm agreed to represent Company B.

Several months later Company B allegedly breached a contract with Company A. Company B then moved to disqualify ABC law firm. Assume the model rules apply. How do you rule on Company B's motion?

# Chapter 4

## Evidentiary Privileges

---

The previous chapters examined the breadth of the tax practitioner's duty of confidentiality. However, that duty is an ethical one that only applies to voluntary disclosures. A practitioner's duty of confidentiality does not provide a legal justification for refusing to disclose information that he is required to disclose by law or court order. In recognition of this fact Model Rule 1.6(b)(4) specifically provides that lawyers do not breach their ethical duties when they disclose information in order to comply with a court order or other law. To shield a client's confidential information from a compelled disclosure, a practitioner must refer to the rules of evidence to determine whether any evidentiary privilege can be asserted. In this chapter we discuss three such privileges: The attorney-client privilege, the tax practitioner-client privilege and the work product doctrine.

As we study these privileges, consider their appropriateness in the tax context. If a privilege applies, then relevant evidence will be excluded from consideration, which directly impedes the search for the truth. In allowing an evidentiary privilege, a societal decision has been made that the purposes of the privilege outweigh the detriment to uncovering the truth. The federal tax system is based on a premise of self-assessment where each taxpayer must review their own situation, apply the relevant law and report their tax liability to the government. In such a system the government is arguably at a disadvantage in uncovering the salient information necessary to apply the tax laws appropriately to each taxpayer. In recognition of this fact, Congress has given the Service broad summons authority to obtain information from taxpayers and third parties. Should the societal decision regarding the appropriateness of allowing an evidentiary privilege be weighed differently in the context of federal taxation?

# A. The Attorney-Client Privilege

## 1.    OVERVIEW OF THE PRIVLEDGE

The attorney-client privilege is one of the oldest evidentiary privileges recognized under the law. However, despite being an accepted privilege since Elizabethan times, its application is still evolving and variations exist in the application of the privilege from state to state. Even the Federal Rules of Evidence specifically leave the law of evidentiary privileges open to common-law development. Those rules do however supply a choice of law mechanism. Federal Rule of Evidence 501 provides that the federal common-law of privileges applies to federal law questions and federal criminal cases, while state law privilege rules are applicable to cases in federal courts where state law is at issue. Further, section 7453 of the Code makes the Federal Rules of Evidence applicable to Tax Court proceedings. Consequently, the federal common-law attorney-client privilege generally applies to all federal tax matters.

In its classic formulation the common-law attorney-client privilege applies "(1) [w]here legal advice of any kind is sought (2) from a professional legal adviser in his capacity as such, (3) the communications relating to that purpose, (4) made in confidence (5) by the client, (6) are at his instance permanently protected (7) from disclosure by himself or by the legal adviser, (8) except the protection be waived." 8 JOHN HENRY WIGMORE, EVIDENCE IN TRIALS AT COMMON LAW § 2292, at 554 (McNaughton rev. ed. 1961). As we will see, these requirements present a number of issues for a tax attorney trying to assert the privilege to prevent disclosure of a client's confidential communications and the lawyer's advice.

## Questions and Comments:

The attorney-client privilege is typically justified because ensuring confidential client communications (1) strengthens our adversarial system of justice (attorneys can better prepare the client's case, assert otherwise overlooked defenses, and prepare in advance for any damaging evidence), (2) enhances judicial economy (attorneys can more realistically appraise the merits of a case and propose more appropriate settlements or advise against litigation), and (3) promotes compliance with the law (attorneys can educate clients regarding the law's requirements and attempt to dissuade illegal or questionable plans before they are undertaken). How would you weigh the significance of these three benefits of the privilege in the federal tax context? How significant is the harm to the government under a self-assessment tax system if it cannot seek the information from tax attorneys? Is it relevant whether the confidential communication occurred before the client's tax return was filed or whether it only occurred after the IRS raised the issue on audit?

## 2. CLIENT IDENTITY

### (a) Overview

Almost every case examining whether a client's identity is considered privileged information begins with the basic proposition that such information is generally *not* privileged. This rule follows from the fact that a client's name is not typically conveyed with an expectation of confidentiality and therefore it fails to meet the *prima facie* requirements for applying the privilege. Nevertheless, in certain extreme situations, the courts have found a client's identity privileged. While the courts have stated various justifications for these decisions, the modern trend is to treat a client's identity as privileged only if such identification would in substance constitute the disclosure of a confidential attorney-client communication. The following case aptly illustrates this "confidential communication exception" in a tax context.

## ALVA C. BAIRD
### v.
## LAURENCE P. KOERNER
279 F.2d 623 (9th Cir. 1960)

\* \* \*

Before STEPHENS, BARNES and JERTBERG, Circuit Judges.

\* \* \*

As government counsel stated in oral argument, the one real issue is: Is there here a valid claim of the attorney-client privilege?

I. Factual Background

\* \* \*

Early in August 1956 appellant [Baird, a well respected tax attorney and former IRS Regional Counsel for eight states,] consulted with certain accountants and gave advice concerning certain undisclosed taxpayers' income tax. There was a discussion of defenses and steps to be taken to place the undisclosed taxpayers in the most favorable position in the event criminal charges were to be brought against them by the Internal Revenue Service.

The accountants determined the undisclosed taxpayers' returns were incorrect and the taxes understated. No investigation was then being made, nor had it been made by the government, of taxpayers.

On or about the middle of August 1956 taxpayers' attorney came to appellant's office in Los Angeles and discussed with him in detail the facts and circumstances of the case. After a complete and thorough discussion of procedural steps, and of the moral, legal and tactical advantages of making payment of the tax then due, but without disclosing the identity of the taxpayers, their said attorney delivered to appellant the sum of $ 12,706.85, which had previously been determined to be the amount of the tax due, with interest thereon to September 1, 1956. The taxpayers' general attorney also, as compensation for the consultation and advice given in the various conferences had in regard to the matter, paid appellant a fee commensurate with the value of the services rendered.

On August 20, 1956 appellant transmitted a cashier's check dated August 17, 1956 for $ 12,706.85 to the District Director of Internal Revenue at Baltimore Maryland, with a letter reading as follows:

'August 20, 1956

'Mr. Clarence L. Fox, Jr.
'District Director of Internal Revenue Custom House

'Baltimore 2, Maryland

'Sir:

'There is enclosed Cashiers Check of Citizens National Trust & Savings Bank of Los Angeles No. 241292, dated August 17, 1956, payable to Director of Internal Revenue in the amount of $12,706.85.

'This represents additional amounts due from one or more taxpayers for some past years. Their names have not been disclosed to me. However, I am informed that the aggregate additional amount, together with interest computed to September 1, 1956, is the amount of the check, $ 12,706.85.

'No investigation of any kind is now in process by the Internal Revenue Service. There seems to be no reason to believe that one will be promulgated in the future. However, the attorney representing this group concluded that there were additional taxes due the United States and recommended to his clients that payment be made. The amount transmitted may be deposited in the Deposit Fund Account of the Treasurer of the United States or in such other account as may be appropriate for unidentified collections.

'Yours Respectfully, (s) Alva C. Baird Alva C. Baird

　　* * *

The record shows that the identity of the taxpayers in question, their names and addresses have never been disclosed to appellant. Appellant was advised, however, that the taxpayers are reputable and responsible business men who are now and have always been engaged in a legitimate business, and have not engaged in any unsavory or illegal businesses of any kind.

On November 27, 1957, appellee, as Special Agent, issued a departmental summons, requiring appellant to identify the attorneys, the accountants, and the taxpayers for whom the check was forwarded. On December 16, 1957 appellant appeared in answer to the subpoena, was sworn, and declined to name the taxpayers on the ground he did not know their names, and declined to name the accountants or attorney on the ground that such information came to him as a privileged communication from the unknown client to Baird, as an attorney.

Appellee then filed a petition for enforcement of the Internal Revenue Service summons, and an order to show cause. Appellant moved to dismiss and to quash. These motions were denied. Appellant then answered the petition and order to show cause, pleading as defenses: (1) that no cause of action was stated; (2) the attorney-client privilege; (3) the fifth amendment, and Article I, Section 13 of the California Constitution; and (4) the fourth amendment, and Article I, Section 19 of the California Constitution.

At the hearing of the order to show cause in the district court, appellant refused to answer questions as to the identity and address of his employers and was found guilty of civil contempt. He was committed to custody until he was willing to answer, and a stay was granted to permit this appeal.

II. The Attorney-Client Privilege

We must first consider what the attorney-client privilege is; whether it here exists; to what does it extend; must it be raised, and if so, how; and who is entitled, or required, to raise it?

* * *

Confidential communications between client and attorney were privileged under common law. The privilege is of ancient origin. Prichard v. United States, 6 Cir., 1950, 181 F.2d 326, affirmed, 339 U.S. 974, 70 S.Ct. 1029, 94 L.Ed. 1380. The doctrine is subject to statutory regulation and limitation, but except as so modified the statutes are merely declaratory of the common law rule. 97 C.J.S. Witnesses § 276. The doctrine is based on public policy. While it is the great purpose of law to ascertain the truth, there is the countervailing necessity of insuring the right of every person to freely and fully confer and confide in one having knowledge of the law, and skilled in its practice, in order that the former may have adequate advice and a proper defense. This assistance can be made safely and readily available only when the client is free from the consequences of apprehension of disclosure by reason of the subsequent statements of the skilled lawyer.

The government recognizes this general rule, but urges that it does not apply to the identity of the client, i.e. to the fact of employment as distinguished from the subject matter of the communication.

The government cites VIII Wigmore on Evidence § 2313 (3rd Ed. 1940), in support of its distinction. Wigmore says:

> The identity of the attorney's client . . . will seldom be a matter communicated in confidence; for the procedure of litigation ordinarily presupposes a disclosure of these facts . . . .Every litigant is in justice entitled to know the identity of his opponents. He

cannot be obliged to struggle in the dark against unknown forces . . . . The privilege cannot be used to evade a client's responsibility for the use of legal process; and if it is necessary for that purpose to make a plain exception to the rule of confidence then it must be made . . . ."On the other hand, the litigant is not entitled to ask any more than serves to fix the client's identity. A communication as to . . . the ultimate motive of the litigation, is equally protected with others, so far as any policy of privilege is concerned . . . .There is not entire harmony in the rulings . . . (for this much mooted class of cases) but *no doubt much ought to depend upon the circumstances of each case.'* (Emphasis added.)

In support of this statement, many cases are cited by the government, some upholding the privilege as to identity of the client, some denying it. But as Wigmore says, much ought to depend on the circumstances of each case. In the instant case, a disclosure of the persons employing the attorney-appellant would disclose the persons paying the tax; the fact of payment indicates clearly what is here specifically admitted, that an additional tax was payable and that the unknown clients owed it. But as yet the clients are unnamed. Suppose those unknown clients had related certain facts to their attorney, and asked that attorney for an opinion as to whether the clients, as taxpayers, owed the government additional taxes. Could the attorney be required to state the information given him in confidence by the clients, and the attorney's advice in response thereto? Or could the government require every tax attorney to reveal the name of those clients who had consulted the attorney with respect to possible taxes payable, so that the government could institute investigations of all such taxpayers?

We think the answer is 'no' to both such questions. If it were not, the government could obtain by indirection, through demand for identity of a taxpayer, the information it seeks simply because a certain amount has been paid in as a tax in accordance with a tax law that permits such an anonymous payment. This would disclose the 'ultimate motive of litigation' which Wigmore says the privilege should protect.

Had the taxpayers filed suit against the government, then clearly public policy would require the taxpayers' attorney to reveal for whom the attorney was acting. The government should not, any more than a private party, be required once litigation is commenced "to struggle in the dark against unknown forces."

But here no litigation exists. The taxpayers have sought no judicial determination of the correctness of the amount paid, nor even of the fact that any sum is owed by them. They have merely stated, through an attorney, "I am worried about my position if the government ever investigates my tax return. Hence I deem it wise to pay X dollars to the government now."

In a very recent case, where the difficult balance between "full disclosure" and "privileged communication" was struck the court said:

"Throughout their judicial endeavors courts seek truth and justice and their search is aided significantly by the fundamental principle of full disclosure. When that principle conflicts with the attorney-client privilege it must, of course, give way but only to the extent necessary to vindicate the privilege and its underlying purposes. The matter is truly one of balance." . . . . [The] cases hold that, under their own facts, the objection of one real client, though valid, must yield to any great interest of that body of clients, the public. There is no question but that it is at times vital to the administration of justice to require disclosure of a client's name.

We conclude there is no federal body of law that requires the exclusion of the identity of the client from the extent of the attorney-client privilege. We believe it must be assessed on a case to case basis, depending on the particular facts of each case. We recognize that the policy of full disclosure is a 'more fundamental one' than the policy of the attorney-client privilege; that the latter is not universally regarded as absolute, and is to be strictly limited to the purposes for which it exists. VIII Wigmore on Evidence § 2291, p. 557. If the identification of the client conveys information which ordinarily would be conceded to be part of the usual privileged communication between attorney and client, then the privilege should extend to such identification in the absence of other factors. Such factors are (a) the commencing of litigation on behalf of the client where he voluntarily subjects himself to the jurisdiction of the court; (b) an identification relating to an employment by some third person, not the client nor his agent; (c) an employment of an attorney with respect to future criminal or fraudulent transactions; (d) the attorney himself being a defendant in a criminal matter. In none of these categories, and perhaps not in others, would the suppressing of some truth, so that the general process of administering justice may be furthered, outweigh the desirability of the rule of privilege; itself an exception to the general view 'that the fullest disclosure of the facts will best lead to the truth and ultimately to the triumph of justice.' In re Selser, 1954, 15 N.J. 393, 105 A.2d 395, 401.

\* \* \*

Our problem is thus narrowed, not to whether there are no exceptions to the general rule (that ordinarily the attorney-client privilege does not include the identity of the client), but whether the exception recognized in Ex parte McDonough is here controlling. 97 C.J. Witnesses § 283 e., p. 803, in discussing this exception, states:

"The name of the client will be considered privileged matter where the circumstances of the case are such that the name of the client is material only for the purpose of showing an acknowledgment of guilt on the part of such client of the very offenses on account of which the attorney was employed . . . ."

The facts of the instant case bring it squarely within that exception to the general rule. Here money was received by the government, paid by persons who thereby admitted they had not paid a sufficient amount in income taxes some one or more years in the past. The names of the clients are useful to the government for but one purpose -- to ascertain which taxpayers think they were delinquent, so that it may check the records for that one year or several years. The volunteer nature of the payment indicates a belief by the taxpayers that more taxes or interest or penalties are due than the sum previously paid, if any. It indicates a feeling of guilt for nonpayment of taxes, though whether it is criminal guilt is undisclosed. But it may well be the link that could form the chain of testimony necessary to convict an individual of a federal crime. Certainly the payment and the feeling of guilt are the reasons the attorney here involved was employed -- to advise his clients what, under the circumstances, should be done.

In striking the balance between the public benefit that might be achieved through permitting a government audit of the tax returns against the sacredness of the attorney's obligation to keep inviolate the secrecy of the client's confidence, we must consider the weakness or strength of the attorney's obligation to his client.

\* \* \*

We hold that . . . under the facts existing here . . . . an attorney cannot be compelled to state the names of clients who employed him to voluntarily mail sums of money to the government in payment of undetermined income taxes, unsued on, and with no government audit or investigation into that client's income tax liability pending.

\* \* \*

The judgment of the lower court is reversed so far as it orders appellant Baird to reveal any information regarding the persons who employed him, and affirmed as to those questions which it held appellant Baird need not answer.

## Questions and Comments:

1. In *Baird* the taxpayers approached Baird for advice after their tax returns had been filed but before any audit was anticipated. As discussed in Chapter 2, a taxpayer generally has no obligation to amend a filed tax return that is subsequently found to contain an error, although a practitioner generally should counsel amendment to correct the error. In *Baird* the taxpayers did not amend their returns but did decide to pay the estimated deficiency anonymously. What considerations do you think may have caused them to actually pay their tax deficiencies while refusing to amend the subject tax returns?

2. How would the court's analysis have changed, if at all, had Baird been consulted after the taxpayers had been informed of a pending audit?

### Problem 4.1

Mobster Mike consults Ada Attorney about his tax situation. Mike tells Ada that he is engaged in a significant illegal business operation which generates approximately $1 million of "net" income each year. He knows that he is obligated to file tax returns and pay tax on this illegal income, but fears that such reporting would alert the authorities to his illegal activities. On the other hand, Mike believes strongly in our great country (he's earning $1 million a year after all) and he wants to pay his "fair share" of the tax burden that makes that greatness possible. He gives Ada $350,000 and instructs her to use it to pay his tax liability for the current year (which he has "generously estimated" to be 35% of his "net" income) to the IRS anonymously. Ada sends the amount to the IRS with a letter similar to the one used in Baird. Will Ada be able to successfully assert the attorney-client privilege when the IRS seeks to learn the identity of her client? Is this situation an appropriate one to apply of the attorney-client privilege as a policy matter? How is this situation different from *Baird*, if at all?

### (b) Section 6050I

Section 6050I of the Code provides that "any person who is engaged in a trade or business, and who in the course of such trade or business, receives more than $10,000 in cash in one transaction (or two or more related transactions)" must disclose this fact and relevant identifying information to the Service. This provision's original purpose was to combat underreporting of taxable income by persons with large cash incomes. However, Congress subsequently transformed the provision into a powerful tool for identifying individuals engaged in drug trafficking and other illegal activities. It did so by permitting the IRS to share the information obtained with other federal agencies engaged in criminal law enforcement activities. See Code Section 6103(i).

Because attorneys engage in a trade or business, any cash payments in excess of $10,000 received from clients must be disclosed to the IRS, pursuant to section 6050I. The statute contains no exclusion for payments made to attorneys, and, despite intense pressure from the practicing bar, neither Congress nor the IRS has created such an exclusion in the more than twenty-five years since the provision was enacted. Despite the absence of any specific exception, through the mid-1990s, attorneys frequently attempted to avoid disclosing the identity of their cash paying clients by asserting the attorney-client privilege. However, the courts consistently rejected any assertion of identity privilege, reasoning that a client's method of payment was not itself privileged information and that revealing the client's identity in connection with his mode of payment would not disclose any confidential client communication. This conclusion seems correct as a policy matter since when the IRS seeks to uncover the mode of a client's payment, it is not seeking to determine the reasons why the client sought legal advice. Because clients desiring confidentiality regarding their identity can avoid any risk of identity disclosure under Section 6050I by paying their legal bills in a form other than cash (e.g., by using a personal check or a cashier's check), applying section 6050I to attorneys should not adversely impact the inclination of potential clients to seek legal advice.

**Problem 4.2**

Nefarious Ned comes to Ada Attorney's office to discuss representing him in a pending tax audit. After an initial discussion, Ada determines that the audit is likely to involve a substantial amount of time and effort on her part. She is also aware of Ned's reputation for not paying his bills on time, so she requests a $75,000 retainer before she begins work. To her surprise, Ned immediately opens his brief case and removes $75,000 in cash to pay the retainer. Assuming Ada still wishes to accept Ned as a client, what are Ada's options at this point? You should review section 6050I(f) in considering your answer.

## (c) "Tax Shelter" Advice

Another category of client identity cases arising under the federal income tax laws relates to situations where the IRS knows that a questionable tax minimization transaction exists, but it cannot readily identify the taxpayers involved. In such cases, the Service may attempt to extract client information from the tax attorneys known to have developed the transaction. The situation most frequently arises when an accounting firm, law firm or investment bank acts as a promoter for a particular tax minimization technique. (See Chapter 5 for a detailed discussion of the ethical considerations regarding tax shelters generally.) Unlike traditional tax planning (where tax practitioners review business driven plans presented by a particular client to make them more tax efficient) a promoted transaction is driven largely by its tax minimization effect and is marketed to clients as a means of reducing their tax liabilities. Such transactions are of particular concern to the IRS in its effort to police the integrity and fairness of the self-assessment system since such plans are typically aggressive interpretations of the law designed to be hard to identify on the face of a tax return that are marketed to many taxpayers despite their being unrelated to the actual business planning of the taxpayer. Since these transactions are often intentionally designed to minimize detection, the IRS has significant informational hurdles to overcome to identify the taxpayers engaged in such activity. Since this burden can be significantly reduced if the IRS can obtain client lists from promoters, the IRS now requires tax practitioners to maintain lists of clients engaging in certain types of transactions. See Treas. Reg. § 301.6112-1. When the IRS then seeks such client identity information from a tax practitioner under this provision, the question becomes whether the attorney-client privilege can be invoked to prevent disclosure.

While the law in this area is still developing, the leading case is United States v. BDO Seidman, 337 F.3d 802 (7th Cir. 2003), cert. denied sub nom, Roes v. United States, 540 U.S. 1178 (2004). In that case BDO Seidman ("BDO"), an accounting firm, advised a number of clients regarding certain transactions that the IRS believed were subject to the IRS client list maintenance requirements. In an effort to determine BDO's compliance with obligations under these rules, the Service summoned the client lists for twenty specified types of transactions the BDO was believed to have marketed to clients. Certain BDO clients intervened to prevent the disclosure of their identities, asserting that such information was protected by the attorney-client privilege (as statutorily extended to accountants pursuant to section 7525, discussed *infra*).

On these facts the Seventh Circuit's ruled that the client names were not privileged. Among several rationales for its decision the court discussed the application of the confidential communication exception and concluded that disclosing the clients' identities on these facts would not reveal any privileged information despite the fact that the disclosure would directly link the clients with particular tax motivated transactions. The court stated:

> [T]he Does submit that the IRS' summonses set forth such detailed descriptions about suspect types of tax shelters under investigation that any document produced in response that also reveals a client's identity will inevitably reveal that client's motivation for seeking tax advice from BDO. The Does define their "motive" for retaining BDO's services as the "desire to engage in financial transactions which the government might later decide to be questionable, or . . . 'potentially abusive.'" Appellants' Br. At 16. Because a client's "motive" for seeking legal advice is considered a confidential communication, the Does contend that the [attorney-client] privilege should protect against the disclosure of their motive for seeking tax advice, a motive that would be known if their identities are revealed.
>
> The Does have not established that a confidential communication will be disclosed if their identities are revealed in response to the summonses. Disclosure of

the identities of the Does will disclose to the IRS that the Does participated in one of the 20 types of tax shelters described in its summonses. It is less than clear, however, as to what motive, or other confidential communication of tax advice, can be inferred from that information alone.

*BDO Seidman,* 337 F.3d at 812.

## Questions and Comments:

1. The clients asserting the privilege in *BDO Seidman* clearly believed that connecting their names to the subject transactions would indicate a motive "to engage in financial transactions which the government might later decide to be questionable, or . . . 'potentially abusive.'" Why does the court refuse to treat this clearly demonstrated "motive" as a confidential communication protected by the attorney-client privilege?

2. The court in *BDO Seidman* presented several alternative grounds for denying the claim of privilege based on the prima facie requirements for the privilege. Review the common law requirements for the privilege set forth earlier in this chapter. If you represented the IRS, what arguments would you make to defeat a claim of privilege in a marketed tax avoidance transaction based on these prima facie requirements?

3. Should the scope of the attorney-client privilege be altered depending on the context involved? What bearing, if any, should the fact that BDO was actively marketing tax minimization transactions to its existing clients have on the applicability of the attorney-client privilege?

## 3.     THE LEGAL ADVICE REQUIREMENT

A key requirement for asserting the attorney-client privilege is that the privileged communication must arise as a result of the client seeking "legal advice." As we will discover, for a tax practitioner this requirement raises some special concerns.

## (a)  Tax Advice vs. Legal Advice

The Internal Revenue Code is a highly complex statute that is subject to frequent, sometimes yearly, Congressional revisions. Further, the administrative regulations and decisions interpreting the Code are voluminous.  Nevertheless, the federal income tax system is one requiring self-assessment by individual taxpayers who need to assimilate this complex body of law and apply it to their own factual situations.  Given this daunting prospect, many taxpayers hire a professional, typically an accountant or an attorney, to prepare their tax returns.  Are such professionals performing "legal" work or merely acting as a "scrivener" completing the tax forms for their clients?  Should a client's communication be privileged if it is conveyed with a dual purpose of obtaining tax advice as well as assisting in the preparation of the tax return?  In considering these questions, contrast Judge Posner's view's in the following case with the excerpt below taken from the Restatement (Third) of the Law Governing Lawyers.

# UNITED STATES
## v.
# RICHARD A. FREDERICK
182 F.3d 496 (7th Cir. 1999)

* * *

Before POSNER, Chief Judge, and KANNE and DIANE P. WOOD, Circuit Judges.

Posner, *Chief Judge*. These appeals challenge an order enforcing summonses that the Internal Revenue Service issued to Richard Frederick. Frederick is both a lawyer and an accountant, and he both provides legal representation to, and prepares the tax returns of, Randolph and Karin Lenz and their company, KCS Industries, Inc.  The IRS is investigating the Lenzes and their company, and the summonses directed Frederick to hand over hundreds of documents that may be germane to the investigation. Frederick balked at handing over all of them, claiming that some were protected by either the attorney-client privilege or the work-product privilege (or both). His refusal precipitated this enforcement proceeding. . . .  The district judge examined the documents *in camera* and ruled that some were privileged but others were not. The appeals challenge the latter ruling.

\* \* \*

Whether a particular document is privileged is a fact-specific and case-specific issue, the sort of issue that district judges are particularly experienced in resolving. It is not the sort of issue that lends itself to governance by a uniform rule that a court of appeals might prescribe and enforce. In these circumstances, a light appellate touch is best.

\* \* \*

Most of the documents in issue were created in connection with Frederick's preparation of the Lenzes' tax returns. They are drafts of the returns (including schedules), worksheets containing the financial data and computations required to fill in the returns, and correspondence relating to the returns. These are the kinds of document that accountants and other preparers generate as an incident to preparing their clients' returns, or that the taxpayers themselves generate if they prepare their own returns, though in the latter case there is unlikely to be correspondence. The materiality of the documents to the IRS's investigation of the Lenzes is not in issue.

\* \* \*

Communications from a client that neither reflect the lawyer's thinking nor are made for the purpose of eliciting the lawyer's professional advice or other legal assistance are not privileged. The information that a person furnishes the preparer of his tax return is furnished for the purpose of enabling the preparation of the return, not the preparation of a brief or an opinion letter. Such information therefore is not privileged.

We do not, however, accept the government's argument that there is no issue of privilege here because the information was transmitted to a tax preparer with the expectation of its being relayed to a third party, namely the IRS. It is true that "if the client transmitted the information so that it might be used on the tax return, such a transmission destroys any expectation of confidentiality." United States v. Lawless, supra, 709 F.2d at 487. . . . But the tax preparer here was also the taxpayers' lawyer, and it cannot be assumed that everything transmitted to him by the taxpayer was intended to assist him in his tax-preparation function and thus might be conveyed to the IRS, rather than in his legal-representation function. . . .

We also reject the government's argument that numerical information can never fall within the attorney-client or work-product privilege. . . . Such cases are rare, but they can be imagined. Suppose a lawyer prepared an estimate of his client's damages; the estimate would be numerical, but insofar as it reflected the lawyer's professional assessment of what to ask the jury for it would be attorney work product. Similarly, if the lawyer asked his client how much he had obtained in the theft for which he was being prosecuted and the client answered, "$10,000," the answer would be protected by the attorney-client privilege. But we do not agree with the appellants that the district judge based his ruling on the erroneous view that numbers can never be privileged. He found no basis for privileging these numbers, remarking, rightly, "It cannot be argued that numbers in the hands of the accountant are different from numbers in the hands of a lawyer."

Besides the information supplied to Frederick by the Lenzes, there are the worksheets, which Frederick prepared and which doubtless reflect some of his own thinking. But the Supreme Court has held that an accountant's worksheets are not privileged, United States v. Arthur Young & Co., supra, 465 U.S. at 817-19, and a lawyer's privilege, as we explained earlier, is no greater when he is doing accountant's work. A complicating factor is that when Frederick was doing these worksheets and filling out the Lenzes' tax returns, he knew that the IRS was investigating the Lenzes and their company, albeit in connection with different tax years, and he was representing them in that investigation. But people who are under investigation and represented by a lawyer have the same duty as anyone else to file tax returns. They should not be permitted, by using a lawyer in lieu of another form of tax preparer, to obtain greater confidentiality than other taxpayers. By using Frederick as their tax preparer, the Lenzes ran the risk that his legal cogitations born out of his legal representation of them would creep into his worksheets and so become discoverable by the government. The Lenzes undoubtedly benefited from having their lawyer do their returns, but they must take the bad with the good; if his legal thinking infects his worksheets, that does not cast the cloak of privilege over the worksheets; they are still accountants' worksheets, unprotected no matter who prepares them.

Put differently, a dual-purpose document--a document prepared for use in preparing tax returns and for use in litigation--is not privileged; otherwise, people in or contemplating litigation would be able to invoke, in effect, an accountant's privilege, provided that they used their lawyer to fill out their tax returns. And likewise if a taxpayer involved in or contemplating litigation sat down with his lawyer (who was also his tax preparer) to discuss both legal strategy and the preparation of his tax returns, and in the course of the discussion bandied about numbers related to both consultations: the taxpayer could not shield these numbers from the Internal Revenue Service. This would be not because they were numbers, but because, being intended (though that was not the only intention) for use in connection with the preparation of tax returns, they were an unprivileged category of numbers.

The most difficult question presented by this appeal, and one on which we cannot find any precedent, relates to documents, numerical and otherwise, prepared in connection with audits of the taxpayers' returns. An example is a memo from Frederick to a paralegal asking her for the amount that Mr. Lenz and his corporation had paid Frederick for legal services rendered personally to Lenz in 1992. The memo was prepared to help Frederick respond to questions raised in an audit of the Lenzes' and the corporation's tax returns. An audit is both a stage in the determination of tax liability, often leading to the submission of revised tax returns, and a possible antechamber to litigation. When a revenue agent is merely verifying the accuracy of a return, often with the assistance of the taxpayer's accountant, this is accountants' work and it remains such even if the person rendering the assistance is a lawyer rather than an accountant. Throwing the cloak of privilege over this type of audit-related work of the taxpayer's representative would create an accountant's privilege usable only by lawyers. If, however, the taxpayer is accompanied to the audit by a lawyer who is there to deal with issues of statutory interpretation or case law that the revenue agent may have raised in connection with his examination of the taxpayer's return, the lawyer is doing lawyer's work and the attorney-client privilege may attach. But the documents in issue do not, so far as we are able to determine, relate to such representation.

\* \* \*

We have looked at all the documents that Frederick argues are privileged. Most are dual-purpose documents, about which no more may be said; some were not even submitted to the district judge for consideration of whether they might be privileged; in others as well, privilege was waived. We cannot find any clear errors in the district judge's rulings.

# Restatement of the Law (Third) The Law Governing Lawyers § 72, Comment c, Illustrations 2 & 3[*]

2. As Lawyer has done in past years, Lawyer prepares Client's federal tax returns, using records, receipts, and other information supplied by Client and without discussing any issues with Client. Client's tax returns are not complex, nor do they require a knowledge of tax law beyond that possessed by nonlawyer preparers of tax returns. Client knows that Lawyer is admitted to practice law but has never discussed with Lawyer any legal question concerning taxes or return preparation, nor has Lawyer offered such advice. Client pays Lawyer on a per-form basis and in an amount comparable to what nonlawyer tax preparers charge. The trier of fact may, but need not, infer that Client's purpose was not that of obtaining legal assistance.

3. Client frequently has consulted Lawyer about legal matters relating to Client's growing business. Lawyer drafts documents and provides other legal assistance relating to a complicated transaction having important tax implications that Client and Lawyer identify and discuss. Client later asks Lawyer to prepare Client's federal income-tax return for the tax year in which the transaction occurs. The circumstances indicate that Lawyer is providing legal services in preparing the tax return.

Some tasks commonly performed by lawyers require no distinctly legal skill. Some courts in an earlier era determined that the lawyer was then a mere "scrivener" and that communications relating to such tasks were not privileged. The older decisions reflected a culture in which many clients were illiterate and lawyers were employed because they could read and write rather than because of their legal skills or knowledge. However, in contemporary practice it will be unusual for a lawyer to prepare a document without communication with the client to determine, at a minimum, the client's objectives. Except in unusual circumstances clearly indicating otherwise, no distinction under this Section should be drawn between situations where the lawyer performs perfunctory services and those involving greater complexity or moment.

---

[*] Reprinted with permission. © The American Law Institute (2000).

## Questions and Comments:

1. Are tax lawyers engaged in "real" legal work or are they just number crunchers? How should the line be drawn between "legal" and "non-legal" work? If we conclude that tax lawyers do legal work, then are accountants that do the exact same type of work also engaged in legal work? If so, are they practicing law without a license? Should the definition of legal work differ between practice of law questions and the attorney-client privilege context?

2. If a lawyer is merely preparing typical tax returns for a fee in line with what accountants charge for that service, and no specific legal advice is requested or rendered, most courts have found that the attorney-client privilege is inapplicable. However, when a significant legal issue arises in the course of preparing the tax return, the issue becomes much closer since resolving the issue will require an analysis of the statute, regulations and cases as applied to the facts previously revealed. While such an analysis seems like legal work, some courts have concluded that since the analysis is undertaken by the return preparer for the purpose of properly completing the tax return it should not be eligible for the privilege. See e.g., *KPMG* 237 F. Supp. 2d 35, 42 (D.D.C. 2002). (finding no privilege for legal memoranda prepared by return preparer prior to return's filing). Is this a sound position? Under this approach does all pre-filing legal advice, even if rendered by an attorney that does not prepare the associated tax return, become non-privileged? See Id. at 44. (finding similar pre-filing memoranda on same topic that were not prepared by the return preparer to be privileged). Is there any justification for a denying the privilege to return preparers in such cases even if a court accepts that the advice constitutes legal advice? In light of these concerns, should a client ever have his attorney also act as a return preparer? Should a client ever let his return preparer prepare legal memoranda or written product memorializing their analysis? For a detailed discussion of the applicability of the attorney-client privilege in the tax return preparation context, see Claudine Pease-Wingenter, Does the Attorney-Client Privilege Apply to Tax Lawyers?: An Examination of the Return Preparation Exception to Define the Parameters of Privilege in the Tax Context, 47 Washburn L.J. 699 (2008).

3. When the *Frederick* opinion was released it was immediately criticized by practitioners as not drawing an appropriate line between privileged legal work and non-privileged accounting work. In response, Judge Posner amended his opinion to delete the

following sentence: "Normally, however, taxpayers in audit proceedings are represented by accountants, or not represented at all, rather than by lawyers; and so the principal effect of equating audits to litigation and thus throwing the cloak of privilege over the audit-related work of the taxpayer's representative would be to create an accountant's privilege usable only by lawyers." Why were practitioners upset by this approach to the privilege question?

4. In his revised opinion Judge Posner inserted the following language in place of the deleted sentence: "When a revenue agent is merely verifying the accuracy of a return, often with the assistance of the taxpayer's accountant, this is accountants' work and it remains such even if the person rendering the assistance is a lawyer rather than an accountant." Consider this statement in the context of the following problem.

**Problem 4.3**

Profit Corp. was founded in 1980 to manufacture personal care appliances. While initially profitable, it fell on hard times as the millennium closed. By 2005 it had incurred an aggregate of $200 million in net operating losses (NOLs). At this point management decided to revitalize the company and undertook a diversification plan that involved acquiring a number of profitable businesses. All these acquisitions were carefully structured, with the aid of Profit Corp.'s outside tax counsel Steady & Slow (S&S), to maximize Profit Corp.'s ability to use its NOLs against future income from the acquired businesses. As a result of this planning, some of the acquisition structures were quite complex. In particular, some employed the use of transitory shell companies and single member limited liability companies which in legal form undertook certain transactions that S&S intended would be collapsed or characterized as not occurring for federal income tax purposes. Additionally, while S&S has done its best in structuring the transactions, it has informed Profit Corp. that there are still a number of potential arguments that the IRS could assert that would limit or eliminate Profit Corp.'s use of its NOLs. Profit Corp. is now under audit. While as yet the IRS Agent conducting the audit has not made any proposed adjustments, he has indicated that he is "considering" whether Profit Corp.'s NOLs can be used against income from the acquired companies and whether the NOLs even continue to exist.

Profit Corp has now received an Information Document Request ("IDR") from the Agent. Among other things, the IDR requests the following factual information: (1) a specific description of the transactional form of each acquisition, and (2) the business purpose(s) for each transaction. Profit Corp. hires S&S to represent it in the audit. S&S reviews the IDR's questions carefully, makes a number of detailed inquiries of Profit Corp.'s executives, and drafts several legal memoranda highlighting the relevance of certain facts to the potential NOL exposure issues. Ultimately S&S drafts a written reply to each IDR question which is provided to the Agent. If the IRS demands that S&S provide a description of its conversations with Profit Corp.'s executives and turn over any memoranda or other documents created in responding to the IDR, can S&S successfully assert the attorney-client privilege?

## (b) Business Advice vs. Legal Advice

The attorney-client privilege only applies to communications arising during consultations relating to legal advice. However, in the real world clients often turn to their legal representatives for guidance on proposed transactions that may transcend mere legal analysis. Conversely, in undertaking even a purely legal analysis of a transaction, practical, economic or reputational concerns may occur to an attorney and be discussed with the client. This blending of legal and business advice is particularly relevant to tax practitioners since their tax analysis may become a central consideration in whether the transaction is undertaken, they may need to suggest changes to the structure of a transaction to address tax concerns while attempting to still fulfill the client's ultimate business objectives, and understanding the non-tax business motivations for the transaction may be central to their analysis of whether the desired tax treatment is supportable. It can also have implications for the in-house attorney who may have both legal and business roles.

# BOCA INVESTERINGS PARTNERSHIP
## v.
## UNITED STATES
31 F. Supp. 2d 9 (D.D.C. 1998)

\* \* \*

FRIEDMAN, Judge:

In a Memorandum Opinion and Order entered on June 9, 1998, Magistrate Judge Facciola considered plaintiffs' claim of attorney-client privilege with respect to eleven documents and defendant's motion to compel production of those documents. He granted the motion in part and denied it in part. . . . Plaintiffs moved for clarification. . . . The matter is now before this Court on defendant's motion for reconsideration of the Magistrate Judge's rulings.

\* \* \*

The author of Document No. 5 is Thomas M. Nee, whom plaintiffs identify as "Vice President for Taxes for AHP." Mr. Nee is a lawyer (although not a member of the New York Bar) who does not work in the Legal Department or for the General Counsel of AHP but rather for the Tax Department, a corporate component within AHP's Financial Group. The defendant argues that because Mr. Nee's position was not organizationally within AHP's Legal Department, because he was not under the direction and control of the General Counsel, and because he was not a member of the bar of the jurisdiction in which he was purporting to practice law, he may not invoke the attorney-client privilege. All of these factors, defendant suggests, indicate that Mr. Nee was not engaged in the practice of law or in providing legal advice but, rather, that he was providing some sort of business advice. Since the burden of demonstrating the right to protect material as privileged rests with the party asserting the privilege, the defendant concludes that Magistrate Judge Facciola was wrong not to require disclosure of Document No. 5 in its entirety.

Communications made by and to in-house lawyers in connection with representatives of the corporation seeking and obtaining legal advice may be protected by the attorney-client privilege just as much as communications with outside counsel. By contrast, communications made by and to the same in-house lawyer with respect to business matters, management decisions or business advice are not protected by the privilege. "The possession of a law degree and admission to the bar is [sic] not enough to establish a person as an attorney for purposes of determining whether the attorney-client privilege applies. the lawyer must not only be functioning as an advisor, but the advice given must be predominately legal, as opposed to business, in nature." North Am. Mortgage Investors v. First Wisconsin Nat'l Bank, 69 F.R.D. 9, 11 (E.D. Wis. 1975); see United States v. International Business Machines Corp., 66 F.R.D. 206, 212-13 (S.D.N.Y. 1974) (lawyer must give predominately legal advice, "not solely, or even largely, business advice"). When a lawyer acts merely to implement a business transaction or provides accounting services, the lawyer is like any other agent of the corporation whose communications are not privileged.

A corporation can protect material as privileged only upon a "clear showing" that the lawyer acted "in a professional legal capacity." In re Sealed Case, 737 F.2d at 99. Because an in-house lawyer often has other functions in addition to providing legal advice, the lawyer's role on a particular occasion will not be self-evident as it usually is in the case of outside counsel. A court must examine the circumstances to determine whether the lawyer was acting as a lawyer rather than as business advisor or management decision-maker. One important indicator of whether a lawyer is involved in giving legal advice or in some other activity is his or her place on the corporation's organizational chart. There is a presumption that a lawyer in the legal department or working for the general counsel is most often giving legal advice, while the opposite presumption applies to a lawyer such as Mr. Nee who works for the Financial Group or some other seemingly management or business side of the house. A lawyer's place on the organizational chart is not always dispositive, and the relevant presumption therefore may be rebutted by the party asserting the privilege.

At his deposition, Mr. Nee described his responsibilities as follows:

> I was responsible for the corporation's worldwide tax matters, which included providing tax counsel on all transactions the company might enter into; as well as responsibility for filing all the corporation's tax returns both in the United States -- federal, state and local

returns -- as well as making sure that the laws of all the foreign countries we operated in were adhered to from a tax standpoint, and that the proper filings would be made; handling all of the company's tax audits; possible litigation that might come up on tax issues, whether they be state or federal or foreign.

Deposition of Thomas Nee ("Nee Dep.") at 10-11. With respect to Document No. 5, the memorandum in question, Mr. Nee testified that "the purpose of the memorandum was to give tax advice to American Home Products Corporation. . . . They requested that I advise them on the tax consequences of entering the Investerings Partnership." Nee Dep. at 92-93. Finally, in response to the question whether "any business justifications, aside from tax considerations" were contained in the memorandum, Mr. Nee testified that the memorandum dealt "exclusively with giving tax advice with respect to financial transactions. . . . Business justifications were not set out . . . . The memorandum does not discuss motivation. It gives tax advice on the consequences of certain transactions." Nee Dep. at 112-14.

While preparation of tax returns and handling tax audits are functions that may or may not be performed by a lawyer and memoranda and conversations in connection therewith generally should not be considered privileged, Mr. Nee gave "tax advice with respect to [the] financial transactions discussed in the memorandum" and "on the consequences of certain transactions." Nee Dep. at 112-14. Magistrate Judge Facciola distinguished portions of the memorandum relating to such advice from other portions of the memorandum that "do not discuss the transaction as contemplated . . . [but instead] communicate either the lawyer's opinion as to the technical soundness of the contemplated transactions and information for a third party, Merrill Lynch." Opinion of Magistrate Judge Facciola at 10-11 (June 9, 1998). He found the former privileged and therefore protected, and he required production of the latter. This Court cannot say that Magistrate Judge Facciola's opinion on this score is either clearly erroneous or contrary to law. *See* Rule 72(a), Fed. R. Civ. P.

\* \* \*

ORDERED that the defendant's motion for reconsideration of Magistrate Judge Facciola's ruling on the attorney-client privilege claims is DENIED.

### Questions and Comments:

1. As discussed in the above case, the majority position is that an attorney must be consulted for "predominately" legal advice. However, in practice drawing the exact line regarding what constitutes predominate is often more difficult. Even if it is clear that the client had a clear purpose of obtaining legal advice, the communication may still not be protected by the privilege to the extent that business reasons alone would have been sufficient to prompt the communication. See e.g., McCaugherty v. Siffermann, 132 F.R.D. 234, 238 (N.D. Cal. 1990).

2. An additional area of potential concern is arguably presented in the context of negotiating tax indemnity provisions as part of the acquisition of a business enterprise. If a client reveals to an attorney potential prior year tax issues solely for the purpose of determining the appropriate type of indemnity provisions to negotiate (and not for the purpose of evaluating the actual likelihood of such tax liabilities being successfully asserted), it could be argued that the attorney's advice is predominately non-legal advice regarding typical market practice in similar situations and the economic considerations associated with different approaches to allocating the risk of future tax liabilities being asserted between the buyer and seller. While the actual drafting of an indemnity provision and determining exactly how specific contractual language would be applied to a specific potential liability would constitute legal work, such legal work may turn out to be relatively modest once the decision has been reached regarding how the client desires to allocate the indemnified risks from an economic and business perspective. Consequently, it could be argued that the legal work involved was not the predominate motive of the client's communication, and as a result the client's revelation of the potential tax issues lurking in its past tax returns would not be protected by the attorney client privilege.

## 4.   CONFIDENTIAL COMMUNICATIONS MADE BY THE CLIENT

The attorney-client privilege only protects confidential client communications. As a result, statements which are not intended to be confidential do not qualify for the privilege. Additionally, under the traditional formulation, communications emanating from an attorney are not privileged in their own right. In the view of the majority of courts, an attorney's statements to a client are generally only privileged insofar as revealing them would also reveal a confidential communication from the client. Lastly, the privilege only shelters "communications" from disclosure. As a result, informing an attorney about a particular fact does not shield that fact from evidence if the client herself is called on to disclose such underlying fact. The privilege merely prevents disclosing that the client actually communicated that fact to her attorney. All three of these requirements have resonance when applying the privilege in the tax context.

Regarding confidential communications, we have already seen several instances where this requirement has tax implications. For instance, a client's identity is generally not privileged since it is not been conveyed in confidence. Similarly, if information is conveyed to an attorney in connection with the preparation of a tax return, then it is generally not eligible for the privilege since it was conveyed with the expectation that it would be disclosed on the return rather than be kept confidential. See, e.g., Colton v. United States, 306 F.2d 633 (2d Cir. 1962); United States v. Merrell, 303 F. Supp. 490 (N.D.N.Y. 1969). This illustrates the more general proposition that any communication by the client to his attorney that is intended to be ultimately transmitted to a third party is not covered by the privilege. This is certainly the case with respect to factual information intended to be disclosed on a tax return, but also applies when information is intended to be disclosed to any third party. A common situation is where an attorney prepares an analysis of a client's potential tax liability for disclosure to the client's accountants in reviewing the appropriateness of the client's reserve account for tax liabilities that may be asserted in the future. Such tax accrual workpapers are therefore generally not covered by the attorney client privilege even if they are *not shown* to an outside accountant (which actual disclosure would waive the privilege in any event) if they were prepared with a non-confidential expectation. United States v. El Paso Company, 682 F.2d 530 (5th Cir. 1982). Accord, U.S. v. Arthur Young & Co., 465 U.S. 805 (1984) (holding tax accrual workpapers prepared by independent accountant were obtainable through the Internal Revenue Service's summons authority). As discussed below, however, the Supreme court has not yet ruled on whether such tax accrual workpapers might nevertheless be eligible for protection under the work-product doctrine in certain situations.

In any event, the Internal Revenue Service has historically exercised restraint in seeking a taxpayer's tax accrual workpapers despite its ability to legally obtain them. The current pronouncements of the Service regarding when it will seek to obtain tax accrual workpapers from a taxpayer or his representatives is contained in Announcement 2002-63, 2002-2 C.B. 72 and Internal Revenue Manual 4.10.20 (7-12-2004). In general, the Service will only request tax accrual workpapers if (1) the taxpayer has properly disclosed a "listed transaction" as defined in Treas. Reg. § 1.6011-4 (but generally will request only those papers related to the disclosed listed transaction unless there are financial irregularities with respect to the taxpayer or the taxpayer has engaged in multiple disclosed listed transactions), (2) the taxpayer has failed to disclose a listed transaction (including a transaction which only became a listed transaction after the return was filed), or (3) in cases not involving listed transactions, there are unusual circumstances where there is a need for facts on a specific issue that has been identified by the examining agent and such facts cannot be obtained from the taxpayer's records or from available third parties.

Even if a client reveals information with a confidential intent, the attorney-client privilege only protects the disclosure of the communication; it does not protect disclosure of the underlying facts communicated. However, both oral and written communications are covered. Thus, a client's oral recitation of the facts to his attorney is protected as well as a written document created by the client for the purpose of communicating the facts to his the attorney. However, documents provided to an attorney that were prepared previously for other business purposes generally are not themselves treated as communications protected by the attorney-client privilege, even if given to the attorney for the purpose of providing legal advice, since they were not created as the confidential means for communicating the information. For a discussion of these issues generally, see, Paul R. Rice, Attorney-Client Privilege: Continuing Confusion About the Attorney Communications, Drafts, Pre-Existing Documents, and the Source of the Facts Communicated, 48 Am. U. L. Rev. 967 (1999). As a result, whether or not any particular document in the files of a client or his attorney is protected by the privilege requires an analysis of the nature of the document, its history, and its contents. Courts typically will reject any blanket assertion of the attorney-client privilege and require a client to assert with specificity why particular documents or portions thereof are protected by the privilege.

Finally, in the majority of jurisdictions any documents prepared by, or advice provided by, an attorney to the client is privileged only to the extent that confidential client communications would be revealed by disclosure. The following case sets forth the relevant standard as applied to the legal opinion of a tax attorney.

# BOCA INVESTERINGS PARTNERSHIP
## v.
## UNITED STATES
1998 WL 426564 (D.D.C.)

Memorandum Opinion:

FRIEDMAN, Judge:

* * *

The attorney-client privilege is construed narrowly to protect from disclosure only those communications from the client to the attorney which were intended to be confidential and made for the purpose of seeking legal advice. Communications from the attorney to the client are privileged, therefore, only insofar as they disclose those kinds of communications from the client to the attorney. Evans v. Atwood, 177 F.R.D. 1, 3 (D.D.C. 1997). Thus, the Court of Appeals has held that opinions of counsel, which did not in themselves disclose any information transmitted to the attorney by a client who was expecting that it be kept confidential, were not protected by the attorney-client privilege. Mead Data Central v. United States Department of Air Force, 184 U.S. App. D.C. 350, 566 F.2d 242, 253 (D.C. Cir. 1977). While such opinions might, in a given instance, be protected from disclosure as work product if they were drafted by an attorney in anticipation of litigation, they cannot in themselves be protected by the attorney-client privilege unless they disclose information transmitted by the client with the expectation that it be kept in confidence. It is therefore incorrect to say, as plaintiffs do, that a lawyer's work is protected by the attorney-client privilege if it is based on confidential information from the client. Unless they are wasting their time, lawyers must always base what they do on the information their clients provide. To protect everything they do, because it was based, at least in part, on confidential information provided by the client would protect documents even if they did not reveal anything the client told the lawyer in confidence. That result is impossible in a Circuit which shields a lawyer's work only if it in itself yields the information which the client did not intend anyone but the lawyer to see. The only proper criterion is the one I articulated in my decision in Evans v. Atwood, *supra:* a document created by an attorney is protected by the attorney-client privilege only if the disclosure of its contents will necessarily and inevitably disclose a communication from the client which the client intended to be confidential.

\* \* \*

The \* \* \* documents remaining present a more complicated situation. These documents would, if disclosed, also disclose the process in which the lawyers engaged as they worked to complete the transactions which have led to this lawsuit. To state that the overall transaction at issue was complicated and that attorneys played a most significant role in creating it, in all of its intricacy, does not reveal anything not already known. \* \* \* However, more significant for present purposes is that disclosure of the process leading up to consummation of the transaction would necessarily yield the precise actions [the client] contemplated taking in order to secure favorable tax treatment. Even the government would have to admit that [the client] reasonably expected that its attorneys, equipped with information as to what [it] intended, would not be compelled, before the fact, to disclose what [it] intended any more than it could compel a lawyer to disclose that he drafted a will to fulfill his client's secret desire to make provision for an illegitimate child. In both instances, by knowing what the lawyer did, one necessarily knows what the client intended and learns something that the client intended to keep secret until his intention was realized.

It is no answer in that context to say that once the contemplated transaction is completed, the client has disclosed to the world what he once kept secret and there is no societal benefit in continuing to seal the lawyer's lips. Under that logic, the government would argue that since [the client] completed the transactions, there is no harm in forcing it to disclose what it wound up doing since nothing secret is being disclosed. That analysis is problematic because the completed transaction may have been different from the contemplated transaction or the client may have disregarded the attorney's advice. In the case of a client who disregards counsel's advice, the lawyer's communication to the client--"do not engage in this transaction"—would be disclosed once the contemplated transaction was consummated simply because the client eventually decided to pursue the course of action. Subsequent disclosure of his lawyer's advice, and his rejection of it, would be extremely detrimental to the client's defense of his transaction and would pit the lawyer against the client. Thus, it is clear that permitting discovery of the contemplation phase of a transaction, and the attorney's advice as to it, creates a powerful deterrent to the client telling his lawyer as candidly as possible all the information the lawyer needs to render sound legal advice.

\* \* \*

With that said, I have to conclude that plaintiffs are properly protecting from disclosure to the government certain information which [the client] communicated to its attorneys regarding the transactions it contemplated completing.

[The court then went on to examine a number of documents finding the client's communications regarding the originally proposed transaction to be privileged. In applying the above analysis to a formal legal opinion from the client's attorney concerning a proposed transaction the court held as follows:]

Document Number 11. This is a formal opinion letter as to the tax consequences of the transaction. Again, I have expurgated only those portions of the opinion which disclose the transaction as contemplated; the attorney's opinion in itself is not protected. Additionally, I note that, on occasion, the attorney refers to facts in the past tense which have already occurred and which must have been documented in some way. As I have explained in this opinion and at greater length in my opinion in Evans v. Atwood, *supra*, information which is publicly known does not become transformed into privileged information merely because a client seeks legal advice as to its significance. Such information is not provided to the attorney in confidence and cannot be considered confidential if that word is to continue to have its ordinary meaning. I have therefore not expurgated the attorney's reference to completed financial transactions. I will permit the defendant access to this document as I have expurgated it.

## Questions and Comments:

In the Boca case above, the legal question was limited to whether the attorney-client privilege protected the subject documents. Finding the privilege inapplicable to an attorney's legal analysis which doesn't reveal client confidences is therefore in line with the purpose of the privilege in promoting frank communications from the client. However, as will be discussed below, the legal analysis and impressions of an attorney will often be protected from disclosure under the work-product doctrine even though they are not covered by the traditional attorney-client privilege.

### Problem 4.4

Promoter is in the business of creating tax shelter strategies and marketing them to clients. Promoter consults with Law Firm regarding the tax consequences of various hypothetical transactions Promoter is developing. If the Internal Revenue Service seeks access to the lawyer's files regarding these hypothetical transactions, to what extent can the client assert the attorney-client privilege?

### Problem 4.5

Public Company completes a complicated transaction about which all the factual aspects and documentation is publicly disclosed pursuant to the relevant securities laws. Attorney is asked to review the documentation and provide an analysis of how the transaction should be reported for tax purposes. Attorney sends Public Company a formal legal opinion regarding the tax consequences of the transaction but does not prepare the tax return. Is the opinion covered by the attorney-client privilege? What if in the course of preparing his legal analysis Attorney consults Public Company regarding its subjective motivations for undertaking the transaction and the information received is relevant to the tax advice given? What if the motivations disclosed have only tangential impact on the tax analysis?

## 5.     DEFINING THE PARTIES TO THE ATTORNEY-CLIENT RELATIONSHIP

When an individual client is involved, it is readily apparent whose confidential communications are covered by the privilege. However, prior to the Supreme Court's decision in Upjohn Co. v. United States, 449 U.S. 383 (1981), courts frequently limited the application of the attorney-client privilege in a business entity setting to communications from a small group of employees with the power to control the actions of the entity. In Upjohn the Supreme Court rejected this narrow control group approach and found that communications form even rank-and-file employees could potentially be covered by the attorney-client privilege to the extent they were acting at the direction of their superiors to provide information to attorneys relevant to the provision of legal advice to the entity.

A similar issue arises on the lawyer side of the relationship. Is the client communicating confidentially with her attorney when some third party is somehow involved in the conversation? Clearly some expansion of the privilege beyond the attorney herself is warranted to allow for the delegation of ministerial matters to others. So courts have routinely found that secretaries, paralegals, and messengers who come into contact with privileged information in the course of their employment by the attorney are covered by the privilege. Similarly, courts have readily found the privilege to still apply to situations where an attorney must use an interpreter to communicate with a client who speaks a different language. But what if what is being translated is not the client's language itself, but specialized information being analyzed by an expert? The leading case in this area is excerpted below.

# UNITED STATES
## v.
# LOUIS KOVEL
### 296 F.2d 918 (2d Cir. 1961)

Before CLARK, HINCKS and FRIENDLY, Circuit Judges.

FRIENDLY, Circuit Judge.

[Kovel was a non-attorney accountant employed by a law firm specializing in tax matters. In the course of his employment he reviewed documents and had discussions with a client of the firm (Mr. Hopps) who was being investigated for possible tax violations. Kovel was subpoenaed to appear before a grand jury considering whether to indict Hopps. Kovel appeared as ordered before the grand jury but refused to answer several questions asserting that the attorney-client privilege prevented him from answering. The presiding judge ruled that the privilege was limited solely to attorneys and when Kovel maintained his refusal to answer the subject questions, the judge found Kovel in contempt and sentenced him to one year imprisonment. This appeal followed.]

* * *

Decision under what circumstances, if any, the attorney-client privilege may include a communication to a nonlawyer by the lawyer's client is the resultant of two conflicting forces. One is the general teaching that "The investigation of truth and the enforcement of testimonial duty demand the restriction, not the expansion, of these privileges," 8 Wigmore, Evidence (McNaughton Rev. 1961), § 2192, p. 73. The other is the more particular lesson "That as, by reason of the complexity and difficulty of our law, litigation can only be properly conducted by professional men, it is absolutely necessary that a man * * * should have recourse to the assistance of professional lawyers, and * * * it is equally necessary * * * that he should be able to place unrestricted and unbounded confidence in the professional agent, and that the communications he so makes to him should be kept secret * * *," Jessel, M.R. in Anderson v. Bank, 2 Ch.D. 644, 649 (1876). Nothing in the policy of the privilege suggests that attorneys, simply by placing accountants, scientists or investigators on their payrolls and maintaining them in their offices, should be able to invest all communications by clients to such persons with a privilege the law has not seen fit to extend when the latter are operating under their own steam. On the other hand, in contrast to the Tudor times when the privilege was first recognized, see 8 Wigmore, Evidence, § 2290, the complexities of modern existence prevent attorneys from effectively handling clients' affairs without the help of others; few lawyers could now practice without the assistance of secretaries, file clerks, telephone operators, messengers, clerks not yet admitted to the bar, and aides of other sorts. "The assistance of these agents being indispensable to his work and the communications of the client being often necessarily committed to them by the attorney or by the client himself, the privilege must include all the persons who act as the attorney's agents." 8 Wigmore, Evidence, § 2301; Annot., 53 A.L.R. 369 (1928).

Indeed, the Government does not here dispute that the privilege covers communications to non-lawyer employees with 'a menial or ministerial responsibility that involves relating communications to an attorney.' We cannot regard the privilege as confined to 'menial or ministerial' employees. Thus, we can see no significant difference between a case where the attorney sends a client speaking a foreign language to an interpreter to make a literal translation of the client's story; a second where the attorney, himself having some little knowledge of the foreign tongue, has a more knowledgeable non-lawyer employee in the room to help out; a third where someone to perform that same function has been brought along by the client; and a fourth where the attorney, ignorant of the foreign language, sends the client to a non-lawyer proficient in it, with instructions to interview the client on the attorney's behalf and then render his own summary of the situation, perhaps drawing on his own knowledge in the process, so that the attorney can give the client proper legal advice.

* * *

This analogy of the client speaking a foreign language is by no means irrelevant to the appeal at hand. Accounting concepts are a foreign language to some lawyers in almost all cases, and to almost all lawyers in some cases. Hence the presence of an accountant, whether hired by the lawyer or by the client, while the client is relating a complicated tax story to the lawyer, ought not destroy the privilege, any more than would that of the linguist in the second or third variations of the foreign language theme discussed above; the presence of the accountant is necessary, or at least highly useful, for the effective consultation between the client and the lawyer which the privilege is designed to permit. [3] By the same token, if the lawyer has directed the client, either in the specific case or generally, to tell his story in the first instance to an accountant engaged by the lawyer, who is then to interpret it so that the lawyer may better give legal advice, communications by the client reasonably related to that purpose ought fall within the privilege; there can be no more virtue in requiring the lawyer to sit by while the client pursues these possibly tedious preliminary conversations with the accountant than in insisting on the lawyer's physical presence while the client dictates a statement to the lawyer's secretary or in interviewed by a clerk not yet admitted to practice. What is vital to the privilege is that the communication be made in confidence for the purpose of obtaining legal advice from the lawyer. If what is sought is not legal advice but only accounting service, as in Olender v. United States, 210 F.2d 795, 805-806 (9 Cir. 1954), see Reisman v. Caplin, 61-2 U.S.T.C. P9673 (1961), or if the advice sought is the accountant's rather than the lawyer's, no privilege exists. We recognize this draws what may seem to some a rather arbitrary line between a case where the client communicates first to his own accountant (no privilege as to such communications, even though he later consults his lawyer on the same matter, Gariepy v. United States, 189 F.2d 459, 463 (6 Cir. 1951)), and others, where the client in the first instance consults a lawyer who retains an accountant as a listening post, or consults the lawyer with his own accountant present. But that is the inevitable consequence of having to reconcile the absence of a privilege for accountants and the effective operation of the privilege of client and lawyer under conditions where the lawyer needs outside help. We realize also that the line we have drawn will not be so easy to apply as the simpler positions urged on us by the parties -- the district judges will scarcely be able to leave the decision of such cases to computers; but the distinction has to be made if the privilege is neither to be unduly expanded nor to become a trap.

\* \* \*

[The court then went on to discuss the potential application of the above standards to Kovel's situation and concluded insufficient information existed in the record to show the history of the communications between Hopps and Kovel and the nature of their discussions and therefore remanded the case.]

The judgment is vacated and the cause remanded for further proceedings consistent with this opinion.

## Questions and Comments:

1.  As the court in Kovel expected, the job of implementing the line drawn by the court has fallen heavily on the district courts.  In subsequent cases those courts have used the Kovel logic to permit the privilege to extend to investment bankers, patent agents, psychiatrists, and even public relations firms.  Nevertheless, the overall thrust of Kovel's progeny has been to closely circumscribe the extension of the privilege to only those cases where the non-lawyer is essentially only performing an interpreting function for the attorney or can be seen as an agent of the client acting at the client's instruction to supply confidential information to the attorney (i.e., a situation akin to the extension of the privilege to non-control group employees under the Upjohn case discussed earlier).  Representative of this trend is the court's statement in Cavallaro v. United States, 284 F.3d 236 (1st Cir. 2002), that the expert must be "nearly indispensable or serve some specialized purpose in facilitating the attorney-client communications."  See generally, Kim J. Gruetzmacher, Comment, Privileged Communications with Accountants: The Demise of United States v. Kovel, 86 Marq. L. Rev. 977, 982 (2003); Ann M. Murphy, Spin Control And The High-Profile Client - Should The Attorney-Client Privilege Extend To Communications With Public Relations Consultants?, 55 Syracuse L. Rev. 545 (2005).

2. At the time Kovel was decided there was no independent accountant-client privilege.  Section 7525 now creates such a privilege.  As a result, the literal holding in Kovel as it relates to accountants is arguably of less relevance today.  Nevertheless, since,

as discussed in detail below, the accountant privilege is inapplicable in certain situations where the traditional attorney-client privilege can apply, it is often prudent to have an attorney hire any accountant employed in connection with tax matters in order to preserve the potential privilege claim under Kovel.

### Problem 4.6

Charlie Collector desires to donate a piece of artwork to a local museum and intends to claim a charitable contribution deduction on his tax return. He contacts Arty Attorney to discuss the availability of the deduction and is advised to obtain an appraisal to support his return position. Ignoring the potential application of the work-product doctrine discussed below, how would you advise Charlie to pursue obtaining such an appraisal to maximize his chances of being able to shelter it from subsequent disclosure to the Internal Revenue Service? See Berbardo v. Comm'r, 104 T.C. 677 (1995); Est. of Halas v. Comm'r, 94 T.C. 570 (1989).

### Problem 4.7

Sam has both a law degree and a CPA. Sam provides tax advice to Linda, but does not prepare her tax return. Ignoring the potential application of the Section 7525 privilege, are Linda's communications to Sam protected by the attorney-client privilege? Should it matter whether Sam holds himself out as an attorney or as a CPA to his clients? See, United States v. Threlkeld, 241 F. Supp. 324 (W.D. Tenn. 1965). What if Sam works for the consulting group of a large accounting firm and local rules prohibits accounting firms from "practicing law"?

## 6. WAIVER OF PRIVILEGE

Even if all the other prerequisites exist, a client can waive the protection of the attorney-client privilege. However, the existence of the attorney-client privilege is a fragile thing and a client may find she has inadvertently or impliedly waived the privilege even if she has never made an explicit renunciation of the privilege. Waivers generally take one of three forms: explicit waivers, inadvertent waivers, and implied waivers. The first two categories are relatively straightforward in application. Determining whether an implied waiver has occurred is often a vexing proposition.

Clearly, there are many situations where a client will explicitly waive the privilege. For instance, a taxpayer on audit may decide that the best way to explain the position taken on a tax return to an examining agent is to give the agent a copy of the legal opinion the taxpayer received on the issue. However, explicit waivers also result whenever a confidential communication is revealed to someone not in a privileged relationship with the client. So, revealing a tax opinion to an investment banker or to an accountant in a capacity not covered by the accountant-taxpayer privilege under section 7525, would waive the privilege. Indeed, in most jurisdictions a waiver of the privilege with respect to certain statements or opinions will be treated as a waiver of the privilege for the entire subject matter covered, not just the particular statement or document disclosed. Thus, for instance, disclosing the tax consequences of a merger in proxy materials has been found to "waive[] the attorney-client privilege with respect to all documents which formed the basis for the advice, all documents considered by counsel in rendering that advice, and all reasonably contemporaneous documents reflecting discussions by counsel or others concerning that advice." In re Pioneer Hi-Bred Int'l Inc., 238 F.3d 1370, 1374-75 (Fed. Cir. 2001).

For a waiver to occur it must be the result of a voluntary act of the client. However, there is no requirement that the voluntary act actually be *intended* to waive the privilege. So, if a client shares privileged information with a banker, the privilege is waived even though client was unaware that doing so would waive the privilege. Conversely, when thief steals privileged documents there is no waiver as long as the client takes appropriate steps to recover the documents and shield them under the privilege when they are ultimately located or recovered. Similarly, a waiver generally does not occur when an agent reveals privileged information without actual or apparent authority as long as the client acts promptly to assert the privilege and recover any copies of the disclosed information. So, a messenger who without authority delivers a privilege document to the government would not waive the privilege due to his lack of authority. Even an agent with apparent authority (e.g. an attorney delivering a privileged document to an adversary as discussed in detail in Chapter 2) may sometimes avoid having waived the privilege if it is shown that the disclosure was inadvertent, it occurred despite taking reasonable measures to prevent disclosure, and the privilege is promptly asserted when the inadvertent disclosure is discovered.

Despite the general rule that the disclosure of a privileged communication to a third party operates as an explicit waiver of the privilege, there are some limited circumstances where a disclosure to "third parties" is deemed to further, rather than undercut, the policies behind the privilege. Consequently, no waiver occurs when privileged communications are disclosed to joint clients, joint litigants and parties sharing a "common interest". See generally, James M. Fischer, *The Attorney Client Privilege Meets Common Interest Arrangement*, 16 Rev. Litig. 631 (1997). Joint client (multiple clients on the same side in a matter represented by the same attorney) and joint litigant (multiple clients on the same side in a matter represented by multiple attorneys) situations in which the parties share information for their mutual benefit represent fairly straightforward instances where the attorney-client privilege should continue to apply despite the technical exposure of communications to a "third party" since the attorneys involved can educate the clients about the scope of the privilege and the agreement of mutual confidentiality in the context of a legal representation where full disclosure of the information from all the clients facilitates providing the most complete legal advice to each.

The "common interest" exception is somewhat harder to define. As a general matter the exception applies where two parties share "an identical legal interest with respect to the subject matter of the communication." Duplan Corp. v. Deering Milliken, 397 F. Supp. 1146, 1164 (D.S.C. 1974). However, in practice issues often arise regarding whether legal issues that arise in the context of a broader business transaction should be covered by the doctrine. For instance, assume Target Company has engaged in some aggressive tax planning in the past. Acquiring Corporation is considering acquiring Target in a tax-free reorganization (as a result of which Acquiring would become liable for any tax deficiencies asserted against Target) and has questioned the appropriateness of the contingent liability reserves that Target has established on its books in respect of its past aggressive tax transactions. In negotiating the terms of the acquisition, Target shows Acquiring copies of the relevant legal opinions received. Has Target waived the attorney-client privilege in respect of all its tax advice on these transactions? Should it matter whether or not the merger is actually consummated? Courts have reached divergent conclusions in similar fact patters. While some courts would take an expansive view and find a common interest here, many courts contend that this type of fact pattern merely represents a "concurrent" legal interest arising from a common *commercial* interest. Such courts limit the common interest exception to situations where the parties are truly forming some common legal strategy, rather than just having an economic interest in a particular legal outcome. For instance, contrast the foregoing illustration with a situation where Target and Acquiring are seeking to start a new joint venture and share separately obtained privileged information in order to facilitate the most tax efficient structuring for creating the new joint venture.

In contrast with explicit and inadvertent waivers, an implied waiver deals with the situation where the nature of the legal matter being litigated itself is said to have impliedly waived the privilege. The courts have yet to develop a uniform approach for when an implied waiver will be found. Some courts take the position that a litigant automatically waives the privilege upon assertion of a claim, counterclaim, or defense that raises a matter to which otherwise privileged material is relevant. Other courts find that in such situations the privilege is waived only when the information sought is both relevant to the issues raised in the case and vital or necessary to the opposing party's defense of the case. Still other courts assert that an implied waiver is only appropriate if a litigant directly puts the attorney's advice at issue in the litigation.

In the tax context, it is not uncommon for taxpayers to seek to prove that they had reasonable cause and good faith for their tax return position in order to avoid a penalty. As a result, a taxpayer's mental state may automatically be at issue, in which case any legal advice relevant to that mental state may be discoverable by reason of an implied waiver of privilege. The following case explores the relevant considerations in such situations.

# THOMAS E. JOHNSTON
## v.
# COMMISSIONER OF INTERNAL REVENUE
### 119 T.C. 27 (2002)

Before Judge Arthur L. Nims, III.

[Facts: Thomas E. Johnston was involved in a number of real estate transactions that ultimately led to the assertion of federal income deficiencies and penalties. As part of his defense he asserted his reliance on "experts" in preparing the relevant tax returns. In making this claim he attempted to limit his reliance claim to advice received from his accountant and affirmatively tried to exclude from his defense reliance on advice received from his legal counsel, Mr. O'Keefe. The government moved immediately for a ruling that the assertion of the reliance on experts defense also implied waived the attorney-client privilege with respect to the advice of Mr. O'Keefe.]

Discussion

I. Motion in Limine

Respondent's motion in limine asks the Court to enter an order in advance of trial ruling that "petitioner Thomas E. Johnston is not entitled to assert attorney-client privilege to prevent his former attorney, Thomas O'Keefe, from testifying about or producing records pertaining to certain confidential communications made by petitioner during the course of the representation". Framed more narrowly, respondent's request is principally concerned with notes made by Mr. O'Keefe regarding the June 28, 1989, meeting with Mr. Johnston * * *. Respondent alleges that these notes are not protected by the attorney-client privilege [since there was a] * * *waiver by petitioners' having placed the nature of attorney-client communications at issue through claimed reliance on counsel's advice * * * .

As construed under Federal common law, the attorney-client privilege exists "to encourage full and frank communication between attorneys and their clients and thereby promote broader public interests in the observance of law and administration of justice." Upjohn Co. v. United States, 449 U.S. 383, 389, 66 L. Ed. 2d 584, 101 S. Ct. 677 (1981). The privilege applies to communications made in confidence both: (1) By a client to an attorney for the purpose of obtaining legal advice, and (2) by an attorney to a client where containing legal advice or revealing confidential information on which the client seeks advice. The burden of establishing that the attorney-client privilege is applicable to particular communications or documents rests with the party asserting the privilege.

As previously indicated, one of the grounds on which respondent alleges that Mr. O'Keefe's notes are not protected here is that petitioners waived the privilege by claiming reliance on advice of counsel. This contention invokes the doctrine of what is referred to as implied waiver. While the precise reach of the theory can be a subject of some controversy, courts typically employ some version of one of several general approaches. These include the so-called automatic waiver rule, under which a party automatically waives the privilege by asserting a claim or defense to which otherwise privileged matter is relevant, see Indep. Prods. Corp. v. Loew's Inc., 22 F.R.D. 266, 276-277 (S.D.N.Y. 1958); a balancing test that weighs the need for discovery against the need to protect the secrecy of the communication, see Greater Newburyport Clamshell Alliance v. Pub. Serv. Co., 838 F.2d 13, 20-22 (1st Cir. 1988); the three-pronged test of Hearn v. Rhay, 68 F.R.D. 574, 581 (E.D. Wash. 1975); and a purportedly more restrictive test where waiver is effected only if a litigant directly injects an attorney's advice into issue, see Rhone-Poulenc Rorer, Inc. v. Home Indem. Co., 32 F.3d at 863-864.

\* \* \*

Hearn v. Rhay, supra 68 F.R.D. 574 at 581, sets forth the following three factors which must be extant for a finding of implied waiver:

(1) assertion of the privilege was a result of some affirmative act, such as filing suit, by the asserting party; (2) through this affirmative act, the asserting party put the protected information at issue by making it relevant to the case; and (3) application of the privilege would have denied the opposing party access to information vital to his defense. \* \* \*

To similar effect, this Court stated in Bernardo v. Commissioner, supra 104 T.C. 677 at 691 (fn. ref. omitted), that the taxpayers did not impliedly waive the privilege where they did not "affirmatively raise a claim that can only be effectively disproven through the discovery of attorney-client communications". Given this precedent and section 7453, we structure our discussion here within the three criteria of the foregoing test.

The statutory notices issued to Mr. Johnston determine deficiencies and section 6663 fraud penalties for each of the years 1989, 1991, and 1992. After petitions were filed in these cases, respondent submitted answers affirmatively setting forth the facts upon which respondent relied in support of the fraud determinations, as required by Rule 36(b) with respect to issues on which respondent bears the burden of proof. Mr. Johnston, in accordance with Rule 37(b), then followed with replies denying the majority of respondent's affirmative allegations. The replies also included additional material addressing affirmative defenses. The reply relating to Mr. Johnston's 1989 tax year stated:

By way of Affirmative Defense to the matters affirmatively alleged by Respondent in its answer, Petitioners allege as follows:

\* \* \*

12) In preparing Petitioner's returns for 1989, Petitioners relied upon advice of qualified experts for the underlying information developed and reported on Petitioner's income tax return for 1989.

A nearly identical reference to the "advice of qualified experts" was made in the reply dealing with the 1991 and 1992 tax years. It is on the above-quoted statement pertaining to 1989 that respondent bases contentions of implied waiver.

Petitioners' response to respondent's argument consists, in its entirety, of the paragraph reproduced below:

Respondent argues that the Petitioner relied on Advice of Counsel in his defense of the within proceeding in his Reply referring to "qualified experts" assisting him in preparing his 1989 tax return. However, the Petitioner's reference in his Reply to "qualified experts" assisting him was his accountant who assisted him in the filing of his Form 1040X for the calendar year 1989 [1-R]. He does not refer to a lawyer. Therefore, there has been no defense of advice of counsel and Respondent's argument is misplaced.

It is within the just-described context that we turn to consideration of the three requirements for implied waiver. As previously indicated, the first mandates that the privilege be asserted as the result of some affirmative act. Here, Mr. Johnston asserted reliance on qualified experts as an affirmative defense to respondent's fraud penalty allegations.

In Hearn v. Rhay, 68 F.R.D. at 576-577, the plaintiff brought suit claiming that his civil rights were violated during his incarceration in a State penitentiary. The defendants asserted the affirmative defense of qualified immunity based upon having acted in good faith, and the plaintiff sought discovery of legal advice the defendants received with respect to his confinement. Id. at 577-578. In those circumstances, the court held that asserting the privilege in furtherance of an affirmative defense satisfied the first element for qualified waiver. Id. at 581. Other courts have similarly opined that raising affirmative defenses can result in a waiver of the attorney-client privilege. The United States District Court for the District of

Columbia, for instance, has refused to uphold the privilege where the defense "of good faith reliance was affirmatively pleaded by the party seeking to use the attorney-client privilege as a shield against discovery." United States v. Exxon Corp., supra at 248. Accordingly, the first requisite is met here if Mr. Johnston's reference to qualified experts is deemed to encompass legal counsel.

We conclude that to now narrow "advice of qualified experts" solely to assistance received from the accountant aiding Mr. Johnston in preparing his amended return would be to support a belated characterization belied by the record. We initially note that Mr. Johnston's reply for the 1989 tax year was filed on September 22, 1997. Petitioners' opposition to the motions in limine was filed on May 31, 2001, more than three and one-half years later. In addition, the incongruity between the original plural "experts" and the subsequent singular "accountant" is difficult to reconcile.

Moreover, petitioners elsewhere in the opposition state: "Thomas O'Keefe, Esq., a certified tax specialist, represented the Petitioner as tax counsel rendering tax advice over a period of many years, and in particular in 1989, the period during which events occurred that are raised in Respondent's Motion in Limine herein." To similar effect, petitioners remark that "Thomas O'Keefe, Esq., a certified tax specialist, had been a long time attorney for Mr. Johnston and entities owned and controlled by him", and at yet another location characterize Mr. O'Keefe as "long time tax counsel of Petitioner, Mr. Johnston". Additionally, the bill from Mr. O'Keefe to * * * Mr. Johnston for legal fees incurred in June of 1989 contains the following description dated "06/28/89":

"Meeting with Tom Johnston, Darrell Spence and Frank Nish re Shorecliffs; Review of sale transaction; Prepared demand on escrow and notice and acknowledgement [sic] regarding earth subsidence issues to Buyer; Tax research and strategy planning regarding basis, installment deal, sub-s and Exchange issues."

There is also the fact that income from the [real estate] sale was reported on neither the original nor the amended 1989 return. Hence, to the extent that reliance on expert advice can excuse the alleged fraudulent failure to report this transaction, such reliance was not only or in the first instance on the accountant aiding in preparation of the amended return. We are satisfied that petitioners' affirmative defense contemplated more than just the cited accountant and is appropriately read to include Mr. O'Keefe, who concededly provided tax advice in 1989.

The second requirement asks whether through this affirmative act the asserting party puts the protected information at issue by making it relevant to the case. This element, too, has been satisfied here. As the Court of Appeals for the Ninth Circuit explained in an analogous context: "to the extent that * * * [the defendant] claims that its tax position is reasonable because it was based on advice of counsel, * * * [the defendant] puts at issue the tax advice it received." Chevron Corp. v. Pennzoil Co., 974 F.2d 1156, 1162-1163 (9th Cir. 1992).

Likewise, petitioners seek to defend against the fraud allegations on grounds of reliance on experts. That defense places at issue the tax advice Mr. Johnston received with respect to his 1989 return. Petitioners have also admitted that Mr. O'Keefe rendered tax advice to Mr. Johnston during 1989. Given these circumstances, petitioners, by raising the affirmative defense of reliance, must be said to have placed at issue in the present proceeding all tax advice received with respect to the 1989 transactions in dispute, including communications with Mr. O'Keefe.

Finally, the third inquiry is directed toward whether allowing the privilege would deny the opposing party access to information vital to its defense. The Courts of Appeals have cautioned that privileged communications do not become discoverable where they simply are relevant to issues raised in the litigation or where they are only one of several forms of indirect evidence about an issue. Rather, the information must be "vital", Hearn v. Rhay, 68 F.R.D. at 581, such that it would be "manifestly unfair" to deny access due to consequent prejudice to the opposing party's defense, Home Indem. Co. v. Lane Powell Moss & Miller, 43 F.3d at 1326-1327. Stated otherwise, the attorney- client privilege "may not be used both as a sword and a shield." Chevron Corp. v. Pennzoil Co., supra at 1162.

In connection with the affirmative defense posture presented in Hearn v. Rhay, supra 68 F.R.D. 581 at 581, the court explained that "one result of asserting the privilege has been to deprive plaintiff of information necessary to 'defend' against defendants' affirmative defense, for the protected information is also germane to plaintiff's burden of proving malice or unreasonable disregard of his clearly established constitutional rights." The analogous scenario in United States v. Exxon Corp., 94 F.R.D. at 249, led the court to observe as follows:

> Exxon's affirmative defenses necessarily revolve around whether Exxon did, in fact, primarily or solely rely upon a particular DOE regulation or communication when the company made its pricing decisions. Thus, the only way to assess the validity of Exxon's affirmative defenses, voluntarily injected into this dispute, is to investigate attorney-client communications where Exxon's interpretation of various DOE policies and directives was established and where Exxon expressed its intentions regarding compliance with those policies and directives. * * *

A parallel situation exists here.

Under section 7454(a) and Rule 142(b), respondent bears the burden of establishing fraud by clear and convincing evidence. Petitioners have asserted reliance on professionals as an affirmative defense to the fraud allegations. To "defend" against this defense, respondent must show that such reliance either was unreasonable or did not in fact occur. Respondent can do so only through knowledge of what tax advice Mr. Johnston received, and such would include communications from Mr. O'Keefe. Additionally, having invoked reliance on "experts", petitioners cannot now be entitled selectively to withhold communications from particular experts, especially those who petitioners concede provided tax advice, while allowing communications from others to be disclosed. Rebuttal of the affirmative defense will depend on the sum of tax advice received on the disputed transactions; respondent will be prejudiced if only portions (presumably those not detrimental to petitioners' position) are available.

To rephrase a conclusion of the Court of Appeals for the Ninth Circuit, petitioners "cannot invoke the attorney-client privilege to deny . . . [respondent] access to the very information that . . . [respondent] must refute in order to demonstrate" the unreasonableness or nonexistence of the claimed reliance. Chevron Corp. v. Pennzoil Co., supra 974 F.2d 1156 at 1163. Doing so would engender precisely the sort of unfairness that the implied waiver doctrine was devised to avoid.

We therefore hold that all three elements of the Hearn v. Rhay, supra 68 F.R.D. 574, test for implied waiver have been established. We shall grant respondent's motion in limine on this basis.

\* \* \*

To reflect the foregoing,

Appropriate orders will be issued granting respondent's motion in limine. . . .

## Questions and Comments:

The voluntary disclosure of a privileged communication will typically waive the attorney-client privilege for all communications related to the same subject matter. Conversely, if a non-privileged communication is revealed by a client, then the disclosure of that communication cannot be said to have waived the privilege with respect to the related subject matter. A typical illustration is a statement to an attorney that was never intended by the client to be kept confidential. So, where client instructs attorney to make a particular settlement offer on a specific issue to the Internal Revenue Service, the client has not waived any privilege that might attach generally to the attorney-client communications about that issue generally since the terms of, and the client's authorization to present, the settlement were never intended to be confidential. What if Mr. Johnston had instructed Mr. O'Keefe to draft an opinion at the time of the real estate transaction that was intended solely for the purpose of being disclosed to the Service if the tax treatment transaction was ever questioned? Since the opinion was created with the intention that it be disclosed, should this yield a different result in the Johnston case?

## Problem 4.8

Client receives a legal opinion from his attorney and shares it with his accountant, who agrees to keep it confidential (but to whom no privilege is extended either by section 7525 or by the Kovel case), to support a position taken in preparing certain financial statements. Does the common interest exception prevent a waiver of the privilege?

## Problem 4.9

Doc Cheatum is a partner in the law firm of Dewey, Cheatum & Howe. His partner Slim Jim asks for Doc's advice on a complex tax issue for a new client. Doc recalls dealing with similar issues for an unrelated client several years ago and provides Slim with a copy of the legal opinion and research done for the earlier client. Has the attorney-client privilege relating to the earlier client's matter been waived? What if Slim ultimately delivers to the new client a legal opinion on the matter that "cribs" large sections of the legal analysis from the earlier opinion?

## B.    The Tax Practitioner-Client Privilege

In 1998 Congress changed the game in terms of accountant provided tax advice by statutorily creating an evidentiary privilege for non-lawyer tax practitioners under Code section 7525. Prior to that time numerous courts had rejected any privilege for communications with accountants even if the tax advice sought was clearly unrelated to tax return preparation. However, while Congress sought to level the playing field between accountants and attorneys, it still left important distinctions between the protection afforded attorney-provided advice and tax advice provided by other tax practitioners.

Section 7525(a)(1) contains the general rule that for communications made on or after July 22, 1998 "the same common law protections of confidentiality which apply to a communication between a taxpayer and an attorney shall also apply to a communication between a taxpayer and any federally authorized tax practitioner to the extent the communication would be considered a privileged communication if it were between a taxpayer and an attorney." Thus, the section generally extends the attorney-client privilege to any individual authorized to practice before the Service, such as CPAs and enrolled agents to the extent the advice they are asked to provide is within the scope of their authority to practice or would be privileged if they were an attorney. As a result, all the rules discussed above regarding the requirements for, and waivers of, the attorney-client privilege have equal applicability to the Section 7525 privilege.

However, Section 7525 goes on to place certain limitations on the reach of the Section 7525 privilege. In particular, Section 7525(a)(2) provides that the Section 7525 privilege can only be asserted in (i) noncriminal tax cases that either (ii) are before the Internal Revenue Service or are brought by or against the United States in Federal court. The limitation to noncriminal tax cases is particularly troublesome. If a civil tax proceeding ever evolves to become a criminal proceeding, then the client would lose any evidentiary privilege for communications with his non-attorney tax advisor.  Conversely, if a matter begins as a criminal tax proceeding and the government obtains client-tax advisor communications that would be privileged in a civil tax matter, it is likely that the disclosure would result in a waiver of the privilege in a subsequent civil tax proceeding even if the government ultimately drops the criminal case.  Consequently, clients relying on non-attorney tax advisors face a potential trap for the unwary if the government ever decides to challenge their tax positions criminally.

Similarly, the limitation of the privilege to federal cases raises waiver issues for non-attorney tax advice that would not be present in attorney advisor situations.  For instance, the federal privilege provides no protection from disclosure of client-accountant communications in the context of a state tax proceeding or other litigation not involving the United States government.  As a result, the disclosure of communications in a state proceeding would seem to waive any Section 7525 privilege otherwise available in a federal proceeding.  Further, the limitation on the privilege only applying to cases brought by or against the United States seems to technically make the section 7525 privilege inapplicable to federal tax issues that happen to be litigated in the federal bankruptcy courts or to a disclosure of an otherwise privileged communications in a federal court proceeding where the client's federal tax liability is not actually being litigated with the government.

Finally, Section 7525(b) explicitly makes the privilege inapplicable to any written communications in connection with the promotion of participation in a "tax shelter."  For these purposes a tax shelter is very broadly defined to include any entity, plan or arrangement if a significant purpose of such entity, plan or arrangement is the avoidance or evasion of federal income tax.  The broad scope of this definition arguably makes _all_ tax planning advice ineligible for the section 7525 privilege.  However, some legislative history appears to imply to the contrary.  See H.R. Conf. Rep. No. 105-599, 269 (1998) (indicating that *promotion* of tax shelters was not considered "part of the routine relationship between a tax practitioner and a client").

The combined result of the above described limits on the section 7525 privilege is that at the time of any client-tax practitioner communication there will be significant uncertainty as to whether the evidentiary privilege will ultimately apply to such communications in light of the possibility that the communication might someday be asserted to relate to a criminal matter, a tax shelter, or tax return preparation and due to the increased waiver risks resulting from possible disclosure of the communication in non-federal tax contexts. As such, many clients still continue to favor using attorneys for their tax advice, and continue to employ Kovel-type arrangements to obtain accountant advice, despite the existence of section 7525.

**Problem 4.10**

Eveready Accountants specializes in reducing its clients' taxes. Upstanding Corporation was a new Eveready client. Eveready reviewed Upstanding's business and tax history and designed several possible tax reduction strategies tailored to Upstanding's situation. Upstanding ultimately executed several of these proposed strategies. On audit the Service is seeking access to Eveready's memoranda and files regarding the executed transactions on the grounds that the transactions represent tax shelters. Will the section 7525 privilege apply to protect these materials? See, Valero Energy Corp. v. United States, 569 F.3d 626 (7th Cir. 2009).

# C.    Work Product Immunity

When the attorney-client privilege applies to a communication, the communication is shielded from discovery despite the fact that this may impede the search for the truth. By contrast, work product immunity is not an absolute privilege and even if it would otherwise apply, the protection can be overcome if sufficient need is demonstrated. Conversely, the work product doctrine covers a significantly broader range of materials. Unlike the attorney-client privilege, it is not limited to confidential client communications or legal advice, and therefore can preclude discovery of a wide range of documents created in anticipation of litigation, even if not created by an attorney. Additionally, waivers of the work product immunity are less common and even where a waiver has occurred, it does not trigger a broad subject matter waiver.

The reason for these stark differences traces to the divergent purposes underlying each doctrine. The attorney-client privilege is aimed at promoting frank client communications with the ultimate goal of improving compliance with the law and ensuring that clients receive legal advice based on complete information. By contrast, work product immunity is based on notions of general fairness. The work product doctrine was originally judicially developed to prevent a party in litigation from gaining an unfair advantage over an opponent by obtaining the fruits of the opponent's litigation preparations. Today, the concept of work product immunity is codified in the federal rules of civil procedure.

Rule 26(b)(3) generally provides that "documents and other tangible things that are prepared in anticipation of litigation or for trial by or for another party or its representative" are shielded from discovery unless the seeking "party shows that it has substantial need for the materials to prepare its case and cannot, without undue hardship, obtain their substantial equivalent by other means." Further, even if this showing is made, the court must still "protect against disclosure of the mental impressions, conclusions, opinions, or legal theories of a party's attorney or other representative concerning the litigation." Essentially the federal rule identifies two types of protected work product: "factual work product" that reflects the collection and development of the facts related to the anticipated litigation, and "opinion work product" that reflects the mental impressions, legal theories, analysis and opinions of an attorney or other representative. Factual work product is normally protected since the seeking party could still uncover the same material through its own efforts and therefore should not be allowed to free-ride on its opponent's legwork. Still, factual work product remains discoverable if substantial need is demonstrated and the relevant information cannot be obtained without undue hardship. Opinion work product by contrast is generally only discoverable in rare circumstances.

The central question in determining whether a document is protected by the work product doctrine is whether it was created "in anticipation of litigation." How should this standard be applied in tax cases? Does the mere possibility that a tax return position may be challenged by the Service in a future audit constitute "litigation?" How certain must the "litigation" be? What if a document is created with dual purposes of supporting a tax return position and laying the groundwork for a potential litigation? Consider these questions in the context of the following case.

# UNITED STATES
## v.
# PATRICK J. ROXWORTHY
457 F.3d 590 (6th Cir. 2006)

Before KEITH and COLE, Circuit Judges; MILLS, District Judge. *

R. GUY COLE, JR., Circuit Judge. Defendant Patrick J. Roxworthy, in his capacity as Vice President of Tax at Yum! Brands, Inc. ("Yum"), appeals the district court's order enforcing an Internal Revenue Service (IRS) administrative summons demanding production of two memoranda that Yum argues are protected by work product privilege. For the reasons set forth below, we reverse the district court's order to compel their production and remand to the district court for entry of an order granting Roxworthy's motion to quash.

## I

The IRS is conducting an investigation of Yum's tax liability for fiscal years 1997, 1998, and 1999. As part of Yum's response to an informal document request, it produced a "privilege log" listing seven documents that it believed were protected from turnover to the IRS by the work product doctrine. * * * Five of the seven documents were ultimately produced to the IRS after the parties entered into a limitation of waiver agreement. The remaining two documents are memoranda prepared by KPMG, LLP, an audit and consulting firm, analyzing the tax consequences of certain transactions entered by Yum pertaining to the creation of a captive insurance company and related stock transfers, including possible arguments that the IRS could mount against Yum's chosen tax treatment of the transactions and possible counter-arguments. The IRS filed a petition in the United States District Court for the Western District of Kentucky to enforce its summons as to the KPMG memoranda. After a show-cause hearing, a magistrate judge entered a report and recommendation that the summons be enforced, concluding that the KPMG memoranda were created not in anticipation of litigation but rather to assist Yum in the preparation of its taxes and yearly audit.

Roxworthy filed objections * * * [and] introduced additional affidavits clarifying that the memoranda at issue were not prepared to assist Yum in the preparation of its taxes, but rather were created because Yum anticipated litigation due to its upcoming recognition of a $112 million loss for tax purposes but not book purposes, the conspicuousness of such a tax treatment, the certainty of an IRS audit due to Yum's size, the unsettled nature of the law in that area, and Yum's belief that the IRS was inclined to litigate such matters. After hearing oral arguments on Roxworthy's objections, the district court adopted the magistrate judge's report and recommendation as the opinion of the court.   * * * This appeal follows.

## II

* * *

B.      Meaning of "in anticipation of litigation"

The "work product privilege" * * * protects from discovery documents and tangible things prepared in anticipation of litigation by or for a party or by or for that party's representative.

* * *

We have yet to define "in anticipation of litigation." Other circuits have adopted the standard first articulated in Wright and Miller's Federal Practice and Procedures, asking whether a document was "prepared or obtained *because of* the prospect of litigation." [Citations omitted.] Today, we join our sister circuits and adopt the "because of" test as the standard for determining whether documents were prepared "in anticipation of litigation."

Adopting this standard prompts the further question of when documents can be said to have been created because of the prospect of litigation. It is clear that documents prepared in the ordinary course of business, or pursuant to public requirements unrelated to litigation, or for other nonlitigation purposes, are not covered by the work product privilege. Thus, a document will not be protected if it would have been prepared in substantially the same manner irrespective of the anticipated litigation. Furthermore, courts applying the "because of" test have typically recognized both a subjective and objective element to the inquiry; that is, a party must "have had a subjective belief that litigation was a real possibility, and that belief must have been objectively reasonable." *Sealed Case*, 330 U.S. App. D.C. 368, 146 F.3d 881 at 884; We therefore embrace the test used by a number of the district courts in our circuit, including the district court in this case, which asks (1) whether a document was created because of a party's subjective anticipation of litigation, as contrasted with an ordinary business purpose, and (2) whether that subjective anticipation of litigation was objectively reasonable.

C.      Subjective anticipation of litigation

The two memoranda at issue here were made available to us for *in camera* review. The documents appear to be two versions of the same memorandum. * * * Both bear a designation of attorney-client privilege but do not bear any work-product designation.

Yum argues that the documents themselves are the best evidence that they were created in anticipation of litigation. Indeed, apart from eleven pages of background facts * * * the memoranda contain dense legal analysis of current tax law, including arguments and counter-arguments in certain areas of law that the memoranda argue are unsettled. * * * The "Discussion" section of each memo sets forth "the rationale for [KPMG's] conclusions and some of the more likely theories that could be asserted by the IRS in challenging [KPMG's] conclusions." [T]he IRS would appear to obtain an unfair advantage by gaining access to KPMG's detailed legal analysis of the strengths and weaknesses of Yum's position. This factor weighs in favor of recognizing the documents as privileged.

Nevertheless, the key issue in determining whether a document should be withheld is the function that the document serves. Because documents are not protected if they were created for nonlitigation purposes, regardless of content, "[d]etermining the driving force behind the preparation of each requested document is therefore required in resolving a work product immunity question." *Nat'l Union*, 967 F.2d at 984. Thus we must examine not only the documents themselves, but the circumstances surrounding the documents' creation.

* * *

The magistrate judge concluded that Yum's "bare, conclusory affidavit allegations" failed to show it "had a subjective belief that litigation was a real possibility" at the time the memoranda were completed. The magistrate judge further concluded that the memoranda were more likely prepared to assist Yum in the preparation of its taxes and the avoidance of understatement penalties if the IRS disagreed with Yum's tax treatment, and therefore concluded that the documents were part of the regular course of business and would have been created irrespective of any potential for litigation.

\* \* \*

While the original record may have left doubts regarding whether Yum subjectively believed litigation was likely, and whether Yum commissioned the KPMG memoranda because of that belief or merely to assist with a business purpose, the affidavits introduced to expand the record clarify these questions.

\* \* \*

We find no evidence in the record to controvert the affidavits supplied by Yum. Although the memoranda do not bear a work-product designation, we agree with the magistrate judge's observation that the absence of a designation alone does not settle the inquiry of whether the documents were created in anticipation of litigation. \* \* \* Yum's uncontroverted assertions that it anticipated litigation because of the uncertainty surrounding the area of tax law at issue are also corroborated by the memoranda's highly detailed discussions of hypothetical legal arguments. Finally, the additional specifics regarding why Yum anticipated litigation, particularly its explanation that it planned to claim a $112 million tax loss with no corresponding book loss, that KPMG had advised the company that the law surrounding captive insurance companies was unsettled, and that the IRS had demonstrated an inclination to litigate in that area, provide more than bare self-serving conclusions. Thus, Yum's unambiguous sworn affidavits and deposition testimony satisfy its burden of demonstrating that the memoranda were prepared due to Yum's subjective anticipation of litigation and not in the ordinary course of business.

\* \* \*

We are persuaded by Yum's argument that even if the KPMG memoranda were prepared in part to assist Yum in avoiding underpayment penalties during an audit, the documents do not lose their work product privilege "merely because [they were] created in order to assist with a business decision," unless the documents "would have been created in essentially similar form irrespective of the litigation." *Adlman II*, 134 F.3d at 1202; United States v. ChevronTexaco Corp., 241 F. Supp. 2d 1065, 1082 (N.D. Cal. 2002) ("[E]xcept where a document would have been generated in the normal course of business even if no litigation was anticipated, the work product doctrine can reach documents prepared 'because of litigation' even if they were prepared in connection with a business transaction or also served a business purpose."). As other courts have noted, a document can be created for both use in the ordinary course of business and in anticipation of litigation without losing its work-product privilege. To the extent that the magistrate judge's findings turned on a requirement that the primary or sole purpose of the KPMG memoranda be in preparation of litigation, we conclude that the magistrate judge relied upon an incorrect interpretation of the law.

\* \* \*

Because the magistrate judge's conclusion is unsupported by both the record and the law, we conclude that the district court committed clear error in adopting the magistrate judge's conclusion that Yum has not demonstrated subjective anticipation of litigation.

D.     Objectively reasonable anticipation of litigation

The magistrate judge further concluded that Yum had failed to show "particular facts that would reasonably give rise" to a belief that "litigation was a real possibility." The district court adopted the magistrate judge's conclusion, noting that "any possibility of litigation was too far removed to be concrete or significant."

Courts have articulated various tests for determining when anticipation of litigation is too speculative to be objectively reasonable. The D.C. Circuit has required the objecting party to prove that a document was "prepared with a specific claim supported by concrete facts which would likely lead to litigation in mind," *Coastal States*, 617 F.2d at 865, but has also found the privilege to apply in the absence of a specific claim where an attorney "rendered legal advice in order to protect the client from future litigation about a particular transaction,"   \* \* \*

The Fourth Circuit has stated that the protection only applies when the "preparer faces an actual claim or a potential claim following an actual event or series of events that reasonably could result in litigation." *Nat'l Union*, 967 F.2d at 984. Although not every audit is potentially the subject of litigation, *see Coastal States*, 617 F.2d at 865, a document prepared "in anticipation of 'dealing with the IRS' . . . may well have been prepared in anticipation of an administrative dispute and this may constitute 'litigation' within the meaning of Rule 26," Hodges, Grant & Kaufmann v. IRS, 768 F.2d 719, 719-22 (5th Cir. 1985).

Here, Yum argues that it anticipated litigation because a yearly IRS audit of Yum was a certainty due to the company's size, the transaction at issue involved a $112 million discrepancy between tax loss and book loss, and the company had been advised by KPMG that the area of law was unsettled and that the IRS had recently targeted this type of transaction. Yum points to a case with analogous facts in which a district court upheld the work-product privilege. In *ChevronTexaco*, as here, the company's tax returns were routinely examined by the IRS, the company was engaged in a transaction involving "a very substantial amount of tax dollars," and the IRS "had previously questioned similar transactions." The court concluded that the withholding party "reasonably believed that it was a virtual certainty that the IRS would challenge the . . . transaction." *Id.*

Likewise * * * Yum has demonstrated that the "expected litigation" here is "quite concrete" despite the absence of any overt indication from the IRS that it intends to pursue litigation against Yum. Yum has identified a specific transaction that could precipitate litigation, the specific legal controversy that would be at issue in the litigation, the opposing party's opportunity to discover the facts that would give rise to the litigation, and the opposing party's general inclination to pursue this sort of litigation. We believe that Yum has established that the memoranda at issue sought to protect Yum "from future litigation about a particular transaction," that Yum has also established that KPMG and Yum had in mind a "specific claim supported by concrete facts which would likely lead to litigation," and that Yum has established that it "face[d] an actual or a potential claim following an actual event or series of events that reasonably could result in litigation," Because we believe that Yum's circumstances clearly constitute objectively reasonable anticipation of litigation under any of the tests we have seen employed by our sister circuits, we need not decide which of these articulations is most useful.

We therefore conclude that the district court committed an error of law in determining that Yum's anticipation of litigation was too remote to constitute a reasonable anticipation of litigation.

* * *

## Questions and Comments:

1.  The scope of the term "litigation" has not been conclusively determined in the tax controversy context, but most courts appear to focus on the expectation for actual trial litigation. In Roxworthy the court did not have to directly face this issue since the taxpayer was under constant audit by the Service and subjectively and objectively believed that the Service would take the matter all the way to trial given the legal uncertainty and the multi-million dollar tax savings involved. If Yum had anticipated that it was likely the issue would be settled with the Service prior to actually suing in court, would the work product immunity have applied? In this regard, consider the Restatement (Third) of the Law Governing Lawyers (section 87 comment h) which provides that:

> Litigation includes civil and criminal trial proceedings, as well as *adversarial* proceedings before an administrative agency, an arbitration panel or a claims commission, and alternative-dispute-resolution proceedings such as mediation or mini-trial. . . . In general, a proceeding is *adversarial* when evidence or legal argument is presented by parties contending against each other with respect to legally significant factual issues. [emphasis added]

The phrase "adversarial" is typically used in the context of a proceeding between two adversaries held before some type of decisional body, rather than the direct negotiation between two opposing parties. See e.g., United States v. American Tel. & Tel. Co., 86 F.R.D. 603, 628 (D.D.C.1979) (defining "litigation" as "a proceeding in a court or administrative tribunal in which the parties have the right to cross-examine witnesses or to subject an opposing party's presentation of proof to equivalent disputation"). When does a tax issue become adversarial? Should the Service's internal Appeals Office function represent an "adversarial" proceeding? On the other hand, some courts seem willing to find arguably "non-adversarial" proceedings within the scope of the term "litigation". See, e.g., Martin v. Monfort, Inc., 150 F.R.D. 172, 173 (D. Colo. 1993) (holding the work-product privilege applied to studies prepared by a corporation in response to an investigation by the Department of Labor alleging violation of the Fair Labor Standards Act). Similarly, as discussed in Chapter 1, ABA Opinions 314 and 85-352 (discussing when an attorney can ethically recommend requesting position) noted that the filing of a tax return can be viewed as the first step toward future litigation, and therefore can be seen as an adversarial act. Consider how dramatically the scope of the work product doctrine would be impacted by these differing approaches to the definition of "litigation." Which approach makes more sense in light of the purposes of the privilege? Which makes more sense in terms of fair tax administration?

2. As the Roxworthy court notes, work product immunity does not extend documents created in the ordinary course of business that would have been prepared in substantially the same manner even if no litigation risk existed. However, a document that was created because of anticipated litigation does not lose its immunity merely because the document also proves useful for some other non-litigation or business related purpose. Thus, the treatment of so called "dual purpose" documents under the work product doctrine requires an analysis of a separate causation test, that is, it requires determining whether the document would have been created in substantially the same form in any event for a non-litigation purpose in the absence of pending or possible future litigation. See, e.g., In re OM Group Sec. Litig., 226 F.R.D. 579, 587 (N.D. Ohio 2005).

3. The Sixth Circuit in Roxworthy joined the majority of the court of appeals in adopting the "because of" test for applying the work product doctrine. However, it is important to note that this causality test must be met in the context of the entire document, not just specific sections. While the fact that certain paragraphs or sentences were written with an eye toward possible future litigation may be evidence that the document was created "because of" litigation, the mere existence of such passages is not itself conclusive. So, as discussed above, a dual purpose document that would have been prepared in substantially the same manner even if no litigation risk existed, would not be protected by work product immunity merely due to some litigation related statements, nor would those particular statements be eligible for the privilege if the document as a whole was not covered.

4. Businesses, accountants and attorneys are often called on to prepare, or contribute to the preparation of, documents supporting the appropriateness of the tax reserve shown on the financial statements for the business. Earlier in this Chapter we saw that while the Service exercises restraint in requesting such tax accrual workpapers, as a matter of law these materials have been found to be ineligible for either the attorney-client privilege or the section

7525 privilege. Recently the First Circuit ruled in a 3-2 enbanc opinion that tax accrual workpapers are not covered by the work product doctrine even if they reflect attorney opinions regarding the likelihood of success if the identified tax issues are litigated. United States v. Textron Inc., _F.3d_, 2009 WL 2476475 What are the arguments you would make for and against the application of the work product doctrine in the context of tax accrual workpapers? Which position is more supportable in light of the policy of the work product privilege and the interests of fair tax administration?

5. As mentioned briefly above, unlike the attorney-client privilege, the voluntary disclosure of a document to a third party does not automatically waive the work product immunity for such document. Such a third party disclosure will only cause a waiver of the privilege if there is a substantial risk that the document would be revealed to an adversary. Additionally, even if the immunity is waived for a particular document, there is no subject matter waiver, so only the specific document revealed is subject to discovery. Regarding inadvertent waivers, courts generally undertake a multi-factor balancing test to determine if a waiver should result as a matter of fundamental fairness. Implied waivers of the work product immunity can also result, as in the attorney-client context, where a taxpayer claims reliance on the advice of counsel as a defense.

## Problem 4.11

Honest Abe owns a small pawn shop. He is considering selling his business to Pawn-It, Inc. and has hired Vicky, a local attorney, for help in structuring and negotiating the transaction. Abe's goal is to maximize his after-tax proceeds from selling the business, in which he has a low tax basis. As part of her work, Vicky prepares a memorandum reviewing the tax consequences of several alternative structures for the transaction (the "Tax Memo"). The Tax Memo goes into detail regarding Vicky's opinions regarding the legal strength of the described tax positions and the various challenges that might be raised by the Service. After reviewing the Tax Memo, Honest Abe opts to use one of the more conservative acquisition strategies. Nevertheless, on audit the Service challenges his tax reporting of the transaction and seeks to obtain a copy of the of the Tax Memo. Honest Abe claims the Tax Memo is protected by both the attorney-client privilege and work product immunity. Who wins and on what theory or theories?

**Problem 4.12**

Use the basic facts from Problem 4.11 except that, instead of selecting a conservative alternative, Honest Abe decided to use the most aggressive tax structuring alternative in implementing the transaction. Is the Tax Memo now more or less likely to be protected from disclosure to the Service? Is society benefited more by applying the privilege in contexts like this or not?

**Problem 4.13**

Ted Taxpayer was recently audited and a deficiency of $20,000 was asserted by the Service. Ted refused to pay and the matter was litigated in the Tax Court which found there was no deficiency owed. Ted has now sued the government for the costs of the litigation under section 7430. The government has defended on the ground that its position in the litigation was "substantially justified" and therefore section 7430 does not allow for recovering the costs of the litigation. Ted seeks to obtain legal memoranda prepared by the government attorneys in connection with the Tax Court suit that set forth their legal thinking and weights. The government asserts work-product privilege. Should the government be forced to disclose the memoranda to Ted?

# Chapter 5

## Tax Shelters

---

The long and the short of it all is that the parties demeaned themselves in entering so dishonest a venture, unquestionably structured to garner for each of the taxpayers tax advantages to which they were not entitled and devoid of any realistic business purpose. * * * [T]hey, by their conduct, nevertheless reveal a malaise which a healthy United States of America cannot sanction. It is a frightening prospect when our wealthy citizens, those in the highest income tax brackets, seek to take indefensible advantage of the country and their fellow citizens, especially those who have far less from which to meet their tax responsibilities.[23]

---

Tax administration has long been hampered by taxpayers who seek deceptive and fraudulent means of avoiding tax. These types of transactions are obviously illegal and a lawyer's participation in advising, adding or marketing such transactions clearly violates ethical and statutory rules.

A much more difficult question arises, however, when the transaction is not simply a fraudulent transaction, but is instead a complicated transaction that achieves significant tax savings by manipulating various tax provisions. These transactions are also often built on fanciful profit projections that almost never materialize. In common parlance these transactions are referred to as tax shelters. Abusive tax shelters can drain the public fisc, threaten tax administration, and create severe inequities in the tax system. Because of the major problems brought on by tax shelters, Congress and the IRS have sought ways to curtail taxpayer participation in these shelters. In truth, taxpayers cannot participate in these shelters without the help of accountants and lawyers. The transactions are simply too complicated and require too much knowledge of the Code and its regulations to be accomplished by unsophisticated taxpayers.

---

[23] Barnard v. Commissioner, 731 F.2d 230 (4th Cir. 1984).

This chapter discusses the statutory and regulatory rules governing lawyers' activities with regard to tax shelters.

# COBRA STRIKES BACK:
# ANATOMY OF A TAX SHELTER[*]

62 Tax Law 59 (2008)
Karen C. Burke
Grayson M.P. McCouch

Like sellers of treasure maps, promoters of tax shelters promise that for a large fee one can navigate a secret route. What clinches these deals is not the chart itself but [an opinion letter] that appears to warrant that the map is as good as gold. . . . Written by tax lawyers using the embossed stationery of their firms, the letters typically cost $50,000, $75,000 or more, and require a signed promise to keep the contents secret, like the treasure map, lest the Internal Revenue Service discover where untaxed fortunes lie. But . . . opinion letters may not be worth the paper they are written on.[24]

## I. Introduction

Paul M. Daugerdas has gained notoriety for himself and his erstwhile firm, Jenkens & Gilchrist, as the designer of a tax shelter technique that uses contingent liabilities to generate artificial tax losses on a grand scale. For all its surface complexity and sophistication, the basic shelter transaction is surprisingly simple in concept. In essence, it uses offsetting options to inflate the basis of property that is distributed by a partnership and then contributed to and sold by another partnership, resulting in a large tax loss without any corresponding economic loss. In principle, this type of shelter could be replicated indefinitely and generate unlimited tax losses. Mr. Daugerdas is by no means unique. The transactions that he approved as shelter counsel on behalf of Jenkens & Gilchrist differ

---

[24] David Cay Johnston, Costly Questions Arise on Legal Opinions for Tax Shelters, N.Y. TIMES, Feb. 9, 2003, at 25.

only in trivial details from myriad other transactions peddled by other lawyers and accountants.

\* \* \* Mr. Daugerdas and others like him have reaped enormous rewards for themselves and their clients, but some of the tax shelters they designed for credulous and wealthy clients have backfired spectacularly. Congress and the Treasury have taken remedial action to shut down abusive tax shelters, and several courts have invoked longstanding judicial doctrines to strike down transactions that lack economic substance and have no real business or investment purpose, despite purported compliance with the literal terms of the tax laws. The proliferation of abusive tax shelters could never have gotten off the ground without the active participation of high-priced counsel—some of them at highly reputable firms—who issued reassuring legal opinions concerning the tax consequences of shelter transactions. Upon discovering that the anticipated tax benefits failed to materialize, disgruntled clients have rushed to sue the lawyers, accountants, investment advisers, and banks that created and marketed defective shelters. Mr. Daugerdas is the target of a criminal investigation, and Jenkens & Gilchrist has been disbanded. And they are only the tip of the iceberg.

\* \* \*

II.  Contingent-Liability Tax Shelters

A.  *Background*

In late 1998, Jenkens & Gilchrist, a fast-growing Texas firm, brought Mr. Daugerdas on board as a tax partner in charge of the firm's newly-opened Chicago office.  Mr. Daugerdas brought with him a lucrative specialty in tax shelters and a close working relationship with several accounting firms (including Ernst & Young and KPMG) and the securities arm of Deutsche Bank. During the next five years, Mr. Daugerdas sold at least 600 generic shelters which generated hundreds of millions of dollars in fees for the firm— he personally netted $93 million—and billions of dollars of artificial tax losses for clients. The financial incentives for crossing the line between shelter promoter and shelter counsel were clearly powerful, and Mr. Daugerdas placed himself and his firm in an ethically equivocal position by rendering favorable tax opinions concerning tax shelters that he helped to design and market. Worse still, the shelters were highly risky. If detected, they would inevitably be challenged by the Service and might well be held invalid in court.

The Service became aware of the scope of shelter promoters' activities in the course of an investigation of accounting firms, and in 2002 began serving summonses on promoters and auditing the tax returns of individual investors. One of those investors, Henry Camferdam, and his business partners had purchased a shelter designed by Mr. Daugerdas and known as COBRA (an acronym for "Currency Options Bring Reward Alternatives").[25] Mr. Camferdam soon emerged as a poster-boy for disgruntled shelter investors. Appearing in 2003 before the Senate Finance Committee at a hearing on abusive tax shelters, he recalled being approached by Ernst & Young with a high-pressure sales pitch about "a tax strategy that could virtually eliminate our capital gains taxes." Although he received assurances that the shelter was "completely legal," he was offered two separate tax opinions from purportedly "independent" counsel as "insurance" against the risk of audit by the Service. In addition, he was required to sign a confidentiality agreement and was not allowed to discuss the shelter with outside counsel. Mr. Camferdam and his business partners sued Jenkens & Gilchrist, Mr. Daugerdas, and others, claiming that they had been lured into purchasing a defective tax shelter. Despite their efforts to portray themselves as innocent investors, these clients may find it difficult to show that they reasonably relied on legal advice concerning transactions that appeared too good to be true.

In 2004, the government forced Jenkens & Gilchrist to turn over its client lists and, in 2005, the firm agreed to pay $81.5 million to settle a class action brought by more than 1,000 tax shelter investors, including Mr. Camferdam. By 2006, Mr. Daugerdas had become "the tax lawyer at the heart of a broadening federal investigation into questionable tax shelters." In 2007, Jenkens & Gilchrist was finally forced to close its doors. As part of a landmark settlement, the firm accepted responsibility for criminal wrongdoing

[25]In 1999, Mr. Camferdam and his three business partners paid more than $6 million in fees—$1 million to Ernst & Young, $2 million to Jenkens & Gilchrist, $75,000 to Brown & Wood (for a second tax opinion), and $3 million to Deutsche Bank—to avoid $14 million of taxes on $70 million of gain from sale of their business. *See* Tax Shelters: Who's Buying, Who's Selling, and What's the Government Doing About It?, Hearing Before the Senate Comm. on Finance, 108th Cong. 15, 87 (2004) (statement of Henry Camferdam, Jr.) Following Ernst & Young's disclosure of their names and the ensuing audit, they eventually ended up owing $14 million in taxes plus an additional $11 million in interest and penalties. *See* Sheldon D. Pollack & Jay A. Soled, Tax Professionals Behaving Badly, 105 TAX NOTES 201, 205 n.31 (Oct. 11, 2004).

in connection with its tax shelter activities and agreed to pay a $76 million penalty.

## Questions and Comments:

1. Burke and McCouch set out the particulars of one type of abusive tax shelter. As Burke and McCouch note, the problem with these types of transactions is they allow taxpayers who have significant income to use these abusive transactions to shelter all of their income thus significantly reducing their tax. Because these transactions can be set up for any amount of money, the taxpayer can essential shield as much income as he wishes, based solely on his willingness to pay the high fees involved. The taxpayer, lawyers, and accountants benefit and society loses.

2. Two problems arise in combating tax shelters.

First, although many of us believe we recognize a tax shelter when we see it, others argue that as long as these schemes technically comply with the law, they are legal. But even if one accepts the argument that taxpayers should be allowed to engage in a transaction as long as the transaction technically complies with the statute, one still has to determine if in fact the transaction entered into by the taxpayer does so.

Courts are thus faced with two separate issues. First, courts must determine whether in fact the transaction does technically comply with the Code provisions. In other words, does the statute operate the way the taxpayer claims it operates? The second question is if a strict (or not so strict) reading of the statute provides the tax benefits the taxpayer claims, is the taxpayer entitled to the benefits even if that is not what Congress intended when it passed the statute?

The second problem that the Service faces in addressing tax shelters is that these shelters are often sold on the condition of confidentiality. Confidentiality allows the shelters to go unnoticed and makes it very difficult for the IRS to identify the promoters and the taxpayers taking advantage of the tax shelter plan. In addition, since only a small number of returns are audited, taxpayers may be willing to play the audit lottery. This is especially true if the taxpayer has a legal opinion that the taxpayer believes will shield him from penalties.

Since you cannot have tax shelters without tax lawyers and accountants, Congress and the Treasury have sought to address the rise in tax shelters by placing restrictions on lawyers and accountants who provide opinion letters on tax transactions and on promoters who sell and distribute tax shelters. These restrictions are contained in Circular 230 and in the penalty provisions in the Code.

## A.     Circular 230, Tax Shelter Regulations

In order to address many of the problems with aggressive tax positions and planning, the Treasury promulgated changes to Circular 230 to provide significant restrictions on lawyers, accountants and other tax professionals engaged in aggressive tax planning. The provisions basically have three components. First, they address the requirements for practitioners providing written advice on tax shelters. Second, they address some of the problems created by confidentiality provisions, and third they provide sanctions for firms and attorneys that violate the provisions. This third provision encourages firms to self-police and puts firms on the hook if attorneys in the firm engage in overly aggressive tax practices.

## 1.     COVERED OPINIONS

IRS Circular 230 Disclosure: Tax advice contained in this communication is not intended or written to be used, and cannot be used, by the taxpayer for the purpose of avoiding penalties that may be imposed on the taxpayer, or for the purpose of promoting, marketing, or recommending to another person a transaction.

This is an example of a standard disclosure statement that is now contained in almost every written communication from a lawyer. This disclosure ensures that any advice in the e-mail or other correspondence will not be subject to §10.35's restrictions. This next portion discusses the rules under Circular 230 and why lawyers and law firms have taken such a broad approach to ensuring that e-mails and other communication do not come within § 10.35 of Circular 230.

Section 10.35 provides the requirements for "covered opinions." A covered opinion can be used by taxpayers as a justification for entering into a transaction and as a defense against penalties. The Treasury regulates these opinions to ensure that lawyers investigate a transaction thoroughly before recommending it to taxpayers. It also ensures that a lawyer has a high level of certainty regarding the validity of the transaction before allowing a taxpayer to rely on the attorney's advice.

Section 10.35 addresses the fact that an attorney's work product is often seen as a "seal of approval." If an attorney's work is going to be a seal of approval for a tax shelter, it is important that the work be well thought out and has a high level of certainty.

Section 10.35 provides that three different types of tax advice may be considered a "covered opinion." The first involves classic tax shelters that are specifically identified by the Service or are substantially similar to transactions listed by the Service. The second type of advice involves advice regarding a plan or arrangement when the principle purpose of the transaction is tax avoidance. The third type of advice, and the type that is the most difficult to identify, is advice about a plan or arrangement when a significant purpose of the transaction is the avoidance or evasion of tax *and* the advice is a reliance opinion, a marketed opinion, advice subject to confidentiality provisions, or advice subject to contractual protection.[26]

Section 10.35 thus addresses some of the biggest problems with tax shelters. It attacks known abusive transactions, transactions close to the line, and transactions with confidentiality or contractual protection provisions. It is easy to know whether a transaction is a listed transaction, and it is pretty easy to tell if the principal purpose is avoidance or evasion. It is, however, much more difficult to determine whether tax avoidance or evasion is a significant purpose. Read literally this provision could apply to a host of planning transactions engaged in by taxpayers.

It is too early to tell how the Service will interpret the principal purpose language. Section 10.35 concludes that tax avoidance is the principal purpose if that purpose "exceeds any other purpose." The definition further provides that a transaction will not meet this definition if it has as its purpose the "claiming of tax

---

[26] There are also exceptions for advice from in-house counsel to the client, advice provided after the return is filed (thus it cannot be encouraging investment in a tax shelter), and negative advice opinions (those opinions that say a transaction will not prevail.) See § 10.35(b)(2)(ii)(A).

benefits in a manner consistent with the statute and Congressional purpose."

Therefore, the real problem for practitioners is the third restriction – a plan that has as its significant purpose the avoidance of tax. Some practitioners have expressed serious concern with this provision. They claim that it is their role to help taxpayers legally avoid tax. Encouraging a client to fund a Section 529 plan, for example, may be suggested to avoid tax and thus a significant purpose of the transaction may be to avoid tax. At the moment, there is no evidence that the Service has interpreted this provision that broadly and the funding of § 529 plan is consistent with the statute and Congressional purpose. However, concerns that the lawyer or firm might be subject to § 10.35 have led practitioners to seek ways to make sure that their advice is not considered a "covered opinion."

When the advice has as its significant purpose tax avoidance, the advice will be considered a covered opinion if it is considered a reliance opinion or a marketed opinion. The attorney must also ensure that it is not subject to confidentiality clauses or contractual protection.

## (a) Reliance Opinion

Section 10.35 includes in the definition of a covered opinion transactions where a significant purpose is the avoidance of tax and the written advice is a "reliance opinion." A reliance opinion is an opinion by an attorney that concludes that it is more likely than not that the taxpayer will prevail with regard to the transaction. Such an opinion can be used by taxpayers as a defense against penalties issued by the IRS.

In fact, the main purpose of a reliance opinion is that the taxpayer can rely on the attorney's conclusion in entering the transaction. Once again we see that the attorney is acting as a "seal of approval" for the transaction. If, however, the communication is not intended for that purpose, the attorney can avoid the designation of a "reliance opinion" by clearly indicating to the taxpayer that the opinion is not intended to be used, and cannot be used, for the purpose of avoiding penalties. This is one of the provisions of Circular 230 that led to the general disclaimers that exist in most law firm communication.

It is important to recognize that reliance opinions are legal and important, especially if the attorney believes that the transaction will more likely than not prevail. They provide advice to taxpayers and allow taxpayers to exercise their rights to organize their affairs to minimize their tax liability. Law firms simply want to make sure that quick, general tax advice is not considered a reliance opinion. If a taxpayer needs or wants a reliance opinion, the attorney can still issue one, he just needs to comply with the rules for covered opinions in § 10.35. Section 10.35 clearly makes such advice more expensive, but it also ensures that the advice has been thought through and that the attorney has considered the matter thoroughly before issuing the opinion.

### (b) Marketing Opinion

Marketing opinions are opinions by lawyers that are used by a taxpayer to market or promote a plan or arrangement that has as a significant purpose the avoidance of tax. (Remember, if it is a listed transaction or a principal purpose transaction, it will be a covered opinion and there is no need to determine whether it will be marketed to others).

Advice will not be considered a marketed opinion if the practitioner "prominently discloses" that 1) the opinion was not intended and cannot be used to avoid penalties, 2) the opinion was issued to the taxpayer for the purpose of using the opinion to market or promote the transaction, *and* 3) the taxpayer should seek independent tax advice regarding the transaction.

### Problem 5.1

You work for the Commissioner of Internal Revenue and have just proposed the rules for Marketed Opinions discussed above. The Commissioner asks you why an opinion is not a marketed opinion simply because there is a disclosure statement that clearly indicates that it is going to be used for the purpose of marketing or promoting a transaction. The Commissioners asks "Shouldn't the purpose behind § 10.35 be to crack down on these types of opinions?" What is your response to the Commissioner? What is the justification for exempting opinions that meet the three requirements discussed above?

## (c) Confidentiality and Contractual Protections

To the extent that the advice is not intended to be advice regarding a tax shelter, attorneys can generally avoid the requirements for covered opinions by indicating that it is not intended for use by the taxpayer to avoid penalties, or for promotion to third parties. But if the advice is subject to confidentiality provisions or contractual protections, the disclaimer will not be enough to prevent the advice from being considered a covered opinion.

Advice will be considered a covered opinion if the advice contains confidentiality restrictions or contractual protections. Advice will be considered subject to "conditions of confidentiality" if the practitioner imposes "a limitation on disclosure of the tax treatment or tax structure of the transaction and the limitation on disclosure protect the confidentiality of that practitioner's tax strategies." § 10.35(b)(6) Advice will be considered subject to conditions of confidentiality even if the confidentiality provisions are not legally binding.

Advice will be considered subject to "contractual protection" if the taxpayer is entitled to a refund of some or all of the fees charged by the attorney if the tax positions addressed in the opinion are not sustained on the merits. Similarly, advice will also be subject to contractual protection if the fees charged are contingent upon the taxpayer realizing the stated tax benefits. See § 10.35(b)(7)

## Problem 5.2

You are working for a U.S. Senator. The Senator tells you that he met an old friend at dinner the other night who was complaining about provisions promulgated by the Treasury restricting the right of attorneys to use confidentiality provisions and to allow contractual protections for taxpayers. Explain to the Senator the public policy reasons for the two provisions. Do you think the Senator's friend is right?

## Questions and Comments:

If an opinion is considered a covered opinion, practitioners need to comply with further regulatory requirements or face the possibility of penalties and sanctions. Thus, determining whether something is in fact a covered opinion becomes very important. In some instances, practitioners may be overly cautious about what constitutes a covered opinion and thus disclaimers have appeared in almost all law firm correspondence.

One complaint is that tax attorneys often provide advice about the tax treatment of transactions and that taxpayers should be able to rely on such advice. They argue that the language in § 10.35 dealing with significant purpose transactions is very broad and that many commonplace transactions may come under the gamut of § 10.35. At the moment, there are no indications that the Service is using § 10.35 to address standard tax deferral transactions like investing in a tax deferred college plan, an IRA, or engaging in a like-kind exchange.

The Treasury, has not further defined the term "significant purpose." It may be that the Treasury has seen the creativity and aggressiveness of some tax planners and does not want to create a definition that can be obfuscated. It may desire some flexibility in applying the regulation when it is clear that the purpose of a transaction is abusive. As the Service enforces § 10.35, lawyers will get a better sense of what transactions the Service believes are significant purpose transactions.

**Problem 5.3**

John has been a client of yours for a long time. He e-mails you a note telling you that he is thinking of selling some stock that he purchased 10 months ago so he can buy a vacation home. John's e-mail indicates that he remembers something about long and short-term capital gain. He wants to sell now but will wait 2 months if that will reduce his taxes. You e-mail John back and tell him that if waits 2 months the transaction will be treated as long-term capital gain and taxed at a significantly lower rate. Your e-mail is one sentence. It does not contain any disclaimers. Is your e-mail a covered opinion?

**Problem 5.4**

Assume in the previous problem there is the standard disclaimer at the bottom of the e-mail. How does the disclosure impact your analysis?

**Problem 5.5**

Your client, ABC, wants to merge with XYZ. Both parties want to structure the merger in a manner that allows for a tax free reorganization. You have structured the merger in a way as to achieve that end and have notified your client that the merger will meet the Code's requirements for a tax free reorganization. XYZ is less sure that the plan will work, and is giving your client a hard time. Your client asks you to send her an e-mail that she can show to XYZ indicating why you believe that the merger would qualify as a tax free reorganization. Assume you send an e-mail about two paragraphs long explaining the law and why the transaction would qualify as a reorganization. The e-mail does not include any other information besides the two paragraphs mentioned above. Does sending the e-mail violate Circular 230?

**Problem 5.6**

There is a major energy crisis and Congress passes significant tax credits for the purchase of alternative energy products. You realize that in Congress's haste, it did not write the tax credit provisions very well. You create a complicated transaction involving solar and wind energy equipment that allows taxpayers to purchase the equipment, claim the credit, and completely eliminate all tax liability. You set up the transaction and begin marketing it to wealthy companies. The promotion materials include an opinion from you setting out the details of the plan. The materials also contain a legend that says any tax advice contained in these materials are not to be used by the taxpayer for the purpose of avoiding penalties, and that the advice was written to support the promotion and marketing of this transaction. At the bottom of the material, in normal type, is a legend that says the taxpayer should seek independent legal advice based on the taxpayer's particular circumstances. There are no confidentiality or contractual protection provisions. Is this a marketed opinion?

## (d)　Covered Opinion Requirements

If advice regarding a transaction is a covered opinion, then a practitioner must comply with the requirements in § 10.35(c). These provisions are mainly designed to ensure that the legal opinions are well thought out and that taxpayers are well informed regarding the transaction.

One characteristic of early tax shelter opinions was the assumption by lawyers of certain important facts. The opinions would set out certain factual assumptions and then proceed with the legal analysis. The factual assumptions were almost always not descriptive of the facts in a specific taxpayer's case. Section 10.35 addresses this problem by requiring a practitioner who issues a covered opinion to use all reasonable efforts to identify and ascertain the actual facts. The attorney cannot assume that the transaction has a business purpose or that there is potential profit apart from the tax benefits. Although a practitioner may rely on valuations, appraisals, and financial forecasts, the practitioner cannot rely on information that he knows or should know is inaccurate.

A covered opinion must also relate the law to the facts and evaluate all significant federal tax issues. The practitioner must then provide conclusions regarding "the likelihood that the taxpayer will prevail on the merits with respect to each significant Federal tax issue considered in the opinion." § 10.35(c)(3) The practitioner must provide the basis for her conclusion. If the practitioner cannot reach a confidence level of at least more likely than not with regard to any significant Federal tax issue, the opinion must clearly disclose that fact. In evaluating the likelihood a taxpayer will prevail, the practitioner may not consider the chance of an audit, that the issue will not be raised, or that the taxpayer may obtain some benefit through settlement. See § 10.35(c)(3)

If the practitioner does not have a confidence level of MLTN with regard to each tax issue, the practitioner must make a prominent disclosure that it does not meet the MLTN standard and that the taxpayer cannot use the opinion to avoid penalties that may be imposed.

If the practitioner is providing advice that is classified as a marketed opinion, the opinion must provide that the practitioner believes with a confidence level of more-likely-than-not (MLTN) that the taxpayer will prevail on the merits with regard to each significant Federal tax issue. See § 10.35(c)(3)(iv). If the practitioner does not have a confidence level of MLTN, the practitioner is not permitted to issue the opinion. (He may issue an opinion that complies with the disclosure provisions in (b)(5)(ii) discussed earlier). Finally, a covered opinion must disclose any compensation agreements and referral agreements that deal with marketing or promoting of the transaction or plan.

If a lawyer cannot meet the requirements for covered opinions or a client wants advice concerning only one aspect of a transaction, an attorney may provide a "Limited Scope Opinion." These opinions are limited to one or more specific Federal tax issues addressed in the opinion. The opinion must disclose that it is a limited opinion and that it only addresses the specific tax issues in the opinion and that the opinion does not express advice concerning other issues. Furthermore, it must state that the opinion cannot be used by the taxpayer to avoid penalties for any issue not addressed in the opinion. § 10.35(c)(3)(v)

### Scenario 5.1

Max creates the following transaction and wants to promote it to individuals to reduce their taxes. Max asks his lawyer, Wendy, to write an opinion letter regarding this transaction. Wendy writes the following letter:

To Whom it May Concern:

I have been asked to evaluate the tax consequences of entering into the xxx transaction. My conclusion is that the transaction indicated below will produce the desired tax benefits and will not be considered an abusive transaction by the Service.

Facts:

The facts set out herein have been provided by ABC and are assumed true for purposes of this letter. There has been no attempt to independently verify the facts as provided by ABC. This opinion is only valid if the facts occur as assumed in this opinion.

The transaction involves the leasing of equipment to manufacture ethanol for use as fuel. Participants invest $10,000 in ABC, and the funds were to be designated as "rental." ABC then would borrow $90,000 on investors' behalf to purchase equipment with a fair market value of $100,000. The note would be paid for with the profit from the transaction. ABC would order equipment from XYZ and would pay $100,000 for the equipment. ABC would then sublease the equipment on the investors' behalf to PPP. PPP would manufacture the ethanol and pay a percentage of its profits back to ABC. ABC would then use those profits to pay expenses. The remaining profits will be used to satisfy the $90,000 note taken out on behalf of the participant. Once the notes are repaid, future profits will be paid to the participants.

All transaction will be at arm's length. The equipment will be acquired with an eye towards making a profit. Finally, the opinion assumes that PPP is a viable ethanol manufacturer.

Conclusions:

Investors can deduct on a pro-rata basis $100,000 as an ordinary and necessary business expense. Investors can claim an investment tax credit of $100,000. The transaction is not an abusive transaction, and the Service would have no reason to challenge the transaction. If it did, the transaction would more likely than not be upheld.

Sincerely,
Wendy

It turns out that Max planned on creating and owning ABC, XYZ, and PPP and that the equipment was worth only about $5,000.[27]

Wendy is under investigation by the Office of Professional Responsibility for violating § 10.35. Assume that Wendy did not know that Max owned ABC, XYZ and PPP and that the transactions were not at arm's length. Also assume that Wendy had no idea regarding the cost of the equipment, but that she is a sophisticated tax practitioner. Is Wendy in trouble? Does this comply with § 10.35? Discuss any possible problems and how those problems could be rectified.

## 2.     COMPLIANCE

The tax shelter provisions in § 10.35 have received a lot of focus from the tax bar, and there have been a lot of complaints that the provision goes too far. Since these changes became effective in 2005, it is still too early to tell how much of an impact § 10.35 will have on tax practice, and how it will be enforced. For example, it is still unclear how broadly the Service will interpret the term

---

[27] For a time, leasing tax shelters such as this one were a craze. The actual transactions were far more complicated. This transaction is based on one litigated in Ackerman v. Schwartz, 733 F.Supp. 1231 (N.D. Ind. 1989).

"substantial purpose." The changes in § 10.35 have, however, put the bar on notice that from the Service's perspective, aggressive (and maybe not so aggressive) tax shelter opinions will be examined very carefully.

One of the many reasons that § 10.35 has had a significant impact on the bar is that the compliance provisions in § 10.36 require firms to create systems to ensure that attorneys in the firm comply with § 10.35. In fact, the regulations specifically place compliance with the attorney in the firm with "principal authority and responsibility for overseeing a firm's practice of providing advice concerning Federal tax issues." § 10.36(a) If the attorney with principal authority fails to do so, that attorney may also be subject to sanction if an attorney in the firm violates § 10.35.

The second reason § 10.35 appears effective is that the Office of Professional Responsibility can sanction and fine attorneys and firms that violate Circular 230. See § 10.50.

## B. Statutory Provisions

Congress has also created strict rules regarding the registration and disclosure of tax shelters. Sections 6111 and 6112 and the accompanying regulations require tax shelter organizers or sellers to register tax shelters with the Department of Treasury. Section 6112 requires a material advisor of tax shelters to keep a record of the people he advised regarding the shelter. The list must be provided to the Service upon request.

## AMERICAN JOBS CREATION ACT OF 2004
Conference Report
108 H. Rpt. 755

House Bill

Disclosure of reportable transactions by material advisors

[t]he House bill requires each material advisor with respect to any reportable transaction (including any listed transaction) to timely file an information return with the Secretary. * * *.

The information return will include (1) information identifying and describing the transaction, (2) information describing any potential tax benefits expected to result from the transaction, and (3) such other information as the Secretary may prescribe. It is expected that the Secretary may seek from the material advisor the same type of information that the Secretary may request from a taxpayer in connection with a reportable transaction.

A "material advisor" means any person (1) who provides material aid, assistance, or advice with respect to organizing, managing, promoting, selling, implementing, or carrying out any reportable transaction, and (2) who directly or indirectly derives gross income for such assistance or advice in excess of $250,000 ($50,000 in the case of a reportable transaction substantially all of the tax benefits from which are provided to natural persons) or such other amount as may be prescribed by the Secretary.

Penalty for failing to furnish information regarding reportable transactions

* * * [T]he House bill imposes a penalty on any material advisor who fails to file an information return, or who files a false or incomplete information return, with respect to a reportable transaction (including a listed transaction). The amount of the penalty is $50,000. If the penalty is with respect to a listed transaction, the amount of the penalty is increased to the greater of (1) $200,000, or (2) 50 percent of the gross income of such person with respect to aid, assistance, or advice which is provided with respect to the transaction before the date the information return that includes the transaction is filed. Intentional disregard by a material advisor of the requirement to disclose a listed transaction increases the penalty to 75 percent of the gross income.

The penalty cannot be waived with respect to a listed transaction. As to reportable transactions, the penalty can be rescinded (or abated) only in exceptional circumstances. All or part of the penalty may be rescinded only if rescinding the penalty would promote compliance with the tax laws and effective tax administration. The decision to rescind a penalty must be accompanied by a record describing the facts and reasons for the action and the amount rescinded. There will be no right to judicially appeal a refusal to rescind a penalty. The IRS also is required to submit an annual report to Congress summarizing the application of the disclosure penalties and providing a description of each penalty rescinded under this provision and the reasons for the rescission.

Senate Amendment

The Senate amendment is the same as the House bill, except the Senate amendment also includes in the definition of a "material advisor" any person who provides material aid, assistance, or advice with respect to insuring any reportable transaction (and who derives gross income for such assistance or advice in excess of the amounts specified in the House bill).

Conference Agreement

The conference agreement follows the Senate amendment.

## Questions and Comments:

1. These provisions are designed to provide transparency when it comes to tax shelter plans. Do you think these rules will significantly slow down a lawyers willingness to promote tax shelters? What about advise on the tax consequences of a tax shelter?

2. Section 6662A also provides significant penalties for taxpayers who have an understatement for reportable and listed transactions. Why are individual penalties not enough to deter conduct? Why might Congress have believed regulation of practitioners was necessary?

3. Treasury Regulation 1.6011-4 defines a listed transaction as a transaction "that is the same as or substantially similar to one of the types of transaction" that the IRS has identified, with written guidance, as a tax avoidance transaction. This is reasonably easy to apply and the substantially similar language is not ambiguous in practice. Tax shelters often build on the same core assumptions and techniques and small changes are made to them to achieve slightly different results.

4. Treasury Regulation 1.6011-4 also defines a "reportable transaction." A reportable transaction is one of the following: 1) confidential transaction whereby practitioner places a limitation on disclosure by the taxpayer, 2) transactions with contractual protection, 3) loss transaction generating sizeable losses (around $10 million for corporations and $2 million for partnerships), 4)

transactions of interest (a transaction the IRS has identified as a transaction of interest).

5.  One of the difficulties in regulating tax shelters is that they are hard to define.  Does the Treasury's attempt here in 1.6011-4 do the trick?  If not, what would you do to improve the definition?  Is the definition too broad?  If so, what are the consequences of the broad definition?

## Problem 5.7

You work for a U.S. Senator who is a former tax lawyer.  The Senator is concerned about the growth in tax shelters and wants your advice on what should be done to limit abuse.  Write a short memo indicating what you think is working now and what improvements should be made.  Try to draft a similar memo assuming the Senator believes Congress has gone too far and that the current rules are having a chilling effect on a tax lawyers willingness to provide tax advice.

# C.  ABA Model Rules

Treasury regulations and the Code regulate an attorney's duties when providing advice about tax avoidance transactions and thus there are specific rules that guide tax practitioners in this context. There is still an overarching question. How does aggressive tax planning fit within lawyers' ethical obligations? Obviously, it is unethical for lawyers to violate the current rules and regulations, but statutory tax rules are not the only rules that guide lawyers in this area.

During the height of an earlier tax shelter era, the ABA sought to provide some guidance regarding a lawyer's duty in issuing a tax shelter opinion.

# ABA FORMAL OPINION 346*
Tax Law Opinions in Tax Shelter Investment Offerings
January 23, 1982 (supersedes 1981 opinion)

* * * Because the successful marketing of tax shelters frequently involves tax opinions issued by lawyers, concerns have been expressed by the organized bar, regulatory agencies and others over the need to articulate ethical standards applicable to a lawyer who issues an opinion which the lawyer knows will be included among the tax shelter offering materials and relied upon by offerees.

* * *

A "tax shelter opinion," as the term is used in this Opinion, is advice by a lawyer concerning the federal tax law applicable to a tax shelter if the advice is referred to either in offering materials or in connection with sales promotion efforts directed to persons other than the client who engages the lawyer to give the advice. The term includes the tax aspects or tax risks portion of the offering materials prepared by the lawyer whether or not a separate opinion letter is issued. * * *

## Disciplinary Standards

A false opinion is one which ignores or minimizes serious legal risks or misstates the facts or the law, knowingly or through gross incompetence. The lawyer who gives a false opinion, including one which is intentionally or recklessly misleading, violates the Disciplinary Rules of the Model Code of Professional Responsibility. Quite clearly, the lawyer exceeds the duty to represent the client zealously within the bounds of the law. Knowingly misstating facts or law * * * is "conduct involving dishonesty, fraud, deceit, or misrepresentation" * * *. The lawyer also violates [ethical rules] by counseling or assisting the offeror "in conduct that the lawyer knows to be illegal or fraudulent." In addition, the lawyer's conduct may

---

involve the concealment or knowing nondisclosure of matters which the lawyer is required by law to reveal.

\* \* \*

The lawyer who accepts as true the facts which the promoter tells him, when the lawyer should know that a further inquiry would disclose that these facts are untrue, also gives a false opinion. It has been said that lawyers cannot "escape criminal liability on a plea of ignorance when they have shut their eyes to what was plainly to be seen." United States v. Benjamin, 328 F.2d 854, 863 (2d Cir. 1964). Recklessly and consciously disregarding information strongly indicating that material facts expressed in the tax shelter opinion are false or misleading involves dishonesty as does assisting the offeror in conduct the lawyer knows to be fraudulent. \* \* \* [The opinion goes on to recognize that the lawyer's conduct may also "involve gross incompetence, or indifference, inadequate preparation under the circumstances and consistent failure to perform obligations to the client."]
*Ethical Considerations*

\* \* \*

LAWYER AS ADVISOR

\* \* \*

The lawyer rendering a tax shelter opinion which he knows will be relied upon by third persons, however, functions more as an advisor than as an advocate. Since the Model Code was adopted in 1969, the differing functions of the advisor and advocate have become more widely recognized.

The Proposed Model Rules specifically recognize the ethical considerations applicable where a lawyer undertakes an evaluation for the use of third persons other than a client. These third persons have an interest in the integrity of the evaluation. The legal duty of the lawyer therefore "goes beyond the obligations a lawyer normally has to third persons." Because third persons may rely on the advice of the lawyer who gives a tax shelter opinion, the principles announced in ABA Formal Opinion 314 have little, if any, applicability.

## ESTABLISHING LAWYER'S RELATIONSHIP

The lawyer should establish the terms of the relationship with the offeror-client at the time the lawyer is engaged to work on the tax shelter offering. This includes making it clear that the lawyer requires from the client a full disclosure of the structure and intended operations of the venture and complete access to all relevant information.

## MAKING FACTUAL INQUIRY

ABA Formal Opinion 335 (1974) establishes guidelines which a lawyer should follow when furnishing an assumed facts opinion in connection with the sale of unregistered securities. The same guidelines describe the extent to which a lawyer should verify the facts presented to him as the basis for a tax shelter opinion:

[T]he lawyer should, in the first instance, make inquiry of his client as to the relevant facts and receive answers. If any of the alleged facts, or the alleged facts taken as a whole, are incomplete in a material respect; or are suspect; or are inconsistent; or either on their face or on the basis of other known facts are open to question, the lawyer should make further inquiry. The extent of this inquiry will depend in each case upon the circumstances; for example, it would be less where the lawyer's past relationship with the client is sufficient to give him a basis for trusting the client's probity than where the client has recently engaged the lawyer, and less where the lawyer's inquiries are answered fully than when there appears a reluctance to disclose information.

Where the lawyer concludes that further inquiry of a reasonable nature would not give him sufficient confidence as to all the relevant facts, or for any other reason he does not make the appropriate further inquiries, he should refuse to give an opinion.

\* \* \*

## RELATING LAW TO FACTS

In discussing the legal issues in a tax shelter opinion, the lawyer should relate the law to the actual facts to the extent the facts are ascertainable when the offering materials are being circulated. A lawyer should not issue a tax shelter opinion which disclaims responsibility for inquiring as to the accuracy of the facts, fails to analyze the critical facts or discusses purely hypothetical facts. It is proper, however, to assume facts which are not currently ascertainable, such as the method of conducting future operations of the venture, so long as the factual assumptions are clearly identified as such in the offering materials, and are reasonable and complete.

* * *

## OPINION AS TO OUTCOME -- MATERIAL TAX ISSUES

* * * The clear disclosure of the tax risks in the offering materials should include an opinion by the lawyer or by another professional providing an overall evaluation of the extent to which the tax benefits, in the aggregate, which are a significant feature of the investment to the typical investor are likely to be realized as contemplated by the offering materials. In making this evaluation, the lawyer should state that the significant tax benefits, in the aggregate, probably will be realized or probably will not be realized, or that the probabilities of realization and nonrealization of the significant tax benefits are evenly divided.

* * *

## ACCURACY OF OFFERING MATERIALS

In all cases, the lawyer who issues a tax shelter opinion, especially an opinion which does not contain a prediction of a favorable outcome, should assure that the offerees will not be misled as a result of mischaracterizations of the extent of the opinion in the offering materials or in connection with sales promotion efforts. In addition, the lawyer always should review the offering materials to assure that the standards set forth in this Opinion are met and that the offering materials, taken as a whole, make it clear that the lawyer's opinion is not a prediction of a favorable outcome of the tax issues concerning which no favorable prediction is made. The risks and uncertainties of the tax issues should be referred to in a summary statement at the very outset of the opinion or the tax aspects or tax risks section of the offering materials.

* * *

*Summary of Ethical Considerations*

\* \* \*

1.   Establish in the beginning the lawyer's relationship with the offeror-client, making clear that in order to issue the opinion, the lawyer requires from that client a full disclosure of the structure and intended operations of the venture and complete access to all relevant information.

2.   Make inquiry as to the relevant facts and, consistent with the standards developed in ABA Formal Opinion 335, be satisfied that the material facts are accurately and completely stated in the offering materials, and that the representations as to intended future activities are clearly identified, reasonable and complete.

3.   Relate the law to the actual facts to the extent ascertainable and, when addressing issues based on future activities, clearly identify what facts are assumed.

4.   Make inquiries to ascertain that a good faith effort has been made to address legal issues other than those to be addressed in the tax shelter opinion.

5. Take reasonable steps to assure that all material federal income and excise tax issues have been considered and that all of those issues which involve the reasonable possibility of a challenge by the Internal Revenue Service have been fully and fairly addressed in the offering materials.

6.   Where possible, provide an opinion as to the likely outcome on the merits of the material tax issues addressed in the offering materials.

7.   Where possible, provide an overall evaluation of the extent to which the tax benefits in the aggregate are likely to be realized.

8.   Assure that the offering materials correctly represent the nature and extent of the tax shelter opinion.

## Questions and Comments:

1.   Re-read the guidelines set out in Formal Opinion 346. Should Formal Opinion 346 have been enough to limit a lawyer's involvement in more recent abusive tax shelters? If so, why was further regulation needed?

2.  Re-examine the edited description of the transaction approved by Jenkins and Gilchrest.  Do you think the opinion letter in that case met the above requirements?

3.  Could you draft an opinion letter that would meet the above requirements?  Would such a letter trouble you from a tax policy standpoint?  Why or why not?

**Problem 5.8**

You are an attorney representing a party to a transaction.  You know that the other party is engaging in the transaction as part of a tax shelter that you believe is improper.  Your client, however, is interested in engaging in the transaction for business reasons.  The other party asks you to structure the transaction in a specific way as to facilitate the shelter transaction. Do you have any duty to refrain from entering the transaction or from agreeing to the structure?  See Darryll K. Jones, The Venerable Firms Behind Santa Monica Pictures, 2005 TNT 196-27 (Oct. 10, 2005).

# Chapter 6

## Business Activities

———

Many lawyers today lament that legal practice has turned from a profession into a business. It will be up to you how you practice law, and how you address difficult questions facing the profession. What is clear, however, is that law is still principally regulated as a profession, not a business. There are significant restrictions on how a lawyer may conduct his affairs that are based on professional norms and judgments. For example, lawyers may not charge unreasonable fees, may not engage in some types of advertising activities, and must follow professional rules regarding solicitation of clients. In the tax area, there are additional rules that limit the use of contingency fees in some tax cases.

The rules surrounding the business aspects of the practice of law are taken very seriously by the bar and the Service and violations of these rules often lead to significant sanctions. See Lisa Lerman, Blue-Chip Bilking: Regulation of Billing and Expense Fraud by Lawyers, 12 Geo. J. Legal Ethics 205 (1999).

## A. Attorney Fees

The legal profession has dedicated a substantial amount of time and energy in developing elaborate sets of ethical guidelines for the benefits of its clients. Similarly, the profession has spent extraordinary resources on interpreting, teaching and enforcing these ethics rules. Yet, ironically, lawyers are not generally regarded by the public as particularly ethical. One major contributing factor to the public opinion of the legal profession appears to be the billing practices of some of its members.[28]

---

[28] ABA Formal Opinion 93-379, December 6, 1993.

## 1.    ABA MODEL RULES

Model Rule 1.5 prohibits a lawyer from charging an unreasonable amount for fees or expenses. With recent announcements that some lawyers are charging over $1,000 an hour, and contingency fee arrangements that are sometimes in the millions, it may be difficult to recognize where the line is regarding excessive fees. There is, however, a line and disciplinary authorities have been willing to sanction lawyers for excessive fee arrangements.

The test for determining whether a fee is unreasonable is a multi-factor, facts and circumstances test. Multi-factor tests should be familiar to tax students and lawyers who grapple with the many such tests in the Code (remember the hobby loss and excessive compensation tests). The factors for determining whether a fee is reasonable are the following: (1) Time and effort required (taking into account the difficulty of the issue and the skill required); (2) The likelihood that engagement by the lawyer will preclude other employment; (3) The fee is similar to those customarily charged for similar work; (4) The amount at stake and the results obtained; (5) Time limitations imposed by client or situation (presumably high pressure quick service deserves a higher fee); (6) The nature and length of relationship; (7) The experience, knowledge, reputation and ability of the lawyer; and (8) Whether the fee is fixed or contingent. These factors are not exclusive and are a guide for determining whether the fee is reasonable. We would also suggest that the sophistication of the client plays a part in determining whether the fee is excessive.

Under the ABA Model Rules, the fee must be communicated to the client, preferably in writing. In most cases, an attorney may charge a contingency fee, but contingency fee arrangements *must* be in writing. Contingency fees, however, are not allowed under Circular 230 in certain tax situations, and are prohibited by the Model Rules in domestic relations and criminal cases.

The ABA model rules specifically contemplate contingency fees. In a formal opinion the ABA explains:

> It is ethical to charge contingent fees as long as the fee is appropriate and reasonable and the client has been fully informed of the availability of alternative billing arrangements. The fact that a client can afford

to compensate the lawyer on another basis does not render a contingent fee arrangement for such a client unethical. Nor is it unethical to charge a contingent fee when liability is clear and some recovery is anticipated. If the lawyer and client so contract, a lawyer is entitled to a full contingent fee on the total recovery by the client, including that portion of the recovery that was the subject of an early settlement offer that was rejected by the client. Finally, if the lawyer and client agree, it is ethical for the lawyer to charge a different contingent fee at different stages of a matter, and to increase the percentage taken as a fee as the amount of the recovery or savings to the client increases. Formal Opinion 94-389.

Just because a contingency fee is allowed, however, does not mean that it is reasonable. Courts have been willing to set aside or reduce contingency fees when they are excessive under the circumstances (For example *see In re September 11th Litigation*, No. 21 MC 101, Judge Hellerstein rejected the contingency fee of 25% for lawyer representing families of four September 11th victims finding the fee too high and unreasonable)..

Look at Rule 1.5. Are the fees in the following situations appropriate under Rule 1.5?

## Problem 6.1

Client engaged in a high volume of business with Lawyer. Client negotiated an agreement that he would receive a 15% discount contingent upon the timely payment of his bills. Client continued to pay bills late, and Lawyer did not want a confrontation with Client regarding the 15% discount. Lawyer entered into "self help" and inflated all bills to Client. He then discounted the inflated bill by 15% producing a net bill at slightly below 100%. What, if any, sanction should result?

## Problem 6.2

Attorney agreed to represent client in a district court case involving a tax lien of $10,000. The attorney was an experienced civil litigator but had never handled a tax case. The attorney and client agreed to a billing rate of $200 (assume this is the market rate for a tax attorney in the area). The attorney proceeded to work on the case and spent time and effort researching tax procedure and tax liens.   The attorney also proposed several novel theories that he presented to the court. (Assume these were not frivolous theories). The attorney was successful and the lien was removed.  The attorney then presented the Client with a bill for $30,000, which accurately represented the time spent on the case.  An independent tax attorney testified that this was an easy lien case and would have required 5-10 hours from a tax attorney familiar with tax liens.  According to the expert, had the attorney known what he was doing, the case never would have gone to court.   What, if any, sanctions should result.

## Problem 6.3

ABC filed a frivolous appeal in a case against XYZ.  XYZ had filed a four page jurisdictional memo with the Court of Appeals that cited five cases.  It also filed a motion for sanctions.  The court granted the motion for sanctions, and the attorneys for XYZ submitted a bill to the court for approval. XYZ filed the following motion for fees:  With regard to the jurisdiction memo, XYZ sought 3.5 partner hours at $500 an hour and 10.5 associate hours at $300 an hour.  With regard to the sanctions motion, the firm charged one partner hour and 12 associate hours.  The firm also charged $165 as a filing fee.  (It turns out that no filing fee exists, but that the fee was for one attorney to become admitted to the court.)  The total fees sought were: $9,165.  Is this excessive?  What, if any, sanctions should result.

## Problem 6.4

John graduates from law school and gets his LL.M. in Tax. He then becomes a sole practitioner representing clients in Tax Court. John is good at his job and represents his clients well.  John, however, cannot afford to hire clerical support.  John does not mind doing the clerical work.  He faxes and delivers documents, contacts the clerk's office and does his own filing.  John charges clients for these activities at his hourly rate, but does so only when the activities are directly related to their cases.  Does this violate Rule 1.5?  If so, what sanction should result?

## 2.    CIRCULAR 230

Circular 230 also contains provisions regulating fees. Section 10.27 provides that "a practitioner may not charge an unreasonable fee." This provision coincides with the ethical duty that already exists under state ethics rules. Section 10.27(b), however, places a significant restriction on the use of contingent fees in tax cases. The basic underlying justification is that in a system that relies on voluntary compliance, the fee structure should not encourage attorneys or others to be overly aggressive. If an attorney receives a percentage of the money "saved" in taxes, the attorney would have an incentive to promote aggressive positions with the hope that the return would not be audited. These policy concerns can be seen throughout § 10.27's restrictions.

In its announcement regarding the final amended rules for § 10.27 the Treasury noted:

> The Treasury Department and the IRS continue to believe that a rule restricting contingent fees for preparing tax returns supports voluntary compliance with the Federal tax laws by discouraging return positions that exploit the audit selection process. In particular, the Treasury Department and IRS are concerned with the use of contingent fee arrangements in connection with claims for refund or amended returns filed late in the examination process. (See 2007-2 C.B. 931).

Section 10.27 allows an attorney to charge a contingency fee when the attorney is representing a taxpayer with regard to an already existing examination or challenge. Attorneys' fees are therefore proper when the Service is challenging an original tax return or a claim for refund. It is also proper when the representation is in connection with a judicial proceeding. A practitioner may also charge a contingency fee when the matter involves a "claim for credit or refund filed solely in connection with the determination of statutory interest or penalties."

Circular 230 also provides a broad definition of a contingency fee. A contingency fee is "any fee that is based . . . on whether or not a position taken on a tax return or other filing avoids challenge by the Internal Revenue Service or is sustained either by the Internal Revenue Service or in litigation." The term contingency fee also includes fees that are determined by the percentage of the refund, the percentage of taxes saved, or based on a specific result. Moreover, the fee arrangement is also considered a contingency fee if the practitioner agrees to reimburse the taxpayer for fees if a position taken is challenged by the Service.

## Problem 6.5

A senior associate in your law firm comes to you as partner in charge to approve a fee arrangement for a new client that the associate has just brought in. The agreement states that the firm will receive a non-refundable retainer of $1,000. The fee will be for whatever investigation needs to be done to determine if there is a proper claim for refund due to a prior year characterization of certain foreign tax payments as deductible. The associate believes the foreign tax payments are really entitled to be treated as tax credits based upon certain IRS rulings that the paid preparer was either not aware of or did not understand. If the firm determines that a claim for refund is warranted, the firm will receive 25% of any amount recovered based on the filing of the refund claim (or further litigation if that is necessary). Is this a proper contingency fee arrangement?

## Problem 6.6

Company ABC provides refund anticipation loans to taxpayers after they have filed their returns. In short, ABC provides a loan to a taxpayer based on the amount of refund that the taxpayer shows on his return. ABC charges a percentage fee based on the amount of the loan and thus based on the amount shown on the return. Does this violate Circular 230?

## Problem 6.7

You think you have found a great tax strategy that will save certain businesses millions in income taxes. Assume the strategy is not a tax shelter and does not run afoul of the restrictions in § 10.35 of Circular 230. You are, however, having a hard time convincing businesses that your plan will work. You suggest the following fee arrangement: You will bill clients $10,000 for preparing tax returns that will use your new strategy and will show a significant reduction in the businesses taxable income. If the return is rejected or the client is later audited, you will refund all but $1,000 of the fee to the client. Is this a valid fee arrangement under Circular 230?

**Problem 6.8**

Assume instead in the problem above that you decide to charge clients $100,000 for all services regarding their case. The $100,000 covers filing the refund claim and all future services that may arise, including litigating the case. Is this a valid fee arrangement under Circular 230?

**Problem 6.9**

You have been asked to appear on a local television program as one of three tax advisors. When people call in with a tax question, the tax advisor who presses the buzzer first will answer the caller's question. Instead of paying you to appear on the program, the TV station proposes that whenever you appear on screen an overprint will also appear on the screen with your name and phone number and the statement, "Fast and reliable - available for consultation at a reasonable fee - call for an appointment." What do you do? Why? What disciplinary rules apply? Explain all of the ethical considerations this scenario presents.

# B.    Communication with Perspective Clients

## 1. ADVERTISING

## BATES
## V.
## STATE BAR OF ARIZONA
### 433 U.S. 350 (1977)

Mr. Justice BLACKMUN delivered the opinion of the Court.

As part of its regulation of the Arizona Bar, the Supreme Court of that State has imposed and enforces a disciplinary rule that restricts advertising by attorneys. This case presents two issues: whether §§ 1 and 2 of the Sherman Act, 15 U.S.C. §§ 1 and 2, forbid such state regulation, and whether the operation of the rule violates the First Amendment, made applicable to the State through the Fourteenth. [The Sherman Act challenge is omitted from this opinion and was rejected by the Court].

Appellants John R. Bates and Van O'Steen are attorneys licensed to practice law in the State of Arizona. * * * In March 1974, appellants * * * opened a law office, which they call a 'legal clinic,' in Phoenix. Their aim was to provide legal services at modest fees to persons of moderate income who did not qualify for governmental legal aid. * * *

* * * [A]ppellants concluded that their practice and clinical concept could not survive unless the availability of legal services at low cost was advertised and in particular, fees were advertised. Consequently, in order to generate the necessary flow of business, that is, 'to attract clients,' appellants on February 22, 1976, placed an advertisement in the Arizona Republic, a daily newspaper of general circulation in the Phoenix metropolitan area. * * *

Appellants concede that the advertisement constituted a clear violation of Disciplinary Rule 2-101(B), incorporated in Rule 29(a) of the Supreme Court of Arizona, 17A Ariz.Rev.Stat., p. 26 (Supp. 1976). The disciplinary rule provides in part:

> (B) A lawyer shall not publicize himself, or his partner, or associate, or any other lawyer affiliated with him or his firm, as a lawyer through newspaper or magazine advertisements, radio or television announcements, display advertisements in the city or telephone directories or other means of commercial publicity, nor shall he authorize or permit others to do so in his behalf.

[The lawyers were not allowed to contest the constitutionality of the rule in the disciplinary proceeding, but they were allowed to establish a record on which a challenge could be brought. The Board of Governors of the State Bar recommended a one-week suspension.]

III

The First Amendment

A

Last Term, in Virginia Pharmacy Board v. Virginia Consumer Council, the Court considered the validity under the First Amendment of a Virginia statute declaring that a pharmacist was guilty of 'unprofessional conduct' if he advertised prescription drug prices. The pharmacist would then be subject to a monetary penalty or the suspension or revocation of his license. The statute thus effectively prevented the advertising of prescription drug price information. We recognized that the pharmacist who desired to advertise did not wish to report any particularly newsworthy fact or to comment on any cultural, philosophical, or political subject; his desired communication was characterized simply: "I will sell you the X prescription drug at the Y price." Nonetheless, we held that commercial speech of that kind was entitled to the protection of the First Amendment.

\* \* \*

## B

The issue presently before us is a narrow one. First, we need not address the peculiar problems associated with advertising claims relating to the quality of legal services. Such claims probably are not susceptible of precise measurement or verification and, under some circumstances, might well be deceptive or misleading to the public, or even false. Appellee does not suggest, nor do we perceive, that appellants' advertisement contained claims, extravagant or otherwise, as to the quality of services. Accordingly, we leave that issue for another day. Second, we also need not resolve the problems associated with in-person solicitation of clients at the hospital room or the accident site, or in any other situation that breeds undue influence by attorneys or their agents or 'runners.' Activity of that kind might well pose dangers of overreaching and misrepresentation not encountered in newspaper announcement advertising. Hence, this issue also is not before us. Third, we note that appellee's criticism of advertising by attorneys does not apply with much force to some of the basic factual content of advertising: information as to the attorney's name, address, and telephone number, office hours, and the like. The American Bar Association itself has a provision in its current Code of Professional Responsibility that would allow the disclosure of such information, and more, in the classified section of the telephone directory. We recognize, however, that an advertising diet limited to such spartan fare would provide scant nourishment.

The heart of the dispute before us today is whether lawyers also may constitutionally advertise the prices at which certain routine services will be performed. Numerous justifications are proffered for the restriction of such price advertising. We consider each in turn:

1. The Adverse Effect on Professionalism. Appellee places particular emphasis on the adverse effects that it feels price

advertising will have on the legal profession. The key to professionalism, it is argued, is the sense of pride that involvement in the discipline generates. It is claimed that price advertising will bring about commercialization, which will undermine the attorney's sense of dignity and self-worth.* * * Advertising is also said to erode the client's trust in his attorney: Once the client perceives that the lawyer is motivated by profit, his confidence that the attorney is acting out of a commitment to the client's welfare is jeopardized. And advertising is said to tarnish the dignified public image of the profession.

We recognize, of course, and commend the spirit of public service with which the profession of law is practiced and to which it is dedicated. The present Members of this Court, licensed attorneys all, could not feel otherwise. And we would have reason to pause if we felt that our decision today would undercut that spirit. But we find the postulated connection between advertising and the erosion of true professionalism to be severely strained. At its core, the argument presumes that attorneys must conceal from themselves and from their clients the real-life fact that lawyers earn their livelihood at the bar. We suspect that few attorneys engage in such self-deception. And rare is the client, moreover, even one of the modest means, who enlists the aid of an attorney with the expectation that his services will be rendered free of charge. * * *

2.  The Inherently Misleading Nature of Attorney Advertising. It is argued that advertising of legal services inevitably will be misleading (a) because such services are so individualized with regard to content and quality as to prevent informed comparison on the basis of an advertisement, (b) because the consumer of legal services is unable to determine in advance just what services he needs, and (c) because advertising by attorneys will highlight irrelevant factors and fail to show the relevant factor of skill.

We are not persuaded that restrained professional advertising by lawyers inevitably will be misleading. Although many services performed by attorneys are indeed unique, it is doubtful that any attorney would or could advertise fixed prices for services of that type. The only services that lend themselves to advertising are the routine ones: the uncontested divorce, the simple adoption, the uncontested personal bankruptcy, the change of name, and the like the very services advertised by appellants. * * * We thus find of little force the assertion that advertising is misleading because of an inherent lack of standardization in legal services.

\* \* \*

The third component is not without merit: Advertising does not provide a complete foundation on which to select an attorney. But it seems peculiar to deny the consumer, on the ground that the information is incomplete, at least some of the relevant information needed to reach an informed decision.  \* \* \*

3. The Adverse Effect on the Administration of Justice. Advertising is said to have the undesirable effect of stirring up litigation. The judicial machinery is designed to serve those who feel sufficiently aggrieved to bring forward their claims. Advertising, it is argued, serves to encourage the assertion of legal rights in the courts, thereby undesirably unsettling societal repose. There is even a suggestion of barratry.

But advertising by attorneys is not an unmitigated source of harm to the administration of justice. It may offer great benefits. Although advertising might increase the use of the judicial machinery, we cannot accept the notion that it is always better for a person to suffer a wrong silently than to redress it by legal action. As the bar acknowledges, 'the middle 70% of our population is not being reached or served adequately by the legal profession.' Among the reasons for this underutilization is fear of the cost, and an inability to locate a suitable lawyer.  Advertising can help to solve this acknowledged problem: Advertising is the traditional mechanism in a free-market economy for a supplier to inform a potential purchaser of the availability and terms of exchange.  \* \* \*

4. The Undesirable Economic Effects of Advertising. It is claimed that advertising will increase the overhead costs of the profession, and that these costs then will be passed along to consumers in the form of increased fees. Moreover, it is claimed that the additional cost of practice will create a substantial entry barrier, deterring or preventing young attorneys from penetrating the market and entrenching the position of the bar's established members.

These two arguments seem dubious at best. Neither distinguishes lawyers from others, and neither appears relevant to the First Amendment. The ban on advertising serves to increase the difficulty of discovering the lowest cost seller of acceptable ability. As a result, to this extent attorneys are isolated from competition, and the incentive to price competitively is reduced.  \* \* \*

The entry-barrier argument is equally unpersuasive. In the absence of advertising, an attorney must rely on his contacts with the community to generate a flow of business. In view of the time necessary to develop such contacts, the ban in fact serves to perpetuate the market position of established attorneys. Consideration of entry-barrier problems would urge that advertising be allowed so as to aid the new competitor in penetrating the market.

5. The Adverse Effect of Advertising on the Quality of Service. It is argued that the attorney may advertise a given 'package' of service at a set price, and will be inclined to provide, by indiscriminate use, the standard package regardless of whether it fits the client's needs.

Restraints on advertising, however, are an ineffective way of deterring shoddy work. An attorney who is inclined to cut quality will do so regardless of the rule on advertising. And the advertisement of a standardized fee does not necessarily mean that the services offered are undesirably standardized. * * *

6. The Difficulties of Enforcement. Finally, it is argued that the wholesale restriction is justified by the problems of enforcement if any other course is taken. Because the public lacks sophistication in legal matters, it may be particularly susceptible to misleading or deceptive advertising by lawyers. After-the-fact action by the consumer lured by such advertising may not provide a realistic restraint because of the inability of the layman to assess whether the service he has received meets professional standards. Thus, the vigilance of a regulatory agency will be required. But because of the numerous purveyors of services, the overseeing of advertising will be burdensome.

It is at least somewhat incongruous for the opponents of advertising to extol the virtues and altruism of the legal profession at one point, and, at another, to assert that its members will seize the opportunity to mislead and distort. We suspect that, with advertising, most lawyers will behave as they always have: They will abide by their solemn oaths to uphold the integrity and honor of their profession and of the legal system. For every attorney who overreaches through advertising, there will be thousands of others who will be candid and honest and straightforward. And, of course, it will be in the latter's interest, as in other cases of misconduct at the bar, to assist in weeding out those few who abuse their trust.

In sum, we are not persuaded that any of the proffered justifications rise to the level of an acceptable reason for the suppression of all advertising by attorneys.

* * *

### IV

In holding that advertising by attorneys may not be subjected to blanket suppression, and that the advertisement at issue is protected, we, of course, do not hold that advertising by attorneys may not be regulated in any way. We mention some of the clearly permissible limitations on advertising not foreclosed by our holding.

Advertising that is false, deceptive, or misleading of course is subject to restraint. Since the advertiser knows his product and has a commercial interest in its dissemination, we have little worry that regulation to assure truthfulness will discourage protected speech. * * * And any concern that strict requirements for truthfulness will undesirably inhibit spontaneity seems inapplicable because commercial speech generally is calculated. Indeed, the public and private benefits from commercial speech derive from confidence in its accuracy and reliability. Thus, the leeway for untruthful or misleading expression that has been allowed in other contexts has little force in the commercial arena. In fact, because the public lacks sophistication concerning legal services, misstatements that might be overlooked or deemed unimportant in other advertising may be found quite inappropriate in legal advertising. For example, advertising claims as to the quality of services a matter we do not address today are not susceptible of measurement or verification; accordingly, such claims may be so likely to be misleading as to warrant restriction. Similar objections might justify restraints on in-person solicitation. We do not foreclose the possibility that some limited supplementation, by way of warning or disclaimer or the like, might be required of even an advertisement of the kind ruled upon today so as to assure that the consumer is not misled. In sum, we recognize that many of the problems in defining the boundary between deceptive and nondeceptive advertising remain to be resolved, and we expect that the bar will have a special role to play in assuring that advertising by attorneys flows both freely and cleanly.

As with other varieties of speech, it follows as well that there may be reasonable restrictions on the time, place, and manner of advertising. * * *.

The constitutional issue in this case is only whether the State may prevent the publication in a newspaper of appellants' truthful advertisement concerning the availability and terms of routine legal services. We rule simply that the flow of such information may not be restrained, and we therefore hold the present application of the disciplinary rule against appellants to be violative of the First Amendment.

The judgment of the Supreme Court of Arizona is therefore affirmed in part and reversed in part.

## Questions and Comments:

1. *Bates* opened up the floodgates for legal services advertisements that are now very common. Justice Blackmun discusses some of the reasons why the Arizona Bar was against advertising by lawyers. Did the evils suggested by the Bar come to pass? Has advertising been a net positive or negative? Do you think advertising harms new lawyers or more experienced ones? Does it matter?

2. *Bates*, however, noted that the Bar still might be able to prevent some advertising by lawyers. It noted that false advertising, and in person "pressure" type advertising might be impermissible. Most bars, and the Model Rules, continue to regulate advertising in these types of settings.

Rule 7.2 allows attorneys to advertise services as long as the advertisements are not false and misleading (see Model Rule 7.1). Moreover, a lawyer is not allowed to solicit a client through in-person, live telephone, or real-time electronic contact. Bars have also taken a very broad view of what is false and misleading. For example, the statement "bankruptcy, but keep house & car" in an advertisement was considered misleading because it failed to explain that "obligations to secured lenders must be reaffirmed in bankruptcy for debtor to keep house and car." In re Anonymous, 775 N.E. 2d 1094 (Ind. 2002) (attorney received private reprimand). Advertising has also been found misleading if it does not fully explain the amount a client will have to pay. An advertisement stating "no recovery, no fee" was found to be misleading because it did not explain that clients might be liable for court costs. Va. Ethics Op. 1750 (2001).

3. True statements that might create expectations about future recovery may also be considered misleading. For example, the statement that "Biker Awarded $250,000 for Accident" was considered misleading even if the statement was true because it created an expectation that lawyer could obtain similar awards for another client. Conn. Ethics Op. 88-3 (1988) (opinion based on sample ad). Similarly, Bars have prohibited lawyers from comparing their services to others or by making statements regarding the quality of their service. For example, statements such as "We Do It Well," or "low-cost alternative" have been found to be misleading. See Medina County Bar Ass'n v. Grieselhuber, 678 N.E.2d 535 (Ohio 1997) (public reprimand for advertisement "We Do It Well" because it was an unverifiable claim); see also D.C. Ethics Op. 172 (1986).

An additional issue that often arises for tax specialists is the extent to which lawyers can advertise or at least make known to clients other degrees or certifications that they might have. For example, can a lawyer advertise that she is also a Certified Public Accountant or a Certified Financial Planner? In most cases, the answer is yes.

## IBANEZ
### v.
## FLORIDA DEPARTMENT OF BUSINESS AND PROFESSIONAL REGULATION, BOARD OF ACCOUNTANCY
512 U.S. 136 (1994)

Justice GINSBURG delivered the opinion of the Court.

Petitioner Silvia Safille Ibanez, a member of the Florida Bar since 1983, practices law in Winter Haven, Florida. She is also a Certified Public Accountant (CPA), licensed by respondent Florida Board of Accountancy (Board) to "practice public accounting." In addition, she is authorized by the Certified Financial Planner Board of Standards, a private organization, to use the trademarked designation "Certified Financial Planner" (CFP).

Ibanez referred to these credentials in her advertising and other communication with the public. She placed CPA and CFP next to her name in her yellow pages listing (under "Attorneys") and on her business card. She also used those designations at the left side of her "Law Offices" stationery. Notwithstanding the apparently truthful nature of her communication – it is undisputed that neither her CPA license nor her CFP certification has been revoked – the Board reprimanded her for engaging in "false, deceptive, and misleading" advertising.

The record reveals that the Board has not shouldered the burden it must carry in matters of this order. It has not demonstrated with sufficient specificity that any member of the public could have been misled by Ibanez' constitutionally protected speech or that any harm could have resulted from allowing that speech to reach the public's eyes. We therefore hold that the Board's decision censuring Ibanez is incompatible with First Amendment restraints on official action.

### I

Under Florida's Public Accountancy Act, only licensed CPA's may "[a]ttest as an expert in accountancy to the reliability or fairness of presentation of financial information," Fla.Stat. § 473.322(1)(c) (1991), or use the title "CPA" or other title "tending to indicate that such person holds an active license" under Florida law. § 473.322(1)(b). * * *

[A disciplinary proceeding was instituted against Ibanez]. The hearing officer subsequently found in Ibanez' favor on all counts, and recommended to the Board that, for want of the requisite proof, all charges against Ibanez be dismissed.

The Board rejected the hearing officer's recommendation, and declared Ibanez guilty of "false, deceptive and misleading" advertising. * * *

### II

### A

The Board correctly acknowledged that Ibanez' use of the CPA and CFP designations was "commercial speech." Because "disclosure of truthful, relevant information is more likely to make a positive contribution to decisionmaking than is concealment of such information," only false, deceptive, or misleading commercial speech may be banned.

Commercial speech that is not false, deceptive, or misleading can be restricted, but only if the State shows that the restriction directly and materially advances a substantial state interest in a manner no more extensive than necessary to serve that interest.

The State's burden is not slight; the "free flow of commercial information is valuable enough to justify imposing on would-be regulators the costs of distinguishing the truthful from the false, the helpful from the misleading, and the harmless from the harmful." Zauder v. Office of Disciplinary Counsel of Supreme Court of Ohio, 471 U.S. 626, 646 (1985). Mere speculation or conjecture" will not suffice; rather the State "must demonstrate that the harms it recites are real and that its restriction will in fact alleviate them to a material degree." Edenfield v. Fane, 507 U.S. 761 (1993). Measured against these standards, the order reprimanding Ibanez cannot stand.

B

We turn first to Ibanez' use of the CPA designation in her commercial communications. On that matter, the Board's position is entirely insubstantial.

The Board's justifications for disciplining Ibanez for using the CFP designation are scarcely more persuasive. The Board concluded that the words used in the designation – particularly, the word "certified" – so closely resemble "the terms protected by state licensure itself, that their use, when not approved by the Board, inherently mislead[s] the public into believing that state approval and recognition exists." This conclusion is difficult to maintain in light of *Peel*. We held in *Peel* that an attorney's use of the designation "Certified Civil Trial Specialist by the National Board of Trial Advocacy" was neither actually nor inherently misleading. The Board offers nothing to support a different conclusion with respect to the CFP designation. Given "the complete absence of any evidence of deception," the Board's "concern about the possibility of deception in hypothetical cases is not sufficient to rebut the constitutional presumption favoring disclosure over concealment." * * *

Ibanez, it bears emphasis, is engaged in the practice of law and so represents her offices to the public. Indeed, she performs work reserved for lawyers but nothing that *only* CPA's may do. It is therefore significant that her use of the designation CFP is considered in all respects appropriate by the Florida Bar. See Brief for Florida Bar as *Amicus Curiae* 9-10 (noting that Florida Bar, Rules of Professional Conduct, and particularly Rule 4-7.3, "specifically allo[w] Ibanez to disclose her CPA and CFP credentials [and] contemplate that Ibanez must provide this information to prospective clients (if relevant)"). * * *

Accordingly, the judgment of the Florida District Court of Appeal is reversed, and the case is remanded for proceedings not inconsistent with this opinion.

*It is so ordered.*

## Questions and Comments:

1. The Model Rules take a fairly restrictive approach to communication regarding specializations. Rule 7.4 provides that a lawyer may communicate whether the law practices or does not practice in a particular area of law. Thus communication that indicates an attorney practices tax law is permissible. The Rules, however also provide that "a lawyer shall not state or imply that a lawyer has been certified as a specialist in a particular field" unless the certifying organization has been approved by state authority or the ABA.

2. Would this rule allow a lawyer to communicate that he has an LL.M. degree? How about whether a lawyer is a CPA or a certified financial planner? Would such a prohibition be consistent with *Ibanez*?

## Problem 6.10

ABC law firm has three lawyers, Al Albert, Bess Betler, and Clyde Crain. Albert and Betler are both members of the bar in state A, which is the state in which ABC is organized. Crain is a tax specialist and is not a member of the bar of State A. Instead he is a member of the bar of State B. Crain is an important part of ABC and handles the firm's tax litigation. He is also a prominent member of the community. ABC's stationary lists the names of the partners in the firm and their phone numbers. Is this a violation of the Model Rules?

**Problem 6.11**

Mike Smith is a partner in a tax boutique law firm and is very well known in the community. He is the former President of the local bar association, has won the state bar's "medal of honor" and was listed as one of the nation's top tax attorneys by Who's Who in Tax Law. He wants to place the following ad in a major U.S. Newspaper. "Sophisticated help for Sophisticated People. Mike Smith is an experienced tax attorney. He has won the bar's 'medal of honor' and is considered one of the top tax attorney's in the United States. When you have sophisticated problems, you need a sophisticated lawyer. Mike Smith is for you." Mike Smith shows the advertisement to other partners in the firm for their consent. You are a partner in Mike's firm. Mike is important to the firm and brings in a lot of business. You want to consent to the advertisement if you can. Can you?

## 2.　SOLICITATION

Although the Supreme Court has been very sympathetic to First Amendment concerns in the advertising context, it has been less sympathetic to those concerns when the issue involves solicitation of clients. Notice in *Bates* the Supreme Court specifically indicated that it was not addressing in person solicitation.

In Florida Bar v. Went for It, 515 U.S. 618 (1995), the Court upheld a Florida ban on written solicitation of personal injury and wrongful death plaintiffs within 30 days of an accident. The Court concluded:

> We believe that the Bar's 30-day restriction on targeted direct-mail solicitation of accident victims and their relatives withstands scrutiny under the three-pronged *Central Hudson* test that we have devised for this context. The Bar has substantial interest both in protecting injured Floridians from invasive conduct by lawyers and in preventing the erosion of confidence in the *profession* that such repeated invasions have engendered. The Bar's proffered study, unrebutted by respondents below, provides evidence indicating that the harms it targets are far from illusory. The palliative devised by the Bar to address these harms is narrow both in scope and in duration. The

Constitution, in our view, requires nothing more. *Id.* at 635.

The Model Rules recognize that there is significant potential for abuse when an experienced lawyer solicits business from a perspective client. Rule 7.3 prohibits an attorney from soliciting a potential client "in person, live telephone or real-time electronic contact." There is an exception in the rule when the lawyer is not intending to obtain pecuniary gain from the solicitation. This exception has generally been read to allow non-profit organizations to contact perspective clients. The rule also exempts an attorney's family, close friends, other lawyers, and prior clients from the rule (except if they have told the attorney not to contact them or if the attorney is coercing or harassing them).

An attorney may contact prospective clients through non-real-time communication, but that communication must contain the notation "advertising material" on the envelop (if there is one) and at the beginning and the end of the recorded or electronic communication.

A lawyer may also not pay someone else to solicit clients and may not pay a fee to others to refer cases to the attorney. (See Rule 7.2). She may enter into reciprocal referral arrangements with other attorneys and other professionals.

Finally, while a lawyer may not split a fee with a non-lawyer, a lawyer may split a fee with a lawyer in another firm. (See Rule 1.5(e)). Thus a lawyer who refers a case to another lawyer, may properly receive a part of the fee charged the client. This arrangement must be disclosed and the division must be "in proportion to the services performed" or "each lawyer must assume joint responsibility for the representation." Rule 1.5(e).

**Problem 6.12**

You are a member of the bar of state X. State X is thinking about passing a rule similar to the rule in Florida. You have been hired by a group of lawyers to write a letter to the bar arguing against the rule. What are your best arguments and why?

## Problem 6.13

The solicitation rules in the Model Rules are designed to protect unsophisticated victims. Why might these rules have the opposite results?

## Problem 6.14

You are an attorney in Tax Court representing XYZ Corporation. A litigant in another case is quite favorably impressed with your statement to the Judge, gets your name from the Clerk, and asks you to represent her in her case. Explain whether you can ethically accept the employment?

### Scenario 6.1

Bruce and Clark graduate from law school and decide to create Bruce and Clark LL.P (B&C). Bruce excelled in tax law and Clark preferred torts. Because they are not experienced attorneys, Bruce and Clark handle a lot of small dollar tort cases. Bruce also prepares some tax returns, and advises small business entities about business organization, formation and tax issues.

Bruce and Clark advertise in the local phone book. The advertisement states:

---

**Bruce and Clark Aggressive Lawyers You Can Trust**

Injured? Problems with the IRS? We can help!!!

We have helped people who are hurt on the job or in accidents

We have helped people who are being hounded by the IRS

We specialize in tax free settlements in personal injury cases

We are available around the clock to suit your needs

We will work hard for you!!!

---

The advertisement is very successful. When Bruce and Clark receive complicated or high dollar cases, they refer the cases to more experienced attorneys in another firm. For every referral, Bruce and Clark receive 10% of the amount received by the attorney who handles the case. Bruce and Clark do not work on the cases once they are referred to other attorneys, but they do sometimes stay involved in the cases so they can learn from the experienced attorney.

B&C's business plan is a huge success. It handle lots of smaller dollar personal inquiry cases that settle quickly. It also has significant revenue from the cases that it referred to other firms. B&C decides to expand its advertising campaign and to create a television commercial.

The commercial starts with a car crash and then shows a distressed parent who says "when my child was hurt in a car accident, I didn't know where to turn. B&C helped me through the trauma and enabled me to collect money to help my daughter recover." The scene then moves to a court room where Bruce and Clark are arguing a case before a jury. They seem very lawyerly and look very impressive. They then close with the tag line. If you need a lawyer Bruce and Clark are here for you.

The Bar brings a complaint against Bruce and Clark claiming that the advertisements violate the rules of professional conduct. Assume you are the lawyer for the Bar, what arguments do you make on the Bar's behalf? If you were the lawyer for Bruce and Clark, what would be your defense?

## Problem 6.15

Instead of the above scenario, Bruce and Clark start a law practice. They recognize that they are inexperienced attorneys, and they prefer to handle small cases while they learn the ropes. When they get a more complicated case, they enlist the assistance of a more experienced member of the bar in a different firm. All attorneys on the case assume joint responsibility and B&C and the experienced attorney split the fee 50/50. Does this fee arrangement comply with the model rules?

# C.  Malpractice

## 1. CAUSE OF ACTION

## BATILLA v. RHODES
848 S.W.2d 833 (Tex. App. 1993)

SEARS, Justice.

Ione A. Batilla (Batilla), appellee, brought suit for legal malpractice against Christopher D. Rhodes, appellant. Trial was to a jury which found gross negligence in appellant's handling of Batilla's tax defense from the Internal Revenue Service (IRS). Judgment was entered on the verdict in favor of Batilla, awarding her $125,500 in actual, and $125,000 in exemplary, damages. Appellant raises 22 points of error. We affirm.

Batilla's tax liability arose in connection with her employment at Randolph Office Furniture (ROF). * * * While she was with ROF she was employed as controller. She did the company books, worked with a company called ADP to issue payroll checks, and oversaw the purchasing department. Batilla, however, had no authority to sign company checks, even on the payroll account, without the owner's approval. In 1984 and 1985, the company was having financial trouble and eventually went into Chapter 7 bankruptcy. During this time period, the owner, George Randolph (Randolph), refused to approve any checks to pay the company's FICA payroll taxes. * * * [O]n the advice of the company attorney, Batilla had someone witness her tender of checks for the taxes to Randolph for his signature. Randolph would either refuse to sign the checks or tear them up. As a result, the ROF payroll taxes were not paid.[29]

In January 1986, Batilla received a call from Mr. Bean with the IRS regarding ROF's unpaid FICA taxes for 1984 and the first

---

[29] [Ed. note] Under I.R.C. 6672, if a person is a "responsible person" for paying trust fund taxes and fails to pay those taxes, the responsible person is liable for a penalty equal to the amount of unpaid taxes. Under our system, employers withhold employment taxes from employees. These taxes are held in trust by the employer for the government. When companies are in financial trouble, they sometimes decide to use employee funds to meet other financial obligations. This is a serious breach of trust and the penalty provisions are designed to allow the Service to seek funds from any person who would have had the authority to pay the tax. Here, Batilla appeared to have done what she should have done. That is, she did her part to ensure the taxes were paid.

quarter of 1985. Mr. Bean wanted to determine if Batilla was a "responsible person" for purposes of assessing a 100% penalty against her, i.e., essentially collecting the unpaid company taxes from her. [Batilla contacted her accountant who recommended the Appellant, Christopher Rhodes. Batilla contacted Rhodes who told her he could help her]. Rhodes told Batilla to "go down and talk to Mr. Bean and then come and see him after [she] spoke with Mr. Bean." She testified appellant further advised her "he would call Mr. Bean" and he indicated that "everything would be all right." Further testimony shows Rhodes told her there would be a $500 retainer fee and "that he would help" her. They set an appointment for early February to meet in person.

\* \* \*

[Batilla met with the IRS in what was described by the court as a very "unpleasant experience." After the meeting with the IRS, Batilla met with Rhodes and gave him the facts of her case, including the fact that she did not have signature authority and that she presented checks to the President for signature. Rhodes represented that he was a tax specialist and would handle her case. Rhodes, however, never presented the information to the IRS regarding Batilla's lack of signature authority. Ultamately, the IRS assessed the full amount of unpaid employment taxes, plus penalties against Batilla. The IRS requested that she sign Form 2751 if she agreed to the assessment. Batilla contacted Rhodes and told him she did not want to agree to the assessment, and did not want to sign the Form 2751. She told him to call the IRS and give them the facts. Rhodes indicated that he would do so.]

Appellant's time-slips indicate no further activity until June 6, 1986 when he charged Batilla 1.3 hours for "[p]reparation of Letter of Protest [and] [r]eview of notice received regarding 100% penalty," and 2.0 hours for "[p]reparation of protest [and] [r]eview of files for L'Lani corporation." When Batilla got a copy of the protest letter which appellant sent to the IRS, she immediately called appellant to tell him the information in the letter was incorrect and that he needed to give them the true facts. Appellant told her he would take care of it. However, appellant never corrected any of the facts in the protest letter, and testified at trial he was not concerned that the letter contained totally inaccurate information "because it was to the best of [his] knowledge at that time."

In 1986, appellant also gave Batilla advice on protecting her family from tax liability. Mr. Bean [the IRS agent] had told Batilla he would garnish her wages and her husband's wages. In response, appellant told Batilla the only way she could prevent the IRS from taking her money was to get a "paper divorce," give her assets to her husband, and put any equity that she had in a trust fund for her son. Batilla followed this advice even though her husband was against the idea. Due to the stress of the tax problems and her husband's unhappiness over the divorce, their "paper divorce" became a real divorce.

After the protest letter was sent, appellant's time-slips reflect no further activity on behalf of Batilla until January 20, 1987. In 1987, appellant had several telephone conferences with IRS representatives, met with Larry Fagen (Fagen) of the IRS, talked to Batilla once, * * * spent a maximum of three hours researching the law, and sent a letter to Fagen. At the meeting with Fagen, appellant was requested to bring "facts, arguments, and legal authority" to support Batilla's position. Any statements appellant brought to the meeting were to be "in affidavit form or signed under penalty of perjury." However, appellant presented an argument to Fagen at the meeting unsupported by any facts or legal authority. He took no case authority with him to the meeting, and he failed to obtain affidavits from Batilla or any of the witnesses, therefore he had no statement of facts to present to the IRS. The obvious result was that the meeting was of zero value to Batilla. If the true facts had been given to the IRS, it would have been apparent Batilla had zero liability.

Appellant's time-slips also indicate he had a telephone conference in 1987 with a "witness;" however, none of the witnesses had ever heard from or spoken to appellant. On June 18, 1987, Fagen sent appellant a letter indicating he had tried to contact appellant and follow up on this matter on March 27, 1987, April 8, 1987, April 27, 1987, and May 20, 1987, but all of these attempts had failed. A copy of this letter from Fagen was also sent to Batilla. She was extremely upset when she received the letter, and immediately called appellant. Batilla was concerned that the IRS still did not know the truth of the matter, i.e., Batilla was *not* a "responsible person" and in fact had no authority to issue checks for payroll deductions. Appellant told her he previously had several conversations with Fagen and that he would submit further information to Fagen. On June 25, 1987, appellant sent Fagen a letter indicating he had received the letter of June 18, 1987 and would be submitting further information by July 8, 1987. Appellant took no action, and never gave the IRS the correct facts. Obviously, the IRS assumed Batilla was a "responsible person" for the ROF taxes, and initiated collection procedures.

Sometime in 1987, appellant signed the same Form 2751 that Batilla told him she would not sign, and in doing so appellant agreed to the assessment of the 100% penalty against Batilla. This form was executed without her knowledge or consent. When he signed the form, he drew a line across the bottom and put an asterisk to the right of the line. Then across the middle of the form next to another asterisk he wrote "[t]axpayer retains the option of filing claim and suit for refund." Appellant never obtained Batilla's consent, never informed her he had signed this form on her behalf, and never sent her a copy of the signed form.

On November 27, 1987, the IRS sent Batilla a letter stating the case was closed "on the basis agreed upon" and the file was to be sent to the service center for account adjustment and interest computation. Batilla frantically tried to contact appellant. After several phone calls, she finally tracked him down in December 1987. She told him about the letter from the IRS, and appellant told her he had done "everything he could" for her. He stated the case was closed, there was nothing else he could do for her, and she would have to get another attorney. Batilla asked if appellant had sent her copies of everything in his files, and he assured her she had copies of all documents and correspondence in the file. He still failed to inform Batilla he had agreed to 100% assessment of the taxes against her.

In February 1988, Batilla received a bill from the IRS for $32,124.31 in unpaid FICA taxes for ROF. Batilla went to the IRS in an attempt to clear up the mistake. She was advised to write out the facts of her case and get affidavits from people with personal knowledge of the events. On March 29, 1988, Batilla prepared a letter stating the facts of her case, supported by five affidavits. In early April 1988, Batilla presented her letter and affidavits to the collection officer, Mr. Amdexter (Amdexter), who refused to listen to anything she had to say. He told her he could seize any asset she had to satisfy the debt.

Batilla was subsequently referred to Ben Stevens (Stevens), and she retained him in April 1988 to represent her in this tax matter. In late April 1988, Stevens discovered that appellant had signed the Form 2751, and agreed to the assessment of the 100%

penalty against Batilla. Stevens immediately informed her of the agreement. On May 11, 1988, the IRS filed a Federal Tax Lien against Batilla. She began payment on the tax lien. In January 1989, Batilla retained Mary Heafner to represent her in this malpractice action against appellant.

In points of error one and two, appellant complains the trial court erred in not making a ruling regarding any "legal errors" he committed, and in rendering judgment for Batilla. * * *

Generally, the determination of negligence, causation and damages in a legal malpractice action are questions of fact for the jury. In the professional misconduct case cited by appellant, the court made it clear the jury is to determine these factual issues. After the jury makes its factual determinations, the court then determines the legal question of "whether such facts found by the jury constitute professional misconduct.". If the trial court determines the facts constitute professional misconduct, it then enters judgment in favor of the plaintiff.

Appellant opines that the effect of signing the Form 2751 is uncertain and requires numerous judgment calls, however, this fact does not prevent the jury from finding him negligent in his handling of the case. The fact of the matter is that Rhodes was hired to *defend* Batilla against the tax assessment, and instead he signed a form against her interest which *consented* to the assessment of the tax against her. He signed this form in contravention of his client's instructions that he show the IRS she was not a person responsible for the payment of the tax. Rhodes failed to go to the IRS meeting with the facts and affidavits which would have relieved Batilla of all liability. In fact he presented incorrect information to the IRS. He advised Batilla to get a "paper divorce" to thwart IRS collection attempts, something a first year law student would have known better than to do. Further, Rhodes failed to appreciate the consequences of signing a Form 2751 before he executed the form. He neglected to discuss this form with Batilla or get her consent before he signed it on her behalf. Additionally, even after he signed the form, Rhodes never told Batilla about consenting to the assessment. Finally, Rhodes terminated his attorney-client relationship with Batilla leaving her in ignorance of the status of her case and without taking any steps to protect her interests. These acts are sufficient to constitute negligence on the part of Rhodes. We overrule appellant's points of error one and two.

In point of error three, appellant contends the trial court erred in overruling his objections to the jury charge because it did not contain the controlling questions or instructions necessary to support a recovery for Batilla. Appellant attempts to add questions which Batilla should have asked the jury in order to be entitled to a recovery. He relies heavily on the issues set out in *Cosgrove v. Grimes,* which, unlike this case, was an attorney malpractice case brought by a plaintiff whose lawsuit had not been properly prosecuted.

The Texas Supreme Court in *Cosgrove* stated that "[a]n attorney malpractice action in Texas is based on negligence." Cosgrove v. Grimes, 774 S.W.2d 662, 664 (Tex.1989). There are four elements which must be established by the plaintiff in a negligence action: 1) "that there is a duty owed to [her] by the defendant," 2) "a breach of that duty," 3) "that the breach proximately caused the plaintiff injury" and 4) "that damages occurred."   Id. at 665 (citing McKinley v. Stripling, 763 S.W.2d 407 (Tex.1989)).

Under Texas' broad form submission rule, the definitions, instructions, and questions submitted to the jury in this case satisfy the four elements of negligence. The jury found Rhodes to be negligent and that his negligent conduct proximately caused Batilla $125,500 in actual damages. The jury further found Rhodes to be grossly negligent and awarded Batilla $125,000 in exemplary damages.

* * * The Court in *Cosgrove* stated the damages issues in that case should have been asked in terms of "what would the plaintiff's damages have been if the suit had been properly prosecuted?" In this case, Batilla did not suffer damages because of Rhodes' failure to properly prosecute the case, instead she incurred damages because of his failure to defend the case, his advice on getting a "paper divorce," and his secretly consenting to the assessment of the tax against her. Thus, her damages questions were properly tied to the underlying case by determining *what damages Batilla incurred as a result of Rhodes' negligent conduct, for example, his failure to properly defend the case.*   We overrule appellant's point of error three.

* * *

As a general rule the standard of care for an attorney being sued for malpractice is set out as follows:

A lawyer in Texas is held to the standard of care which would be exercised by a reasonably prudent attorney, based on the information the attorney has at the time of the alleged act of negligence.

In other areas of professional malpractice, such as medical malpractice, a practitioner "who holds himself out as a specialist is generally expected to possess a higher degree of skill and learning than a general practitioner." Other jurisdictions have applied this standard to attorneys and have held that an attorney who holds himself out as a specialist or expert in a field is held to the standard of the reasonably prudent expert attorney in that field.

We see no reason why this standard of care for one who holds himself out as an expert or specialist should not apply to appellant. According to his own testimony, appellant is a "tax expert." Batilla testified he held himself out to her as a tax specialist who was familiar with 100% penalty cases, and that he would have no troubling taking care of her case. Thus, appellant was properly held to the standard of care which would be exercised by a reasonably prudent tax attorney.

\* \* \*

In points of error nine, ten, and eleven, appellant complains the trial court erred in awarding $125,000 in exemplary damages. He alleges the amount of exemplary damages found by the jury is excessive and there is insufficient evidence of his "net worth" on which to base the award. Appellant also contends there is no evidence or insufficient evidence of "gross negligence" upon which to base the award of exemplary damages.

The factors to consider when reviewing exemplary damages are set out in Alamo Nat'l Bank v. Kraus, 616 S.W.2d 908 (Tex.1981). These five factors "are (1) the nature of the wrong, (2) the character of the conduct involved, (3) the degree of culpability of the wrongdoer, (4) the situation and sensibilities of the parties concerned, and (5) the extent to which such conduct offends a public sense of justice and propriety." Further, the amount of exemplary damages awarded must be reasonably proportioned to the amount of actual damages awarded.

Based on the facts discussed earlier in this opinion, we find the nature of the wrong, the character of appellant's conduct, the degree of culpability of appellant, the situation and sensibilities of appellant and Batilla, and the extent to which appellant's conduct offends the public sense of justice and propriety sufficient to support this award of exemplary damages. Additionally, the amount of exemplary damages awarded was $125,000 and the amount of actual damages awarded was $125,500, a ratio of approximately one to one. The award of exemplary damages was not excessive in this case.

\* \* \*

Finally, we address appellant's complaint of no evidence or factually insufficient evidence to establish his "gross negligence."

\* \* \*

The record is replete with evidence sufficient to support the jury's finding of gross negligence on the part of appellant. His conscious indifference in investigating and presenting facts to the IRS, in failing to return phone calls from the IRS, in failing to investigate or correct the false and misleading information he sent to the IRS, in failing to research or present any facts, affidavits, or legal authority favorable to his client in his meeting with the IRS, in failing to recognize the effects of signing the Form 2751 before signing it, in signing the form agreeing to the assessment of the tax against his client in direct contravention to the purpose for which he had been retained, in doing so without his client's knowledge or consent, and in terminating his relationship with his client without even informing her of the status of her case, are sufficient to support a finding of gross negligence on appellant's part.

\* \* \*

## Questions and Comments:

1. Think hard about how this attorney's inaction and malpractice made someone else's life miserable. A little work on the part of Mr. Rhodes could have saved Ms. Batilla a lot of heartache. This was not the case where there were complicated facts and the attorney made some innocent mistakes. Here, the attorney violated the trust that his client placed in him. It is important to recognize that malpractice on the part of attorneys, even in tax collection cases, can have a serious negative impact on people's lives.

2. A tax attorney is an expert. Notice in the opinion the court establishes that Rhodes held himself out as a tax expert. Should tax lawyers be held to a higher standard than non-tax lawyers? In general, if an attorney holds himself out as an expert in a particular field, the attorney will be required to exercise the standard of care that an expert in the field would exercise. See e.g. Bent v. Green, 466 A.2d 322 (Conn. 1983), Wright v. Williams, 47 Cal. App. 3d 802 (1975).

3. Did Rhodes's actions violate the Model Rules of Professional Conduct or Circular 230. Assume you were disciplinary counsel for the Texas bar, would you bring an action against Rhodes? What if you were the Director of the Office of Professional Responsibility at the Internal Revenue Service?

4. How do you prove an attorney violated his duty of care? Most courts require a plaintiff to provide expert testimony to prove a violation of an attorney's standard of care. Courts generally will not require such proof when the violation is obvious. See e.g. Bent v. Green, 466 A.2d 322 (Conn. 1983).

5. The court here notes that the action for malpractice in this case is an action for negligence. Thus, plaintiffs must show duty, breach, proximate cause, and damages. There are some states that also recognize a contracts cause of action for malpractice. In addition, several tax malpractice actions have been litigated as securities violation cases (see Seippel v. Jenking & Gilchrist, 341 F. Supp2d 363 (S.D. NY 2004).

6. Some complicated privity issues arise when it is a third party claiming an attorney's malpractice. Traditionally, courts held that attorneys only had a duty to their clients.

In National Savings Bank v. Ward, 100 U.S. 195, 200 (1880), the Court examined whether an attorney who made a mistake in a title search was liable to a third party for malpractice. The Court held "the obligation of the attorney is to his client and not to a third party, and unless there is something in the circumstances of this case [like fraud] to take it out of that general rule, it seems clear that the proposition of the defendant must be sustained." Courts have traditionally followed this rule. See e.g. Pelham v. Griesheimer, 417 N.E. 2d. 882 (Ill. App. 1981); Hermann v. Frey, 537 N.E.2d 529 (Ind. App. 1989).

Some courts, however, have recognized that an attorney may have a duty to third parties.

# ESTATE OF VERNON R. DRWENSKI,
# V.
# M. SCOTT MCCOLLOCH, ESQ.
### 83 P.3d 457 (Wyo. 2004)

KITE, JUSTICE.

Vernon Drwenski died before his divorce was finalized. As a result, his widow, Trudy Drwenski, inherited money from the estate she would not have inherited if she and Mr. Drwenski had been divorced. Mr. Drwenski's daughter, Erin Connely, sued her father's divorce attorney, Scott McColloch, because he failed to finalize the divorce before Mr. Drwenski died. The district court granted Mr. McColloch's motion for summary judgment finding he owed no duty to Ms. Connely or to the estate. We affirm the district court's judgment.

\* \* \*

DISCUSSION

Duty of Attorney to Third Party

This case requires us to examine the current state of the law and determine whether there are any circumstances in which an attorney owes a duty to a nonclient. Over 120 years ago, the United States Supreme Court held that absent fraud, collusion, or privity of contract, an attorney is not liable to a third party for professional malpractice. Savings Bank v. Ward, 100 U.S. 195, 25 L.Ed. 621, (1879). Almost eighty years later, the California Supreme Court was the first to depart from that strict contractual privity rule. In Biakanja v. Irving, 49 Cal.2d 647, 320 P.2d 16 (1958), the court formulated the "balancing factors" test. This test is "closely related to the analysis and policy reasons used to justify permitting a third-party beneficiary to recover in a contract action." California's balancing test requires the weighing of specific public policy considerations and closely mirrors the factors we adopted in Gates v. Richardson, 719 P.2d 193 (Wyo.1986), to be utilized in considering whether new tort duties should be recognized. The Biakanja court held a duty to a nonclient could be found upon a balancing of the following six factors: (1) the extent to which the transaction was intended to affect the plaintiff; (2) the foreseeability of harm; (3) the degree of certainty that the plaintiff suffered injury; (4) the closeness of the connection between the defendant's conduct and the injury suffered; (5) the moral blame attached to the defendant's conduct; and (6) the policy of preventing future harm. Biakanja, 320 P.2d at 19.

The California court tailored its balancing test three years later in Lucas v. Hamm, 56 Cal.2d 583, 15 Cal.Rptr. 821, 364 P.2d 685 (1961) by replacing the moral blame element with an inquiry into whether expansion of liability to the nonclient would place an undue burden on the legal profession. Id. 15 Cal.Rptr. 821, 364 P.2d at 688. The Lucas plaintiffs were beneficiaries under a will and brought an action against the attorney who prepared it. As a result of a drafting error, plaintiffs received a smaller share of the estate than the testator intended. The court held the lack of privity between plaintiffs and the attorney did not preclude the intended beneficiaries, who lost their testamentary rights because of an attorney's failure to properly prepare the will, from recovering as third-party beneficiaries. Since Lucas, courts all over the country have applied the six factors to determine whether the circumstances warrant finding an attorney owes a duty to a nonclient.

However, the Lucas balancing test is not the only test utilized for determining attorney liability to nonclients. Some courts rely upon a third party beneficiary contract theory similar to that set forth in the Restatement (Second) of Contracts § 302 (1981). Jurisdictions adopting this approach include Illinois, Maryland, Oregon, and Pennsylvania. (Pelham v. Griesheimer, 93 Ill.App.3d 751, 49 Ill.Dec. 192, 417 N.E.2d 882 (1981) aff'd, 92 Ill.2d 13, 64 Ill.Dec. 544, 440 N.E.2d 96 (1982); Goerlich v. Courtney Industries, Inc., 84 Md.App. 660, 581 A.2d 825 (Ct.Spec.App.1990); Hale v. Groce, 304 Or. 281, 744 P.2d 1289 (1987); Guy v. Liederbach, 501 Pa. 47, 459 A.2d 744 (1983)).

Under the third party beneficiary analysis, the inquiry is whether the client's intent to benefit the nonclient was the direct purpose of the attorney-client relationship. The duty does not extend to those incidentally deriving an indirect benefit. Neither does it extend to those in an adversarial relationship with the client. The third party beneficiary test requires the plaintiff to prove clearly that (1) the client intended to benefit the plaintiff by entering into a contract with the attorney, (2) the attorney breached his contract with the client by failing to perform under its terms, and (3) giving the plaintiff the right to stand "in the client's shoes" would be appropriate to give effect to the intent of the contract.

Interestingly, commentators have suggested that even in those jurisdictions that apply California's balancing approach, the predominant inquiry is generally whether a principal purpose of the attorney's retention to provide legal services was to provide a specific benefit to the plaintiff--in other words, the third party beneficiary test.

For example, an Illinois court concluded that the balancing test might be appropriate in some situations, but required the divorced client's children to prove that the attorney-client contract to obtain the divorce was entered into primarily for their benefit. Pelham, supra.. The Maryland court has gone even further in its adoption of the third party beneficiary test and added an additional requirement that the interests of the third party be identical to the interests of the client. Goerlich, 581 A.2d at 827. Arizona clarifies the third party beneficiary test and requires plaintiffs to prove negligence by the attorney toward the client, not just a deleterious effect upon the beneficiary due to the attorney's negligence. Franko v. Mitchell, 158 Ariz. 391, 762 P.2d 1345 (Ct.App.1988).

Only New York, Texas, Ohio and Nebraska continue to hold there is no recovery for nonclients. See, for example, Conti v. Polizzotto, 243 A.D.2d 672, 663 N.Y.S.2d 293 (N.Y.App.Div.1997); Barcelo v. Elliott, 923 S.W.2d 575 (Tex.1996); Simon v. Zipperstein, 32 Ohio St.3d 74, 512 N.E.2d 636 (1987); and St. Mary's Church of Schuyler v. Tomek, 212 Neb. 728, 325 N.W.2d 164 (1982). Weighing whether to adopt such a duty, the South Dakota court explained the disinclination to allow a nonclient to sue an attorney for malpractice:

> There are several reasons courts are reluctant to relax the rule of privity in attorney malpractice cases. First, the rule preserves an attorney's duty of loyalty to and effective advocacy for the client. Simon v. Zipperstein, 32 Ohio St.3d 74, 512 N.E.2d 636, 638 (Ohio 1987). Second, adding responsibilities to nonclients creates the danger of conflicting duties. John H. Bauman, A Sense of Duty: Regulation of Lawyer Responsibility to Third Parties by the Tort System, 37 S Tex L Rev 995, 1006 (1996). Third, once the privity rule is relaxed, the number of persons a lawyer might be accountable to

could be limitless. Nat'l Savings Bank v. Ward, 100 U.S. 195, 198, 25 L.Ed. 621, 624 (1879). Fourth, a relaxation of the strict privity rule would imperil attorney-client confidentiality.

Courts that have refrained from adopting a duty to a nonclient are quickly becoming part of a thinning minority and some would say are being overprotective of the legal profession. As one commentator explains:

> The modern trend in the United States is to recognize the existence of a duty beyond the confines of those in privity and the attorney/client contract. Whatever the legal theory, however, there must be a duty of care owed by the attorney to the plaintiff . . . A duty exists under two principal theories. The first approach is the multi-criteria balancing test, which originated in California. Another approach is the concept of a third-party beneficiary contract. Mallen, supra, at 693-94.

## Questions and Comments:

The court in Drwenski traces the history of the privity requirement for malpractice cases and concludes that some flexibility in the privity requirement is warranted. The court hints that doctrine may be unnecessarily protective of the legal profession. One normally thinks of malpractice as a wrong against one's client; can you think of situations where it might be proper for a third party to sue an attorney. Is there a difference between a malpractice action and a negligence action? Should there be?

### Problem 6.16

Attorney Gilchrest designed a shelter similar to the COBRA tax shelter discussed at the beginning of chapter 5. Gilchrest also provided a tax opinion letter to Jenkins who marketed the shelter. Jenkins paid Gilchrest for his work. Sam Sham bought the tax shelter and offset nearly $5 million in capital gains from taxation. The IRS disputed the deductions and ultimately prevailed in court. Sham owed over $3 million in back taxes and penalties. Sam sued both Jenkins and Gilchrest alleging malpractice. Assume you are the attorney for Sam, what are your best arguments for recovery? What if you represented Jenkins? What if you represented

Gilchrest?   Can you represent both Jenkins & Gilchrest in this action?

**Problem 6.17**

Frank was a tax attorney who specialized in tax controversy work.  Pierce was having a dispute with the IRS about whether an expense was deductible under § 162 or whether it was a hobby.  Pierce had been deducting his son's golf lessons as an ordinary and necessary business expense because his son intended to be a professional golfer.  Frank agreed to take the case and charged Pierce a retainer of $500.  Frank completely forgot about the case.  He never filed a petition in Tax Court, and the period for filing a claim in Tax Court ran.  About four months later, Pierce called Frank about the claim and Frank said the time to file a petition in Tax Court has run.  Frank admitted he forgot to file the petition, but said that Frank would have lost the case anyway.  He agrees to return the $500 Pierce paid him.  Pierce comes to you and wants to sue Frank for malpractice.  Does Pierce have a case?  Did Frank do anything wrong besides failing to file the Tax Court petition?

## 2.    STATUTE OF LIMITATIONS

It is particularly difficult to determine the correct point in which the statute of limitations starts running in malpractice actions involving disputes over tax liability.   The basic question is determining when a specific negligent act occurred that starts the running of the statute of limitations.  Some courts have determined that the statute of limitations starts to run when the attorney commits the negligent act.  This is a particularly harsh rule for clients, since clients will often not learn of the error until the period of limitations has run.  Other jurisdictions have determined that the statute starts to run when the taxpayer receives a notice of deficiency.  This presumably is the point that the taxpayer knows that there was a potential mistake.  Finally, some courts have determined that the statute does not start running, or is tolled, until there is an actual injury (when some action has been taken to allow the tax to be assessed.)  Courts that apply this rule do so because there must be damages for a malpractice claim to be successful.  These courts have held that a client has not suffered damages until it is clear that the client will not prevail on the merits of her underlying claim.

# SEIPPEL,
# V.
# JENKINS & GILCHRIST
341 F.Supp 2d 363 (S.D. NY 2004)

SCHEINDLIN, DISTRICT JUDGE,

This case arises out of tax and consulting services offered by several professional law, financial services and accounting firms. Plaintiffs, William and Sharon Seippel, filed this suit on September 10, 2003, alleging that defendants violated the Racketeer Influenced and Corrupt Organizations Act ("RICO"), and are liable for damages and other relief arising from breach of fiduciary duty, inducing breach of fiduciary duty, fraud, negligent misrepresentation, breach of contract, malpractice, "unethical, excessive, illegal and unreasonable fees," and unjust enrichment.

## II. BACKGROUND

### A. Defendants' Alleged Conspiracy

The following facts are drawn from the allegations in the Amended Complaint and the RICO Statement. For the purpose of this motion, these allegations are assumed to be true.

Between 1996 and 2003, the Sidley Defendants, in concert with the Jenkens Defendants, were engaged in the development and promotion of a variety of tax shelters, including one labelled "Currency Options Bring Reward Alternatives," or "COBRA." In late 1997 and 1998, the Sidley Defendants entered into an alliance to operate, market and promote these tax shelters with a number of other accounting and financial services firms, including, among others, the Deutsche Bank Defendants and Ernst & Young LLP.

Pursuant to this alliance, each of the defendants authorized these firms to represent that the shelters were developed by the accounting firm soliciting the taxpayer, and that they had been independently "vetted" and determined to be "legitimate" and "conservative" by the Lawyer Defendants. In fact, the shelters were developed by the Lawyer Defendants themselves. The soliciting firms promised the taxpayers that the Lawyer Defendants would provide opinion letters attesting to the legitimacy of the shelters, and that these letters would "protect any participant from the imposition of penalties by tax authorities."

Though these letters were "canned" and required little additional work, the Lawyer Defendants charged substantial fees, calculated as a percentage of the capital losses each client would claim on its tax returns.  The defendants agreed that on some transactions, the Jenkens Defendants would provide the first opinion letter and take the "lion's share" of the fees, and the Sidley Defendants would provide a secondary letter and receive a smaller fee, while on other transactions the positions would be reversed.

The Lawyer Defendants' undisclosed role in marketing and promoting the shelters both compromised their objectivity, and "presented a risk that the [tax authorities] would and could claim that the opinion letters . . . would not shield them from the assessment of penalties."  The defendants agreed that "the firms soliciting prospective participants . . . would overstate what those opinion letters would conclude regarding the legitimacy of the tax scheme being promoted and would understate its risks and the likelihood of an audit."  The defendants further agreed that the taxpayer would not receive the opinion letters until after it had engaged in the promoted transactions.  Finally, defendants agreed that the accounting firms soliciting taxpayers would represent that the tax shelter "was a 'proprietary' product of that firm so . . . prospective participants could not take it to their own attorney or accountant for an opinion as to its legitimacy."

The Seippels contend that "defendants either knew or should have known from the outset that the COBRA tax shelter would not pass muster with the IRS or the Virginia tax authorities."  In support of this allegation, the Seippels point to two Internal Revenue Service rulings, IRS Notice 1999-59 and Notice 2000-44, and to a decision of the Third Circuit Court of Appeals, ACM Partnership v. Commissioner,stated that "certain types of transactions ... that are being marketed to taxpayers for the purpose of generating ... artificial losses are not allowable for federal income tax purposes." Notice 2000-44, released on September 5, 2000, "specified [that] the precise transaction marketed ... as the COBRA transaction" was not properly allowable for tax purposes.   Nevertheless, defendants continued to market the transactions.

B. The Seippels' COBRA Transaction

\* \* \*

The Seippels had a series of meetings and telephone and email conversations with Paul in late 1999, during which Paul represented that "COBRA was 100 percent legitimate, and backed by two blue chip law firms (Jenkens & Gilchrist and Brown & Wood) [and] was not only completely legal and based on 'loopholes' created by the IRS, but actually was 'conservative'." Paul represented that the COBRA shelter had been developed by Ernst & Young, not by the Lawyer Defendants. Paul told the Seippels that the Lawyer Defendants would provide opinion letters confirming the propriety of the COBRA transaction, and represented that these letters would "in the event of any IRS audit . . . enable the Seippels to satisfy the IRS auditors as to the propriety of the tax returns [and] would serve as a protection against the imposition of tax penalties."

At some point in late 1999, after being contacted by Ernst & Young, Mr. Seippel sold his stock and realized a large gain. During the same period, the Seippels agreed to participate in the COBRA transaction to reduce their tax liability for that gain. \* \* \*

In February 2000, Mr. Seippel received an opinion letter from Jenkens and Gilchrist "stating that the Seippels could properly and legally claim losses totaling $12,000,000 on their tax returns as a result of the COBRA transaction." In March 2000, Mr. Seippel received a similar opinion from Brown & Wood, stating that "the IRS should not be successful were it to assert a penalty . . . for positions taken in [the Seippels'] U.S. Federal income tax [returns] with respect to the [COBRA] transactions." The Jenkens & Gilchrist opinion letter stated that IRS Notice 1999-59, released on December 27, 1999, did not apply to COBRA. The Brown & Wood opinion letter did not mention the Notice, nor did any other communication from defendants to the Seippels apart from the Jenkens & Gilchrist opinion letter. The defendants never informed the Seippels about IRS Notice 2000-44, released on September 5, 2000.

The Seippels paid the Jenkens Defendants $338,880 for their opinion letter, legal advice and assistance in establishing the entities required to carry out the COBRA transaction. This fee was calculated as a percentage of the $12,000,000 in losses created by the transaction. The Seippels paid Brown & Wood $21,180 for the second opinion letter. The Seippels contend that both payments were "unethically excessive," because the letters were "canned" and the lawyers "expended little, if any, time or effort" in creating them.

Ernst & Young prepared the Seippels' 1999 and 2000 tax returns. These returns used the COBRA losses to offset and reduce the Seippels' tax liability.

In March 2002, Ernst & Young informed Mr. Seippel that it had received subpoenas in an IRS investigation of COBRA. In July 2002, the Seippels retained new tax and legal advisors, and discovered the alleged fraud for the first time. The Seippels allege that they have paid and will continue to incur substantial damages in the form of fees paid to these new advisors retained to "rectify . . . Defendants' wrongdoing." The Seippels' 1999 and 2000 tax returns have been audited by the IRS and Virginia tax authorities, and the Seippels have "had to make tax payments in an amount exceeding $5 million they were promised they would not have to make" and "have paid interest and/or penalties . . . totaling over $1 million and owe additional such amounts." The Seippels also allege various other injuries, including losses caused by having liquidated assets at fire sale prices to meet their tax obligations, and the loss of alternative legitimate tax savings.

* * *

C. The State Law Claims Against the Sidley Defendants

1. Malpractice

* * *

New York's statute of limitations for legal malpractice is three years, regardless of whether the underlying theory is based in contract or tort. The claim accrues "when all the facts necessary to the cause of action have occured and an injured party can obtain relief in court." The claim accrues "even if the aggrieved party is then ignorant of the wrong or injury."

The Seippels argue that their malpractice claim accrued, at the earliest, in July 2002, when they hired new counsel and accountants to investigate the propriety of their 1999 tax returns. Prior to that time, the Seippels argue, they had suffered no damages and so had no cause of action for malpractice.

The Seippels' argument is at odds with the holding of Ackerman v. Price Waterhouse. The *Ackerman* court held that a claim against accountants for malpractice in the preparation of tax returns accrues when plaintiffs first receive and rely on the defendant's work product and "as a consequence of such reliance, can become liable for tax deficiencies." The court rejected the argument that the claim could only accrue if and when the IRS assesses a deficiency, in favor of a "precise accrual date that can be uniformly applied." The *Ackerman* rule has been applied to malpractice claims against attorneys. The Seippels' malpractice claims against the Sidley Defendants thus accrued "on or about March 9, 2000," when they received and relied on Brown & Wood's opinion letter.

The Seippels offer two arguments for tolling the statute of limitations on their malpractice claims. First, they argue that the Lawyer Defendants should be estopped from asserting the statute of limitations defense because of their attempt to "wrongfully induce the plaintiff to refrain from timely commencing an action by deception [and] concealment." But "New York courts have rejected the proposition that fraudulent concealment tolls the statute of limitations in non-medical malpractice cases."

Second, the Seippels argue that the statute should be tolled because the Lawyer Defendants' "Failure To Fulfill Their Duty To Correct Their Advice To Plaintiffs Created A Continuous Wrong." This argument also fails. The theory that a malpractice claim based on false tax advice given in 2000 does not accrue so long as it remains uncorrected is clearly incompatible with the theory of *Ackerman.* Indeed, in McCoy v. Feinman, applying *Ackerman,* the New York Court of Appeals explicitly held that a continuing failure to correct malpractice could not toll the statute: "our law cannot permit a limitations period to depend on a continuing omission that can go on for decades."

The Seippels' malpractice claim is time-barred, and the statute of limitations cannot be tolled. The claim must therefore be dismissed.

## Questions and Comments:

Is this a harsh result? Does this mean that in New York you will rarely have malpractice actions succeed in tax cases? What would the justification be for having this rule? Does this rule make sense in the context of complicated transactions with unsophisticated clients?

## Problem 6.18

How would this rule work in medical malpractice actions? For example, in the television show Grey's Anatomy, a surgeon left a sponge in a patient and it was not discovered for several years (assume five years). Would the statute of limitations have run? Can you distinguish this medical situation from the tax situation?

## Problem 6.19

You work for a member of the New York legislature who is upset by the decision in *Seippel*. He wants to know the policy justifications for the rule, and your advice regarding whether the rule should be changed. If you were going to change the rule, what modifications would you suggest?

# Chapter 7

## Practice of Law

In addition to regulating the conduct of lawyers, state bars also regulate who may practice law, and therefore separate rules exist in each state authorizing an attorney to practice law in a particular state. Because of these rules, attorneys often become members of the bars of different states. The state centered licensure process works well when attorneys are practicing mainly within one jurisdiction, but it is becoming far more problematic as law practice becomes more national and international. The state centered approach also provides some difficulties for those practicing mainly in the Federal arena (such as Federal tax practice), and for government and corporate attorneys. In addition, as part of Sarbanes-Oxley (often referred to as SoX), new restrictions and responsibilities were placed on corporate counsel.

## A.  Unauthorized Practice of Law

States are entitled to regulate the practice of law under their general police powers. Unauthorized practice of law restrictions are often criticized as being paternalistic and designed to protect lawyers' monopoly on legal services. Especially with the expansion of the Internet and word processing, there are services that lawyers perform that probably could be performed by non-lawyers. For example, there have been disputes regarding whether an attorney is necessary for a real estate closing,[30] to represent clients filing patents,[31] and to negotiate deals with insurance companies.[32]

In fact, the Texas Supreme Court held that the sale of Quicken's computer program, Quicken Family Lawyer, was the unauthorized practice of law. Quicken must have had good lobbyists because the Texas legislature quickly amended the statute. It provides "the 'practice of law' does not include the design, creation,

---

[30] In re Opinion No. 26 of Committee on the Unauthorized Practice of Law, 654 A.2d 1344 (N.J. 1995))(Real Estate Closing is the practice of law);  In re Ingalls, 633 S.E.2d 512 (S.C. 2006)(same).

[31] Sperry v. Florida, 373 U.S. 379 (1963).

[32] Professional Adjusters, Inc. v. Tandon, 433 N.E.2d 779 (Ind.1982)(holding that independent adjusters engaged in the unauthorized practice of law when they negotiated on behalf of insured with insurance companies)).

publication, distribution, display, or sale . . . [of] computer software, or similar products if the products clearly and conspicuously state that the products are not a substitute for the advice of an attorney."[33]

There is, however, a very strong state interest in ensuring that its citizens are well represented and that the judicial process in the state runs smoothly. It is often difficult to determine what is the practice of law and some states have been reluctant to be explicit in defining the term.

In People v. Shell, 148 P.3d 162 (Colo. 2006) the Supreme Court of Colorado defined the unauthorized practice of law as:

> acting "in a representative capacity in protecting, enforcing, or defending the legal rights and duties of another and in counseling, advising and assisting him in connection with these rights and duties. . . ." Denver Bar Ass'n v. Pub. Util. Comm'n, 154 Colo. 273, 279, 391 P.2d 467, 471 (1964). Applying this definition, we have held that an unlicensed person engages in the unauthorized practice of law by offering legal advice about a specific case, drafting or selecting legal pleadings for another's use in a judicial proceeding without the supervision of an attorney, or holding oneself out as the representative of another in a legal action.

The Ohio Supreme Court in Land Title Abstract & Trust Co. v. Dworken, 193 N.E. 650 (Ohio 1934) provided the following discussion regarding the definition of unauthorized practice of law:

> The practice of law is, 'as generally understood, the doing or performing services in a court of justice, in any matter depending therein, throughout its various stages, and in conformity with the adopted rules of procedure. But in a larger sense it includes legal advice and counsel, and the preparation of legal instruments and contracts by which legal rights are secured, although such matter may or may not be depending in a court.' 49 Corpus Juris, p. 1313.

---

[33] See Unauthorized Practice of Law Committee v. Parsons Technology, Inc., 179 F.3d 956 (5th Cir. 1999)(vacating district court decision that Quicken Family Lawyer was unauthorized practice of law in light of legislature's action).

This view is supported by substantial authorities, among the cases being People v. Alfani, 125 N. E. 671, where it is held as follows:

'The practice of law is not limited to the conduct of cases in courts. It embraces the preparation of pleadings and other papers incident to actions and special proceedings and the management of such actions and proceedings on behalf of clients before judges and courts, and in addition conveyancing, the preparation of legal instruments of all kinds, and in general all advice to clients and all action taken for them in matters connected with the law. An attorney-at-law is one who engages in any of these branches of the practice of law.'

A very terse definition of the practice of law is announced in the case of People v. Title Guarantee & Trust Co., 180 App.Div. 648, 168 N. Y. S. 278, 280, as follows:

'The 'practice of the law,' as the term is now commonly used, embraces much more than the conduct of litigation. The greater, more responsible, and delicate part of a lawyer's work is in other directions. Drafting instruments creating trusts, formulating contracts, drawing wills and negotiations, all require legal knowledge and power of adaptation of the highest order. Beside these employments, mere skill in trying lawsuits, where ready wit and natural resources often prevail against profound knowledge of the law, is a relatively unimportant part of a lawyer's work.'

A lawyer generally may not practice, and may not assist others in practicing law in a jurisdiction unless he is authorized to do so by that jurisdiction. There are tricky issues that arise in this area regarding multijurisdictional practice, cooperative arrangements with other lawyers, and the work of legal assistants. There are also challenging questions that are specific to those in tax practice regarding work that is done with accountants and work done for accounting firms. Finally, government and corporate counsel face challenges with regard to multijurisdictional practice.

## 1. FEDERAL PRACTICE

States are generally charged with determining the requirements for practicing law within their borders. Thus, a lawyer licensed in one state may be violating the law by practicing law in another state in which he is not licensed. This problem arises often in general legal practice, but is even more complicated for tax lawyers. The question arises whether a tax lawyer can practice Federal tax law in a particular jurisdiction even if he is not a member of the bar of that jurisdiction.

Circular 230 sets out the requirements for being able to practice before the IRS. Enrolled agents, accountants, and lawyers are all authorized to practice before the IRS. Authorization to practice before the IRS., does not, however, authorize practice before the Tax Court. Unlike in most areas, however, you do not need to be a lawyer to litigate a case in Tax Court.

Section 7452 of the Code provides that "no qualified person shall be denied admission to practice before the Tax Court because of his failure to be a member of any profession or calling." In other words, lawyers do not have a monopoly on representation in Tax Court. The Tax Court has established rules on admission and these rules provide that non-lawyers may be admitted to Tax Court upon the passage of an examination. These same individuals are not, however, allowed to litigate tax cases in the district courts or the U.S. Court of Federal Claims. Upon application, lawyers are admitted without taking the exam, as long as they are a member in good standing of a state bar.

Thus it appears that practice in Tax Court is the practice of law, but individuals that meet the Tax Court's requirements are specifically authorized by Federal law to engage in such practice. If non-lawyers are allowed to practice in Tax Court without being a member of a state bar where the case originates, lawyers are likely allowed to do so as well. As you read the following cases, think about whether an attorney may engage in Federal tax practice in a state even though he is not a member of the bar in that state.

# SPERRY v. FLORIDA
## 373 U.S. 379 (1963)

Mr. Chief Justice WARREN delivered the opinion of the Court.

Petitioner is a practitioner registered to practice before the United States Patent Office. He has not been admitted to practice law before the Florida or any other bar. Alleging, among other things, that petitioner "is engaged in the unauthorized practice of law, in that although he is not a member of The Florida Bar, he nevertheless maintains an office . . .in Tampa, Florida, . . .holds himself out to the public as a Patent Attorney . . .represents Florida clients before the United States Patent Office, . . .has rendered opinions as to patentability, and . . .has prepared various legal instruments, including . . .applications and amendments to applications for letters patent, and filed same in the United States Patent Office in Washington, D.C.," the Florida Bar instituted these proceedings in the Supreme Court of Florida to enjoin the performance of these and other specified acts within the State. Petitioner filed an answer in which he admitted the above allegations but pleaded as a defense "that the work performed by him for Florida citizens is solely that work which is presented to the United States Patent Office and that he charges fees solely for his work of preparing and prosecuting patent applications and patent assignments and determinations incident to preparing and prosecuting patent applications and assignments." Thereupon, the court granted the Bar's motion for a summary decree and permanently enjoined the petitioner from [working as a patent attorney].

The Supreme Court of Florida concluded that petitioner's conduct constituted the unauthorized practice of law which the State, acting under its police power, could properly prohibit, and that neither federal statute nor the Constitution of the United States empowered any federal body to authorize such conduct in Florida.

In his petition for certiorari, petitioner attacked the injunction "only insofar as it prohibits him from engaging in the specific activities . . . (referred to above), covered by his federal license to practice before the Patent Office. He does not claim that he has any right otherwise to engage in activities that would be regarded as the practice of law." We granted certiorari.

* * *

We do not question the determination that under Florida law the preparation and prosecution of patent applications for others constitutes the practice of law. Such conduct inevitably requires the practitioner to consider and advise his clients as to the patentability of their inventions under the statutory criteria, as well as to consider the advisability of relying upon alternative forms of protection which may be available under statute law. It also involves his participation in the drafting of the specification and claims of the patent application, which this Court long ago noted 'constitute(s) one of the most difficult legal instruments to draw with accuracy,' And upon rejection of the application, the practitioner may also assist in the preparation of amendments, which frequently requires written argument to establish the patentability of the claimed invention under the applicable rules of law and in light of the prior art. Nor do we doubt that Florida has a substantial interest in regulating the practice of law within the State and that, in the absence of federal legislation, it could validly prohibit nonlawyers from engaging in this circumscribed form of patent practice.

But "the law of the State, though enacted in the exercise of powers not controverted, must yield" when incompatible with federal legislation. Congress has provided that the Commissioner of Patents "may prescribe regulations governing the recognition and conduct of agents, attorneys, or other persons representing applicants or other parties before the Patent Office," and the Commissioner, pursuant to, has provided by regulation that "(a)n applicant for patent . . . may be represented by an attorney or agent authorized to practice before the Patent Office in patent cases." 37 CFR s 1.31. (Emphasis added.) . . .

The statute thus expressly permits the Commissioner to authorize practice before the Patent Office by non-lawyers, and the Commissioner has explicitly granted such authority. If the authorization is unqualified, then, by virtue of the Supremacy Clause, Florida may not deny to those failing to meet its own qualifications the right to perform the functions within the scope of the federal authority. A State may not enforce licensing requirements which, though valid in the absence of federal regulation, give "the State's licensing board a virtual power of review over the federal determination" that a person or agency is qualified and entitled to perform certain functions, or which impose upon the performance of activity sanctioned by federal license additional conditions not contemplated by Congress. "No State law can hinder or obstruct the free use of a license granted under an act of Congress."

\* \* \*

Examination of the development of practice before the Patent Office and its governmental regulation reveals that: (1) nonlawyers have practiced before the Office from its inception, with the express approval of the Patent Office and to the knowledge of Congress; (2) during prolonged congressional study of unethical practices before the Patent Office, the right of nonlawyer agents to practice before the Office went unquestioned, and there was no suggestion that abuses might be curbed by state regulation; (3) despite protests of the bar, Congress in enacting the Administrative Procedure Act refused to limit the right to practice before the administrative agencies to lawyers; and (4) the Patent Office has defended the value of nonlawyer practitioners while taking steps to protect the interests which a State has in prohibiting unauthorized practice of law. We find implicit in this history congressional (and administrative) recognition that registration in the Patent Office confers a right to practice before the Office without regard to whether the State within which the practice is conducted would otherwise prohibit such conduct.

\* \* \*

## Questions and Comments:

*Sperry* is the seminal case in this area. *Sperry* generally stands for the proposition that States do not have the authority to regulate the practice of law before Federal agencies. But the thrust of the opinion was more limited than that. The Court stated that "'the law of the State, though enacted in the exercise of powers not controverted, must yield' when incompatible with federal legislation." Federal law expressly provided that non-lawyers could practice before the Patent Office. Federal law provides that qualified non-lawyers may represent citizens before Federal agencies, and the Tax Court has specific rules authorizing non-lawyers to appear in Tax Court upon the completion of an examination. (Lawyers may appear upon application without an examination).

It is therefore reasonably clear after *Sperry* that a lawyer who is a member of the bar of any State, may represent a taxpayer in Tax Court even if the lawyer is not a member of the bar of the state in which the taxpayer resides. *Sperry*, however, did not settle the issue whether a lawyer may practice "Federal law" in a State even though he is not a member of the bar of that State. For example, is a lawyer allowed to represent a taxpayer in district court even though he is not a member of the bar of the State in which the case is pending? Although some States have remained active in regulating this area and have taken a restrictive view of *Sperry*, the general rule is that as long as the attorney is practicing Federal law, he may do so in a State even if he is not a member of the bar of that state.

## SURRICK v. KILLION
449 F.3d 520 (3d Cir. 2006)

ALDISERT, CIRCUIT JUDGE.

Paul J. Killion, Chief Counsel of the Commonwealth of Pennsylvania's Office of Disciplinary Counsel ("Office of Disciplinary Counsel"), appeals from the United States District Court for the Eastern District of Pennsylvania's order granting summary judgment to Robert Surrick in this declaratory judgment action. The District Court declared that Surrick, an attorney authorized to practice before the Eastern District of Pennsylvania but suspended by the Bar of the Supreme Court of Pennsylvania ("Pennsylvania Bar"), is permitted to maintain a law office in the Commonwealth of Pennsylvania for the sole purpose of supporting his practice before the federal court, subject to certain conditions. * * *

On March 24, 2000, following disciplinary proceedings, Surrick was suspended from the Pennsylvania Bar for five years. The Eastern District of Pennsylvania ordered a reciprocal suspension of thirty months. * * *

Surrick was readmitted to the Eastern District of Pennsylvania Bar on May 17, 2004. On August 16, 2004, the Pennsylvania Supreme Court issued its decision in *Marcone,* which involved disciplinary proceedings against another Pennsylvania attorney. Therein, the Pennsylvania Supreme Court held that an attorney suspended from practice in the Pennsylvania courts but readmitted to the federal district court could not maintain a law office in the Commonwealth so long as he remains unauthorized to practice in the Pennsylvania state courts. * * *

On December 7, 2004, Surrick initiated this declaratory judgment action against Paul Killion, Chief Disciplinary Counsel of the Office of Disciplinary Counsel, and the named justices of the Pennsylvania Supreme Court, alleging that the decision in *Marcone* was contrary to federal law and that he reasonably feared that the Office of Disciplinary Counsel would administer sanctions if he were to open a law office. * * * Surrick's claims were predicated on the Supremacy Clause of the United States Constitution and the First Amendment. The Office of Disciplinary Counsel subsequently moved to dismiss Surrick's complaint, arguing, *inter alia,* that his claims were not ripe and that his complaint failed to state a claim upon which relief could be granted.

The District Court held hearings on January 24 and March 7, 2005. At those hearings, Surrick testified that he intends to open and maintain an office to support his practice before the federal courts. He testified that he intends to practice in the medical malpractice field, suing those who bring "frivolous" malpractice lawsuits against doctors. He testified that such lawsuits would be brought in federal court pursuant to federal diversity jurisdiction. The Office of Disciplinary Counsel responded by presenting expert testimony that, using modern technology, attorneys are now able to practice law without a traditional law office.

On April 20, 2005, the District Court granted limited declaratory relief in Surrick's favor, declaring that Surrick "may open a legal office for the practice of law before the United States District Court for the Eastern District" of Pennsylvania subject to eight conditions: [the conditions included obtaining reinstatement in Pennsylvania, paying fines etc.]

* * *

The question in this case is whether a state may prohibit an attorney admitted to the bar of a federal district court, but suspended from the state bar, from maintaining a legal office for the sole purpose of supporting a practice before the federal court. The starting point for our analysis is the seminal case of Sperry v. State of Florida, in which the United States Supreme Court held that the State of Florida could not enjoin a local patent practitioner, who was not admitted to the State Bar of Florida, from preparing patent applications and other legal instruments that are filed solely in the United States Patent and Trademark Office. The Supreme Court began its analysis by recognizing that the state had a substantial interest in regulating the practice of law within its borders and that, in the absence of federal legislation, it could validly prohibit non-lawyers from preparing and filing patent applications. Under the Supremacy Clause, however, "'the law of the State, though enacted in the exercise of powers uncontroverted, must yield' when incompatible with federal legislation." The Court reasoned that if the state were permitted to enforce licensing requirements contrary to federal law, the state would then have the power of review over federal licensing requirements:

> [a] State may not enforce licensing requirements which, though valid in the absence of federal regulation, give "the State's licensing board a virtual power of review over the federal determination" that a person or agency is qualified and entitled to perform certain functions, or which impose upon the performance of activity sanctioned by federal license additional conditions not contemplated by Congress. "No State law can hinder or obstruct the free use of a license granted under an act of Congress."

*Sperry* therefore stands for the general proposition that where federal law authorizes an agent to practice before a federal tribunal, the federal law preempts a state's licensing requirements to the extent that those requirements hinder or obstruct the goals of federal law. "When state licensing laws purport to prohibit lawyers from doing that which federal law entitles them to do, the state law must give way.").

The Office of Disciplinary Counsel contends that *Sperry* is distinguishable for two reasons. First, the enabling congressional statute in *Sperry* expressly allowed for the prosecution of patents by non-lawyers, whereas here no Congressional statute expressly permits Surrick to maintain a law office. Second, that because Surrick intends to litigate federal diversity actions, he is for all practical matters practicing state law.   * * *

A

Under the Supremacy Clause, when state law conflicts or is incompatible with federal law, the federal law preempts the state law. Preemption generally occurs in three ways: (1) where Congress has expressly preempted state law; (2) where Congress has legislated so comprehensively that federal law occupies an entire field of regulation and leaves no room for state law; or (3) where federal law conflicts with state law. This case indisputably involves "conflict preemption," which arises when "state law stands as an obstacle to the accomplishment and execution of the full purposes and objectives of Congress."

As discussed above, it is well established that "a federal court has the power to control admission to its bar and to discipline attorneys who appear before it." In re Poole, 222 F.3d 618, 620 (9th Cir.2000). * * * This power is rooted in both statute, see 28 U.S.C. § 2071(a), and inherent authority. Pursuant to its exclusive authority over members of its bar, the Eastern District of Pennsylvania promulgated Rule 83.6VII(I) * * * which expressly permits attorneys suspended from a state bar to practice before the Eastern District of Pennsylvania. It is therefore beyond dispute -and the Office of Disciplinary Counsel does not question this point-that the Commonwealth lacks the authority to prohibit Surrick from practicing law before the Eastern District of Pennsylvania.

The more difficult question is whether a state law prohibiting Surrick from maintaining a law office is preempted by this exclusive authority of the Eastern District of Pennsylvania to determine who may practice law before it. The Office of Disciplinary Counsel argues that conflict preemption does not apply here because, unlike in Sperry, where the federal statute specifically authorized non-lawyers to prepare and prosecute patents, there is no federal statute or local rule expressly setting forth the right of federal courts to determine who may maintain an office in a state.

This argument is based on both a misreading of Sperry and a misapprehension of the preemption doctrine. Federal law preempts not only state laws that expressly prohibit the very act the federal law allows, but those that "stand as an obstacle to the accomplishment of the full purposes and objectives" of federal law. Thus, federal and state law need not be contradictory on their faces for preemption to apply. It is sufficient that the state law "impose[s] . . . additional conditions" not contemplated by Congress.

In Sperry, for example, the State Bar of Florida argued that the federal license to practice before the Patent Office was a narrow one, only conferring the right to practice in the physical presence of the Patent and Trademark Office and the District of Columbia. Id. The Supreme Court rejected this contention, stating that Sperry had to be permitted to "perform[ ] tasks incident to the preparation and prosecution of patent applications." Although the Court expressly declined "to determine what functions are reasonably within the scope of the practice authorized" by federal law, it noted that a practitioner "must of course render opinions as to the patentability of the inventions brought to him, and . . . it is entirely reasonable for a practitioner to hold himself out as qualified to perform his specialized work, so long as he does not misrepresent the scope of his license."

The reasons for the broad construction of the Supremacy Clause are plain. If preemption only applied to state laws that directly contradict federal laws, federal laws could be effectively nullified by state laws prohibiting those acts that are incident to, but not specifically authorized by, federal law. Under such a regime, state officials would have a "virtual power of review" over federal laws. Accordingly, the question here is not whether any federal law expressly confers the right to maintain an office, but whether the maintenance of an office is "reasonably within the scope" of the federally-conferred license to practice law.

We agree with the District Court that maintaining a law office is "reasonably within the scope of the practice authorized" by 28 U.S.C. §§ 1654 & 2071 and the local rules and that the state's regulation of such conduct hinders Surrick's federal license to practice law. * * *

B

We reject the Office of Disciplinary Counsel's additional argument that the District Court ignored "the overlay of federal with state practice" and that Surrick's intention to practice solely diversity cases should influence our decision. Although we acknowledge that federal cases, and especially diversity cases, often involve questions of Pennsylvania law, and that the Commonwealth has a legitimate interest in preventing suspended attorneys from practicing state law, preemption analysis does not involve a balancing of state and federal interests. Once it is determined that there is a conflict between a valid federal law and a state law, the state law must give way. The Office of Disciplinary Counsel cannot point to any authority indicating that a federal court's power to determine who may practice law before it depends on the type of cases a lawyer intends to practice. * * * We therefore reject the argument that the intertwining of state and federal law somehow "preclude[s] a finding of federal preemption."

* * *

## Questions and Comments:

Under *Surrick* a lawyer may practice Federal tax law in a state even if he is not a member of the bar of that State, *Surrick,* however, only applies in the Third Circuit and only when the case involving unauthorized practice is brought in Federal court. These cases, however, are usually brought in state court. As the Court notes in the full opinion, the Third Circuit has no authority over State Supreme Courts. State Supreme Courts often take a stricter view of the Supremacy Clause. In Office of Disciplinary Counsel v. Marcone, 855 A.2d 654 (2004), the case that encouraged *Surrick* to file in Federal court, the Supreme Court of Pennsylvania held that the state could prosecute an attorney for unauthorized practice of law if the attorney opened an office in the State and provided legal advice, even if the attorney limited himself to Federal practice. Read *Marcone* and contrast it with *Surrick.*

# OFFICE OF DISCIPLINARY COUNSEL
## v.
# MARCONE
### 855 A.2D 654 (2004)

* * *  That Mr. Marcone's maintenance of a law office is limited solely to his practice before the United States District Court for the Eastern District of Pennsylvania does not alter our conclusion [that Marcone is engaged in unauthorized practice of law].

First, neither our Rules nor our case law have limited the concept of practicing law to Pennsylvania law. * * *

Additionally, current legal practice consists of a complex and interconnected web of legal knowledge, concerns, strategies, and consequences. More specifically, holding oneself out to the public as engaging in a general federal practice and advising clients as part of a federal practice today necessarily implicates counseling clients on state law issues. State law concerns are the foundation of federal diversity actions. Even federal law matters are in many instances "only a federal overlay to applicable state law." Thus, to suggest that because maintenance of an office is limited to federal practice, it does not constitute the practice of law within the borders of a state, is to ignore the realities of current legal practice.

Finally, considerations of public policy undergird our determination. As noted above, this Court's core obligation in regulating attorney conduct is to protect the citizens of our Commonwealth, to secure the public's interest in competent legal representation, and to ensure the integrity of our legal system. The embarkation of advising a client in legal matters includes decision making regarding the status of potential claims and deciding which claims to pursue. This last aspect of counseling clients is especially relevant, as a suspended attorney maintaining a law office dedicated "exclusively" to the practice of federal matters could cant advice artificially in the direction of the attorney's "limited" practice. Thus, pragmatically speaking, to permit within our Commonwealth's borders without regulation the maintenance of a law office by a suspended attorney, dedicated to an "exclusive" federal practice, in which such counseling could take place, would be to leave our citizens vulnerable to misguidance and exploitation. Related thereto, limiting the concept of the practice of law to Pennsylvania law, exclusive from federal matters, would be virtually impossible to apply and enforce, and would defeat our mandate of protecting the public from incompetent or unethical practitioners. Indeed, the operation of a law office by a suspended attorney could be used as a "shield behind which to conduct an unlimited-in-fact law practice."

Our * * * conclusion that a suspended attorney maintaining a law office in our Commonwealth for purposes of practicing before a federal court is engaging in the practice of law are buttressed by similar decisions from our sister states. The few courts that have addressed issues akin to the one sub judice have been consistently and notably hostile to the notion of an attorney who is not a member of the state bar maintaining a law office for purposes of a federal practice. These courts have concluded that maintaining such an office constitutes the unauthorized practice of law for purposes of state law. See, e.g., In the Matter of Perrello, 386 N.E.2d at 179 (attorney suspended from practice of law in Indiana engaged in unauthorized practice of law when maintaining law office for purposes of federal practice); Attorney Grievance Commission of Maryland v. Harris-Smith, 356 Md. 72, 737 A.2d 567 (1999)(attorney maintaining an office and advising clients for practice of federal and non-Maryland law constituted the unauthorized practice of law); In re Peterson, 163 B.R. at 673 (attorney admitted in federal court in Connecticut could not maintain his sole office in that state and hold himself out to residents of Connecticut as a practitioner in bankruptcy law); In re Roel, 3 N.Y.2d 224, 165 N.Y.S.2d 31, 144

N.E.2d 24 (1957)(maintaining law office and giving advice solely on Mexican law enjoined as unauthorized practice of law in New York). Accord, Wolfram, Sneaking Around in the Legal Profession: Interjurisdictional Unauthorized Practice By Transactional Lawyers, 36 S. Tex. L.Rev. at 698.

Mr. Marcone, however, raises a number of arguments as to why we should not find him in contempt of our prior order. We find none of these contentions to be meritorious.

\* \* \*

Mr. Marcone relies upon In re Desilets, 291 F.3d 925 (6th Cir.2002) in support of his conclusion that it is solely for the federal courts to regulate the lawyers admitted to federal practice. Mr. Marcone's reliance on Desilets is misplaced for a number of reasons. First, that decision dealt with whether an individual was an "attorney" for purposes of the bankruptcy code with respect to practice in a Michigan federal bankruptcy court and did not deal with the maintenance of a law office in a state by a suspended attorney. The Desilets court concluded that federal standards control admission to the federal bar. Nothing herein is contrary to this principle. Second, that decision did not deal with an attorney that was suspended from the practice of law in the state in which he wished to practice. Indeed, the attorney at issue was admitted to the bar of the state of Texas. Finally, to the extent that Desilets can be read to be contrary to our decision today, we are not bound by the decisions of lower federal courts. As noted above, we find that the discussions of the practice of law contained in In re Peterson, 163 B.R. at 673 and In re Lite Ray Realty Corp., 257 B.R. at 155, more accurately reflect the realities of the practice of law and bankruptcy law in particular. Mr. Marcone also offers as "[o]f interest" the United States Supreme Court's decision in Sperry v. Florida. Sperry dealt with a lay person who represented patent applicants before the United States Patent Office. The United States Supreme Court held that the state of Florida could not prohibit this layperson from representing individuals with respect to patent applications. The Court's decision was based upon a federal statute which specifically permits the Commissioner of Patents to authorize practice before the Patent Office by non-lawyers. Unlike the situation at bar, Sperry dealt with the ability of a layperson, expressly authorized by federal statute, to work in a specialized area of federal law-patent law, before an agency, the Patent and Trademark Office, which had a long tradition of regulating practitioners before it. Thus, it is clearly distinguishable from the circumstances in this case regulating a suspended attorney's maintenance of a law office and does not compel a result different from the one we reach today.

The Supremacy Clause of the United States Constitution prohibits states from enacting laws that are contrary to the laws of our federal government: "This Constitution and the Laws of the United States . . . shall be the supreme Law of the Land; and the Judges in every State shall be bound thereby, any Thing in the Constitution or Laws of any State to the Contrary notwithstanding." U.S. Const. art. VI, cl.2. It is through this clause that the United States Congress may preempt state law. In determining whether a state regulation is preempted by federal law, we start "with the assumption that the historic police powers of the States [are] not to be superseded by ... Federal Act unless it [is] the clear and manifest purpose of Congress.".  There are three ways in which a state law may be preempted. First, state law may be preempted where the United States Congress enacts a provision which expressly preempts the state enactment.. Likewise, preemption may be found where Congress has legislated in a field so comprehensively that it has implicitly expressed an intention to occupy the given field to the exclusion of state law.. Finally, a state enactment will be preempted where a state law conflicts with a federal law. Id. Such a conflict may be found in two instances, when it is impossible to comply with both federal and state law, or where the state law "stands as an obstacle to the accomplishment and execution of the full purposes and objectives of Congress."

First, Mr. Marcone fails to offer any statute or rule that expressly preempts our state regulation of the practice of law in general or of Mr. Marcone's maintenance of a law office within our borders in particular. Furthermore, the statutes and rule offered by Mr. Marcone fall far short of establishing that the federal enactments are so comprehensive that they demonstrate that Congress has intended to occupy regulation of the field to the exclusion of our state. Simply because federal statutes allow for the promulgation of rules, and permit one to conduct cases by counsel in federal courts, certainly does not evidence a Congressional intent to divest state courts of their authority to regulate the practice of law by suspended attorneys within their borders. Likewise, while under the local rules for the United States District Court for the Eastern District of Pennsylvania an attorney may be reinstated to "practice before this court notwithstanding the refusal of a state court to reinstate the attorney to practice," E.D.Pa.R.Civ.P. 83.6 VII(I), this does not evidence an intent to prohibit our Court from regulating the maintenance of a law office by a suspended attorney for the proffering of himself to the public or for client consultation and advice. In light of the historical licensing and regulation of attorneys by the states within their respective jurisdictions, and the failure of Mr. Marcone to offer a federal statute or rule that even minimally suggests an intention by Congress to limit the breadth of our Rules in this regard, we simply cannot find support for the proposition that Congress has expressed the sweeping intention of occupying the field to the exclusion of the states.

Finally, we find no conflict between the federal statutes and rules and our state rules. While an attorney's admission to federal court may permit him to represent clients in federal court, it is not impossible or even inconsistent in the least for Marcone to comply with our Court's authority to regulate a suspended attorney's maintenance of a law office within our borders from which he holds himself out to the public and consults with clients, even if "limited" to a federal practice. In re Lite Ray Realty Corp., 257 B.R. at 156 (federal court admission does not permit attorney to open a local office and practice generally, even if practice limited to bankruptcy); In re Peterson, 163 B.R. at 675 (attorney admitted in federal court in Connecticut could not maintain his sole office in that state and hold himself out to residents of Connecticut as a practitioner in bankruptcy law).

For these same reasons, we cannot say that our regulation of the maintenance of a law office significantly frustrates the accomplishment of the purposes of Congress. While regulation of the maintenance a law office through which one holds himself out to the public and counsels clients may place some burden on one who has been suspended from the practice of law in a particular state but who is nevertheless admitted before a federal court, our regulation of those who maintain a law office within our borders simply does not, without more, result in conflict pre-emption. Indeed, we find that in these circumstances, the regulation of a suspended attorney's law office where he holds himself out to the public and counsels clients is an area in which the applicable federal statutes and rules and this Court's Rules coexist. Based upon the above, we conclude that our regulation of Mr. Marcone's maintenance of a law office within our Commonwealth is not preempted by federal statute or local rule, and thus, does not run afoul of the Supremacy Clause of the United States Constitution. * * *

## Scenario 7.1

Max is a partner in a boutique law firm in Washington, D.C. He is well known as one of the top tax controversy lawyers in the United States. Emma, a well known business person in Pennsylvania approaches Max and asks him to represent her in a tax refund action in district court. Since Emma lives in Pennsylvania, the refund action would normally be filed in Pennsylvania. (She could file in the Federal Court of Claims). Max researches the law and finds a great case in the Third Circuit so he is especially excited about filing in district court in Pennsylvania. Max litigates the case in Pennsylvania and uses his hotel room as a temporary office. Max wins the case, and Emma is happy with the result, decides that she does not want to pay Max and believes she is not obligated to do so because Max was not a member of the Pennsylvania bar and therefore his representation amounted to the unauthorized practice of law. Max sues Emma in Pennsylvania state court. Who will prevail and why?

## 2.    MULTIJURISDICTIONAL TAX PRACTICE

Multi-Jurisdiction legal practice is now very common, and the new model rules recognize this trend and provide far more flexibility to lawyers who are temporarily practicing law in another state.

The model rules were amended in August 2002 and Rule 5.5 now provides more flexible rules for multijurisdictional practice. Rule 5.5 permits lawyers to practice in other jurisdictions on a limited basis without becoming licensed in the jurisdiction. These rules were hotly debated within the ABA and recognize that multijurisdictional practice is becoming the norm.[34]

Under these rules, a lawyer may provide temporary legal services in a State even though he is not licensed in that state in the following circumstances:

1)    The lawyer partners with a lawyer who is licensed in the jurisdiction and both lawyers actively participate in the case;

---

[34] For a more in-depth discussion of multijurisdictional practice and the influence of Rule 5.5, see Arthur F. Greenbaum, Multijurisdictional Practice and the Influence of Model Rule of Professional Conduct 5.5 – An Interim Assessment, (forthcoming Akron Law Review 2010).

2) The lawyer is authorized by law to appear in a proceeding (for example when authorized to appear by an agency or tribunal or when appearing pro hac vice);

3) The representation is reasonably related "to a pending or potential arbitration, mediation, or other alternative dispute resolution proceeding; or

4) The representation arises out of or is related to a lawyer's practice in another jurisdiction.

The above exceptions apply only in temporary circumstances. They are designed to allow practice when it would be impractacle, based on the limited contact with the jurisdiction, to require bar membership. In contrast, Rule 5.5(d) provides two situations where multijurisdictional practice is allowed on a more permanent basis. Under Rule 5.5(d), a lawyer may provide services to her employer even if she is not licensed in the specific jurisdiction. This allows corporate counsel to work on issues in a particular state even if the lawyer is not licensed in that state.

In addition, Rule 5.5(d) recognizes the problem faced by attorneys engaged in Federal practice and specifically allows a lawyer to provide services in a jurisdiction even though he is not licensed in that jurisdiction if the lawyer is authorized by Federal law to provide such services. This clearly would apply to a lawyer representing a client in Tax Court, but it still might not apply to tax practice in district court.

## 3.    PROFESSIONAL INDEPENDENCE

The legal profession has traditionally viewed lawyer independence as a cornerstone of good representation. A lawyer's professional independence, judgment and decision making should not be influenced by financial arrangements with non-lawyers. Obviously a lawyer receives fees from a client. In almost all cases, the lawyer's interests align with the client's and the client is paying the lawyer for her independent judgment. What the legal profession is generally concerned about is when a third party who is not a lawyer might have some incentive to influence the independent judgment of the lawyer. Thus state bars and the model rules generally limit an attorney's ability to share fees with a non-lawyer, and place restrictions on when an attorney may receive payment from a third party.

Model Rule 5.4 provides that "a lawyer or law firm shall not share legal fees with a nonlawyer." The Rules provide for some exceptions almost all of which deal with the payment to an estate when a legal practice is purchased, dissolved, or a partner or associate dies.

A lawyer may also not form a partnership with a nonlawyer "if any of the activities of the partnership consist of the practice of law." A lawyer also is prohibited from practicing in a professional corporation if a nonlawyer owns an interest in the corporation or is a director of the corporation, or if a nonlawyer has the right to control the professional judgment of the lawyer.

The Rules of Professional Conduct for the D.C. Bar allow for lawyers in some instances to form partnerships with nonlawyers. The comments to Rule 5.4 of the D.C. Rules of Professional conduct explains:

> [3] As the demand increased for a broad range of professional services from a single source, lawyers employed professionals from other disciplines to work for them. So long as the nonlawyers remained employees of the lawyers, these relationships did not violate the disciplinary rules. However, when lawyers and nonlawyers considered forming partnerships and professional corporations to provide a combination of legal and other services to the public, they faced serious obstacles under the former rules.

> [4] This rule rejects an absolute prohibition against lawyers and nonlawyers joining together to provide collaborative services, but continues to impose traditional ethical requirements with respect to the organization thus created. Thus, a lawyer may practice law in an organization where nonlawyers hold a financial interest or exercise managerial authority, but only if the conditions set forth in subparagraphs (b)(1), (b)(2), and (b)(3) are satisfied, and pursuant to subparagraph (b)(4), satisfaction of these conditions is set forth in a written instrument. The requirement of a writing helps ensure that these important conditions are not overlooked in establishing the organizational structure of entities in which nonlawyers enjoy an

ownership or managerial role equivalent to that of a partner in a traditional law firm.

### Problem 7.1

Big accounting firm hires lawyers to work in the accounting firm. The lawyers assist in the firm's tax work. Are the lawyers who work for the accounting firm in violation of the Model Rules?

### Problem 7.2

Big accounting firm realizes that its clients are generating a lot of tax controversy work. The firm prepares the clients' returns and represents the clients at audit. It wants to represent the clients in Tax Court as well. Big accounting firm recognizes that many of the best tax controversy people are lawyers. The firm wants to hire lawyers to represent the firm's clients in Tax Court. Is the accounting firm guilty of unauthorized practice of law? Has the attorney violated the Model Rules by agreeing to be employed by the accounting firm and represent its clients in Tax Court?

### Problem 7.3

Jack is an accountant engaged in tax controversy work. He wants to recruit Paul, a tax litigator with the Department of Justice to join him in his practice. The idea is that Jack and John will be partners and will share profits. They will only represent clients in Tax Court. Both Jack and John are members of the bar of the Tax Court and are authorized to represent clients in Tax Court. Are they in violation of the Model Rules?

### Problem 7.4

You have been appointed by the State bar to represent it in a proceeding involving any violations of the Model Rules that occurred in Problems 7.1 through 7.3. What are your best policy arguments in support of sanctions? What policy arguments give you the most pause? What do you think the proper rule should be?

## B.    Government Lawyers

Government lawyers are bound by Rules of Professional Conduct, but their unique role as lawyers for the Government often raises questions regarding which rules apply (which State rules), and how those rules apply in a specific situation. Moreover, in the Government context, there is significant disagreement over who the attorney represents. Who is the client? Finally, Government Ethics rules place further restrictions on government attorneys both while they are in government and once they leave government.

## 1.    WHAT RULES APPLY?

Prior to 1998 the Justice Department argued that its lawyers were not bound by state ethics rules. The theory was that the Department of Justice attorneys were representatives of the United States, and States could not regulate Federal government attorneys.[35]

The Government's position was not outrageous. It argued that preemption rules prohibited States from regulating Federal Government attorneys. The Attorney General argued that Government attorneys should comply with State ethics rules, but that the Attorney General had the right to waive that requirement.

In 1998, Congress passed the "McDade Amendment," named after its sponsor, Joseph McDade (R-Pa.), who was displeased by the conduct of government lawyers investigating him (McDade was acquitted). McDade complained that Government lawyers violated State ethics rules as part of the investigation. The McDade amendment provides that a Government attorney must comply with State laws and rules "in each State where such attorney engages in the attorneys duties. . ." 28 U.S.C. §530B.

In addition to the McDade Amendment, Federal government attorneys must comply with general ethics rules that apply to government employees. For example, employees may not receive gifts from parties doing business before the employee's agency, may not engage in some types of outside employment, and may not use their public office for private gain. See 5 C.F.R. § 2635.101. In addition, agencies of the Federal government have the authority to promulgate additional ethics rules. (See 5 C.F.R. § 3101.101 for the Department of Treasury and 5 C.F.R. § 3801.101 for the Department of Justice). Finally, IRS attorneys must comply with guidelines set out by the Chief Counsel. The Internal Revenue Manual indicates

---

[35] For a thorough discussion of this issue see Ethical Standards for Federal Prosecutors Act of 1996; Hearings Before the Subcomm. On Courts and Intellectual Property of the H. Comm. On the Judiciary, 104th Cong. 7 (1996).

that IRS attorneys are bound "by the professional codes of the states where they are admitted to the bar" and that the ABA Rules of Professional Conduct are the "generally accepted ethical standard for attorneys." Moreover, Tax Court Rule 201(a) provides that attorneys must comply with the letter and spirit of the ABA Rules of Professional Conduct.

Thus an attorney for the IRS is governed by the ABA Model rules, the rules in the jurisdiction in which he practices, and the rules in the jurisdiction or jurisdictions in which he is a member of the bar. Who knows what happens if these rules conflict?

## 2. WHO IS THE CLIENT?

### GOVERNMENT LAWYERS AND CONFIDENTIALITY NORMS
85 Washington U.L. Rev. 1033 (2007)
Kathleen Clark[*]

\* \* \*

Government officials, courts, and commentators have identified a wide variety of possible clients that the government lawyer might represent. One can find some support for the following as clients: the "public interest," the public at large, the entire government, the branch of government employing the lawyer, the particular agency employing the lawyer, and a particular government official (such as the head of a government organization) in his official or individual capacity.

In some situations a government lawyer is assigned to defend an individual government employee rather than represent a government entity. Such is routinely the case for Judge Advocate General military defense lawyers, who take on a traditional lawyer-client relationship with their individual clients. Justice Department lawyers representing government officials who have been sued in their individual capacity face a more complex situation. Federal government lawyers represent individual government officials only if the Attorney General has determined that it is "in the interest of the United States" to provide such representation. Under Justice Department regulations, the government lawyer's confidentiality duty toward her individual client is more limited than in a

---

[*] Reprinted with permission. Washington University Law Review (2007).

traditional lawyer-client relationship. The lawyer must keep confidential only that information that is covered by the attorney-client privilege.[36] Any nonprivileged information need not be held confidential, and Justice Department attorneys have been required to disclose information adverse to their individual client where the lawyer learned it from a source other than a client communication.

In most situations, the government lawyer represents a government entity rather than an individual government employee. While the professional rules provide guidance for entity representation, they generally leave open the key question for government lawyers: which government entity does the lawyer represent?

The identity of the client has important implications for lawyer confidentiality. If a government lawyer represents "the people," then presumably she could disclose information to anyone who is one of "the people." If a government lawyer represents an agency, then the entity exception to confidentiality will apply, but if she is representing the agency head, then it will not. If a Justice Department lawyer represents the entire government, then she can reveal information to a member of Congress, but if she represents the executive branch, she cannot. If a state natural resources department lawyer represents her agency, then she cannot reveal information about wrongdoing at the department to anyone outside of the department, including the state attorney general. If a lawyer in the California Insurance Department * * * represents the entire government of California, then she can reveal information to state legislators. But if she represents only the Insurance Department, then she cannot - unless an exception to confidentiality applies.

Writing years before the American Bar Association adopted its Model Rules of Professional Conduct - including its rule specifically dealing with entity clients - Robert Lawry argued that client identity was the wrong question for government lawyers to ask. Lawry correctly noted that identifying the client does not end the inquiry regarding a government lawyer's confidentiality duty. But client identity is an appropriate starting point for an inquiry about confidentiality. Correctly identifying the government lawyer's client will help the lawyer determine the set of individuals to whom she can reveal information.

---

[36] 28 C.F.R. § 50.15(a)(3)(2007).

Some have attempted to provide a universal answer to the question of the identity of the government lawyer's client. Politicians often claim that the government lawyer's client is "the public," and a few commentators assert that government lawyers should pursue "the public interest." But these formulations fail to identify who can give direction to the lawyer on behalf of the client. Some assert that the government lawyer represents the government as a whole, but Geoffrey Miller persuasively rebuts that notion as it pertains to a government with separated powers. Miller notes that lawyers in the executive branch do not generally represent Congress or the judiciary. Many assert that the client is the particular agency that employs the lawyer, but this approach is singularly inappropriate for the hundreds of Justice Department lawyers who represent other government agencies and departments in court.

**Questions and Comments:**

1. The Rules of Professional Conduct for the District of Columbia provide specific rules regarding the attorney-client relationship when an attorney works for the Government. Rule 1.6(k) states "the client of the government lawyer is the agency that employs the lawyers unless expressly provided to the contrary by appropriate law, regulation, or order."

2. The Federal Bar Association adopted Model Rules of Professional Conduct for Federal Lawyers. These rules are not binding on lawyers and were designed to provide guidance to agencies and other entities designing ethical rules for lawyers. The Rules are well thought out and worth reading and thinking about if you are going to become a government lawyer.

## 3.   POST-GOVERNMENT EMPLOYMENT

There are several different issues facing lawyers who leave Government service and enter the private sector. Attorneys must comply with statutory restrictions on post-government employment and ethical rules regarding conflicts of interests. The conflict of interest rules also apply to lawyers moving from the private sector to the Government.

Federal law places restrictions on former government employees. For example, a former federal employee is prohibited from attempting to influence the government on behalf of a third party if: 1) United States is a party or has a "direct and substantial interest," 2) the former employee participated "personally and substantially" in the matter, and 3) the issue involved a "specific party or specific parties at the time of such participation." See 18 U.S.C. 207)(a). This rule thus prohibits an employee form working on a refund case on behalf of the IRS, leaving the IRS, and assisting the party in the refund suit with the claim. Former employees are permanently barred from this representation and violation of 18 U.S.C. § 207(a) is a crime punishable by up to 1 year in jail (5 years for a willful violation).

Federal law also places a restriction on some activities for two years post government employment. In this regard, a former employee may not attempt to influence the government on behalf of a third party for two years if: 1) The United States is a party or has a "direct and substantial interest," 2) the former employee reasonably knew or should have known the issue was pending under her official responsibility within 1 year of the termination, and 3) the issue involved "a specific party or specific parties at the time it was so pending." See 18 U.S.C. § 207(b). This prohibition is somewhat broader than subsection (a), but the prohibition lasts for only 2 years. Under subsection (b), if you were a supervising attorney at the Department of Justice and one of the attorney's you supervised was litigating a refund action, you could not represent the opposing party in the refund action even if you barely participated in the case. A violation of subsection (b) is also a crime punishable by up to a 1 year in jail (5 years for a willful violation).

Section 207 applies to both attorneys and non-attorneys. The conduct set out in section 207, however, is also prohibited by the Model Rules and most State rules dealing with conflicts of interest. Model Rule 1.11 prohibits a former government attorney from representing a client in connection with an issue that the "lawyer participated personally and substantially" as a government employee unless the former employer gives informed consent in writing. Section 10.25(b) of Circular 230, similarly prohibits a former employee "who personally and substantially participated in a particular matter involving specific parties" from representing or assisting those parties in the same matter upon leaving government service. Moreover, the attorney continues to have obligations to its former employer under Model Rule 1.9.

In addition, not only is the former employee barred from representation, but the former employee's firm is barred unless the former employee is screened from the matter and timely notice is provided to the government.

## Problem 7.5

Anne Lorry works in the chief counsel's office at the Internal Revenue Service. She litigates cases in Tax Court and has developed a specialty for cases involving the taxation of damages under § 104 of the Code. Anne is such an expert on the subject that she is temporarily assigned to another division at the IRS to help write regulations on the topic. Soon after the regulations are published, Anne leaves the IRS and represents clients before the IRS and in Tax Court. Anne is approached by Max Schlier who has a particularly interesting case involving §104(a)(2). Anne wants to take the case. Is she barred by statute or by the ABA Model Rules?

## Problem 7.6

Tony works for the Department of Justice and is currently litigating a case against a major corporation involving international tax credits. The General Counsel of the corporation is very impressed and approaches Tony about coming to work for the company. The General Counsel understands that Tony cannot work on this case. Tony is a little uncomfortable but is interested in the job and wants to get more information. At what point, if any, is Tony required to tell his employer about the contact?

## Problem 7.7

Julie JD worked for the IRS Chief Counsel's Office as an attorney. While with Chief Counsel, she prepared and drafted a "refund litigation defense letter," sent to the Department of Justice setting forth the IRS's position in defense of the refund case commenced by the XYZ Corporation seeking a refund of more than 50 million dollars for taxable years 2007 and 2008. Thereafter, she leaves government service to work for a law firm. Coincidently, that very firm represents the XYZ Corporation in its refund litigation case in United States District Court for the Southern District of Ohio involving a claim for more than 50 million dollars for taxable years 2007 and 2008. The firm asks if Julie will work on this case. In this regard, does Julie have any ethical obligations or related considerations? Can the firm continue to handle the case and allow Julie to work on it? Can the firm continue to handle the case?

## C. Corporate Counsel

Recent corporate scandals have highlighted the importance and ethical duties of corporate counsel. What is the role of corporate counsel when she discovers wrongdoing within her organization? Who is her client? To whom does she owe a duty? The Model Rules and provisions of Sarbanes-Oxley (SoX) help answer some of these questions.[37]

Model Rule 1.13 provides that a lawyer employed by an organization represents the organization, not an individual employee or manager in the organization. Communication to the attorney related to official business by employees or officers of the organization is determined to be client communication and is protected by Rule 1.6. It is, however, the organization, not the individual, who has the right to protect that communication.

If a lawyer detects wrongdoing in the corporation, the lawyer may have an obligation to report that wrongdoing to higher authorities in the organization. Under Rule 1.13(b) if a lawyer knows that an officer or employee of an organization is engaged in, or plans to engage in, a violation of legal obligation or violation of law "that reasonably might be imputed to the organization," then the lawyer should act in the best interest of the organization. Unless the lawyer determines that it is not necessary, the lawyer "shall" contact higher authorities within the corporation.[38]

By contacting higher authorities within the organization, the lawyer ensures that the corporation is aware of the potential wrongdoing and can take action to remedy the problem. The problem gets far more difficult for the attorney if higher authorities within the organization fail to take action or are involved in the wrongdoing. Rule 1.13(c) provides that if the highest authority within the organization does not remedy the situation, and the lawyer believes that the violation "is reasonably certain to result in substantial injury to the organization" then the lawyer *may* disclose

---

[37] Pub. L. No. 107-204, 116 Stat. 745 (2002).

[38] For example, an attorney might determine that the employee is engaging in the improper conduct due to a misunderstanding of the law. In that case, the attorney might determine that she should contact the employee to correct the problem.

the information but only to the extent necessary to prevent substantial injury.

Section 307 of Sarbanes-Oxley build on the requirements in the Model Rules. Section 307 of Sarbanes-Oxley requires lawyers representing public companies to report to higher authorities when they have "credible evidence" of a material violation of federal securities laws or breach of fiduciary duty by the company or its agents. The Securities and Exchange Commission has issued regulations for attorney's appearing and practicing before the Commission. These regulations require attorneys to report a material violation to the chief legal officer or to the chief legal officer and the chief executive officer. 17 C.F.R. § 205.3. The chief legal officer must then either investigate to determine whether the material violation occurred, is ongoing, or is about to occur or must refer the matter to a qualified legal compliance committee that was set up by the board of directors. If the chief legal officer determines there is not a material violation, the officer must then inform the attorney and advise the attorney of the basis for the decision. If the chief legal officer determines there is a violation, he must take reasonable steps to cause the company to adopt an appropriate response. 17 C.F.R. §205.3(b)(2)

If the attorney believes that the chief legal officer is not taking appropriate steps, or believes that reporting to that officer would be futile, the attorney may report such evidence to the audit committee of the board of directors or to the board of directors. 17 C.F.R. § 205.3(b)(3).

## Problem 7.8

Peter is General Counsel for Big Corporation. Peter realizes that the Chief Executive of the organization is using corporate resources for private gain. The CEO has Big Corporation maintenance employees work on his private residence, has the company's graphic designers make fliers for his child's play, and often goes golfing on company time.

Does Peter have an obligation under the Model Rules or Sarbanes-Oxley to report this activity to the Board of Directors or any other company employee?

**Problem 7.9**

You are corporate tax counsel for a major corporation. Your corporation has decided to invest in a tax shelter similar to the COBRA transaction discussed in Chapter 5. You advise the corporation that you think the transaction will not be upheld by the IRS and that the corporation could be subject to significant tax liability if the IRS audits the company's returns. The company is about to file disclosures with the SEC that do not mention its participation in the shelter and do not disclose the potential tax liability. What action do you take and why?

# Index

References are to pages